RED GUARD
The Political Biography of Dai Hsiao-ai

Red Guard

THE POLITICAL BIOGRAPHY
OF DAI HSIAO-AI

by **Gordon A. Bennett**
and **Ronald N. Montaperto**

LONDON · GEORGE ALLEN & UNWIN LTD
Ruskin House   Museum Street

First published in Great Britain in 1971

ISBN 0 04 920035 6

Printed in Great Britain
by Compton Printing Ltd.
London and Aylesbury

FOR DAI HSIAO-AI

CONTENTS

PREFACE

Although the mobilization of youth in turmoil has recently disturbed societies around the world, in no place was the effect more dramatic than in China, where millions of Red Guards roamed the country in late 1966 and early 1967. The movement was heralded by Chairman Mao Tse-tung in August 1966 when he appeared at the Gate of Heavenly Peace in Peking wearing a red armband. Within days millions of youths throughout China proclaimed themselves Red Guards. Universities were closed down and turned into Red Guard headquarters. Before the end of the year over 11 million youths had traveled to Peking to proclaim their loyalty to Chairman Mao and to exchange experiences with other Red Guards. In a series of parades in Peking millions of students, young workers, and soldiers passed the reviewing stands. Red Guards around the country who had traveled to Peking then led other Red Guards in their localities in an attack on intellectuals and others who were pursuing the "bourgeois path." Bulletin boards throughout China were

covered with huge posters denouncing leading Party officials. Leading members of the almost sacred Communist Party were paraded in
dunce caps and accused in front of mass rallies. Before the end of
the Cultural Revolution thousands of Party leaders had been denounced, factions had fought it out both verbally and physically,
and ultimately the Army moved in to preserve order.

Unlike the student movements which were attacking authorities in other countries, the student movement in China was stimulated and encouraged by the nation's highest leader. The Red
Guards were utilized by Chairman Mao as a way of attacking opponents within the Communist Party. But if attacking his opponents
was the only aim Chairman Mao had in mind, there were other
means at his disposal. He clearly wanted to mobilize the energies of
youth, to enhance their revolutionary fervor and to strengthen their
commitment to the building of a strong China. Whatever Mao and
other leaders in Peking might have intended, the Red Guards themselves assumed leadership in the local community. Even if Red
Guards had been adequately informed of the intentions of the
Peking leaders, they carried out the movement in a way that was in
keeping with their own hopes and ambitions.

The events of the Cultural Revolution were inadequately covered by the Western press not only because of the lack of accurate
information available from China but because Western reporters
were so poorly prepared in terms of their understanding of Communist China to provide adequate coverage. Western newspapers
reported rumors or stray incidents or occasional news releases without providing the context necessary to make a story meaningful.
Books have since appeared on the Cultural Revolution but most of
them tell more about their authors than about the Cultural Revolution. Some represent the author's romantic notions of how he would
like his own society to be. Others represent the author's nightmares.
Other accounts are garbled reports adding up to confusion. It is
refreshing to have at last an authentic account by a thoughtful
participant of the Cultural Revolution, carefully prepared by two
young American China specialists. When I met former Red Guard
leader Dai in Hong Kong in the summer of 1969, he was still _

engaged in the careful job of checking his recollections with available documents to be more precise about dates and names. He is a sensitive but serious youth. If one had not known of his background, he could have passed for an innocent high school youth who has never strayed far from the classroom and the library.

Gorden Bennett and Ronald Montaperto have given Dai's recollection the serious attention it deserves. They began interviewing Dai only after they acquired considerable background in Chinese language and Chinese studies. They went over and over the record to eliminate possible confusion, to expand recollections, to iron out inconsistencies and to produce a rounded, coherent story. They then translated Dai's interviews into English and provided the contextual background necessary to make sense out of the documents. As one who has gone over available documents from Canton before and during the Cultural Revolution, I can testify to the carefulness of Montaperto's and Bennett's work and the extent to which it is consistent with the documentation available.

The result is the richest, most human account of the Red Guard period yet to appear in English. This document contains none of the stereotypes found in many refugee accounts. It is the story of a subtle mind which captures the enthusiasm for Chairman Mao, the confusion of the Red Guards about what really was happening and which side was the true representative of Mao, petty squabbling between factions and between Red Guards of one locale and another, the excitement of sight-seeing and traveling, the thrill and righteousness felt in denouncing backward Party leaders.

It is comforting for people trying to cope with an overly complex world to devise a set of categories which will give them an intellectual grasp on China. It is tempting to think of Chinese as Communists, as current versions of traditional Chinese, as romantic utopians, as totalitarians. Anyone who reads the following document and ponders its implications will not be satisfied with such simple categories. He will find that the Chinese government is powerful and at times coercive, but far from totalitarian. He will find that youths are self-centered but moved by their respect for Mao and their hope for China, and that the Cultural Revolution was filled with chaos, but not with anarchy. In short, he will find that the Chinese cannot be classified simply as black or white, red or yellow.

PROFESSOR EZRA F. VOGEL
Associate Director, East Asian Research Center,
Harvard University, Cambridge, Mass.

ACKNOWLEDGMENTS

During our stay in Hong Kong we met and spoke with many
people, all of whom, in retrospect, have made contributions to this
book. Frequently, what began as a casual conversation led to some
new insight or to the sudden recognition of questions or issues
which might otherwise have been neglected. While we cannot re-
pay our debt to all these colleagues and friends, we do acknowledge
it and express our thanks to them.

We are most grateful of all to John Gittings. Without his
original interest and encouragement, Dai's essays might still remain
in our files. His frequent questions and his welcome advice on
matters of fact and style were crucial in bringing this project to
fruition.

Many other people, especially colleagues at the Universities
Service Centre, offered suggestions, criticisms, and judicious teasing
when our own inability to keep pace with events in China caused
us to become discouraged. They helped us a great deal to improve

our understanding of the Cultural Revolution. Thus, we offer thanks to Richard Baum, Parris Chang, John Despres, Victor Falkenheim, Sidney Greenblatt, Martin Whyte, and Akira Yamagiwa. "Lao Yang" kept both Dai Hsiao-ai and us alert with his frank criticism; Teng Wah never failed to raise interesting points for discussion. Jayne Montaperto offered many suggestions which improved the clarity of our prose. She also typed the manuscript. Finally, we are grateful to Ezra Vogel for his willingness to share his time and advice with us.

Thanks to the effort of all of these people, the errors in this book are undoubtedly fewer than might otherwise have been the case. For those which remain, we assume full responsibility. Similarly, we hope that no commentator will fail to separate us from the Fulbright-Hays Fellowship program and The University of Michigan Center for Chinese Studies, whose support made our stay in Hong Kong possible. In the following pages we speak only for ourselves.

INTRODUCTION

The Great Proletarian Cultural Revolution was a political "happening." Whatever China's leaders may have had in mind, for most of the nation's seven hundred million people, it existed as a sometimes frightening, sometimes inspiring, but always mysterious fact of life whose ultimate purpose remained hidden. Accordingly, popular reaction to it reflected a variety of changing patterns. Some individuals, while continually striving to predict how changes in the movement might influence their own lives, decided to seize what they viewed as an opportunity for advancement by participating actively. Others participated equally actively but were motivated . by more idealistic feelings of loyalty to Mao Tse-tung and to the fulfillment of the Chinese revolution. Perhaps the majority of individuals in this category were students. Finally, still other Chinese preferred to avoid the risks of political participation entirely and displayed only the minimum level of activism required for their own survival.

In this book we will explore the inner workings of the Cultural Revolution as a mass-oriented, political instrument by following the adventures of one young Chinese student whose commitment to principle dictated that he choose the path of active participation. To general readers, our effort is offered as an account of the movement which highlights its human side. To specialists, it is offered as a single detailed experience which may throw some light upon broader interpretations of the Cultural Revolution.

Dai Hsiao-ai, the pseudonym the Chinese student has chosen for himself, had in June 1966 completed all but one year of his senior middle school (senior high school) curriculum in the city of Canton, Kwangtung Province. He had just passed his seventeenth birthday when the Cultural Revolution began there in earnest in May. Over the next eighteen months, until he left for Hong Kong in November 1967, Dai served as head of one of his school's numerous Red Guard organizations, and thus was far more than a mere bystander or passive participant in the Cultural Revolution. His experience was accordingly rich in spite of his relatively low station in China's power hierarchy.

We asked Dai to write his memoirs soon after he settled down with relatives in Hong Kong, long before time might have blurred his recollections. We prompted his memory with fifteen broad questions, such as: "What was the relationship of your student group to workers?" "What kinds of persons became Red Guard leaders, and how were they chosen?" "Why did student factionalism produce such high tensions, and finally evolve into bloody fighting?"

Dai immediately balked. He preferred, he said, to follow the chronological development of the movement and to write more anecdotally. We effected a compromise in which Dai treated each of our crosscutting topical questions more or less chronologically. Ultimately we managed to obtain a series of ten- to fifteen-page essays outlining those experiences and impressions that he thought were most important and most relevant to each issue. Points which needed additional clarification, or which we expected would elicit sufficient interest to warrant pursuing in greater length, were afterward taken up in supplementary interviews. By the time of actual writing, Dai was spending nearly all of his waking hours in our office, and gaps in his narrative which only then became apparent were promptly filled as they appeared.

From the very beginning our purpose has been to present the events of the Cultural Revolution as they were seen through the eyes of an observer-participant. Thus, we have tried to reproduce Dai's story essentially as he told it. We have neither used his experiences as a point of departure for analyzing the movement as a whole, nor have we translated his vocabulary into more neutral, analytical terms in order to "correct" his biases. When we felt that his views on a given matter were too one-sided or that they differed markedly from other sources, we asked him to reconsider his position. If he expressed inability or unwillingness to change his stance, we felt obligated to remain true to his viewpoint. In the two or three cases where Dai was intransigent, we have tried to explain why this may have been so. In sum, the advantages of presenting one detailed, personal account of the Cultural Revolution seemed to outweigh the polluting of Dai's original materials with the current theories and fancies of either of us, even at the cost of failing to exploit them for all their interpretative worth.

Our own contributions, apart from translation, have therefore centered upon correcting chronological errors and inconsistencies in Dai's original account, rearranging his wandering, episodic essays into more topically unified chapters, adding supplementary text that serves to relate his particular experiences to over-all trends in the Cultural Revolution, providing explanatory notes, and probing for detail on points which, while second nature to him, remain unclear to non-participants. Inevitably, much of the book is written in our own third-person narrative to describe those parts of Dai's story which either were not cogently presented in his own essays or had to be assembled from several different discussions. Throughout the book, we have tried to clearly identify our words so that the reader will encounter minimum difficulty in distinguishing Dai's comments from our own.

The remainder of the work is expressed in Dai's own words. Two small but necessary liberties were taken in rendering these direct quotations. First, statements made originally in essay form and later amplified through supplementary interviews were combined into one "quotation." Second, Dai's highly repetitive style of Chinese prose was abbreviated and written in more readable English. We did not tamper in the least with his concepts, his language style (polite, vulgar, sarcastic, tongue-in-cheek, etc.), or content of statements.

An alternative to this book's approach to studying the Cultural Revolution is to try to reconstruct the larger picture by patiently piecing together statements from thousands of newspapers and radio broadcasts in combination with reports of visitors and other such sources. The single biography approach, which produces a lone, detailed, in-depth sample of the conduct of the movement, cannot be regarded as a substitute for such a systematic and comprehensive investigation. It is rather a supplementary exercise which portrays in microcosm the broad outlines suggested by official documentation. Practitioners of other, broader approaches will find that our in-depth information, far from challenging the conclusions drawn from their less personal sources, tends usually to verify their findings.

Dai's reasons for ultimately rejecting the Cultural Revolution late in 1967 are discussed fully in the concluding chapter. It need only be noted here that after arriving in Hong Kong, he moved into a protective environment of relatives. Thus, he was largely spared the experience of having been set adrift in a world that does not care, a common feeling among refugees from Communist society. The Communists could be as paternalistic as they were demanding or repressive. Regardless of what most refugees recall of the difficult aspects of life in China, they do seem to miss the care and concern expressed for them by the "small groups" and protective institutions to which they had to belong. By comparison, family life in Hong Kong was undoubtedly less encompassing (although definitely more so than the pattern familiar in the West).

In his less family-influenced attitudes toward the student life he left behind, Dai remains introspective. His position can only be described as vacillating. He often talks as if he is still a Red Guard fighting for the ultimate and absolute victory of Chairman

Mao's correct revolutionary line. When in such a mood he disdains the "rotten eggs" who opposed Mao in a variety of devious and subtle ways. He criticizes "revisionists" and "reactionaries" who failed to adopt the proper Maoist political spirit, and describes "mistakes" committed by people in factions not allied with his own. He even wrote one article in a (right-leaning) Hong Kong newspaper harshly criticizing the colony's own Communists for failing to absorb Mao's thought in a meaningful way. In short, he is still capable of a solid doctrinal, indeed at times doctrinaire, approach to analyzing political life in China.

On other occasions, by complete contrast, he rails against the overly doctrinaire Maoists for unnecessarily plunging their country into chaos for the purpose of petty political ambition. When in these moods, he doubts the sensitivity of mainland China politicians, satirizes absurdly simplistic Communist propaganda, and speaks regretfully of the arbitrary and unkind aspects of Mao's high-conflict politics. While changing his stance from day to day, Dai seems over the long run to be growing measurably more cynical about the Revolution. His questioning frame of mind, however, stops far short of accepting most non-Communist interpretations of recent events in China. After passing through a brief stage of examining analyses of the Cultural Revolution featured in Hong Kong's right-wing press, he rejected such sources entirely and took to reading the local Communist *Ta Kung Pao* exclusively. He did feel, to cite a single exception, that the research articles published in the Union Research Institute's relatively objective journal, *Tsu Kuo*, had improved considerably by mid-1967, after having failed miserably, in his view, to capture the spirit of the Cultural Revolution in its earlier stages.

For several reasons, we must regretfully avoid discussing many aspects of Dai Hsiao-ai's personal background and current situation which are relevant to interpreting his attitudes and his credibility. Risking the safety and tranquillity of people still living in China is too high a cost to pay for including such information. We should point out that once Dai learned his accounts would be constructed into a book-length manuscript, he took an even keener interest in the research project than he had displayed at first. He voluntarily supplied a higher level of detail in his essays; he went to greater lengths to verify exact quotes, dates, and names which could be located in available documentary sources in Chinese; and he revised a few episodes that he had written in rathec sketchy form at the beginning of the project. This will explain his apparent total recall of the content of central directives, the number of people present at meetings, and other smaller points as well.

Can Dai Hsiao-ai be believed? Overall, yes. On those occasions when an outside source could be found to corroborate his version of events, the high degree of correspondence was most reassuring. Most deviations in his account occurred in matters of chronology, which led us to invest a heavy proportion of our effort in firmly establishing the order of events in China. A second difficulty with his reportage we discovered (duplicating a similar difficulty in dealing with the Chinese Communist press) was Dai's tendency to mask important particulars of episodes by describing them in overly general terms. Thus, in translating Dai's statements into English we attempted to go behind the curtain of general expression ("they did," or "they thought . . .") to ask and find out exactly what individual or group in question was actually involved in a given situation. A third and final factor to consider in estimating (and accepting) Dai's credibility was his practice of keeping a diary in which notes on many episodes described in this book were originally entered shortly after they occurred. Even though one of the two volumes he filled during the Cultural Revolution (the later one) was left behind in China, the very act of taking notes itself undoubtedly constituted an important aid to his recall.

Having thus considered the approach's limitations, we hope readers will join us in viewing Mao Tse-tung's Great Proletarian Cultural Revolution through the eyes of this one young southern Chinese student who himself played an active part in it. We will follow Dai Hsiao-ai's course from May 1966 until November 1967, when his revolutionary path came to an end.

GORDON A. BENNETT
RONALD N. MONTAPERTO
August 1970

PROLOGUE

Dai Hsiao-ai: School Life Before the Cultural Revolution

The Kaochung Upper Middle School lies on a flatland in suburban Canton. Although the area is administered by the city, its farms and fishponds lend it a thoroughly rustic air, particularly when the students are away on vacation. Usually, the only sounds are those of farm animals blended with shouts from the athletic fields and the occasional lorry on its journey to or from Canton. It is a peaceful scene.

Viewed from a distance, the school might be mistaken for a cluster of farm buildings. One turns off the main road and enters through a high gate. A short drive leads to the auditorium, which lies within the U-shaped structure housing the classroom wings and the administrative offices. Behind the "U" are two dormitories for male and female students, the dining hall, and a group of storage sheds. The land falls away on both sides and behind to a high fence which forms the border of the school compound. Here are located the athletic fields and the vegetable patches which the students cultivate in their spare time. When not otherwise occupied, many students like to relax by strolling about the grounds. They are all proud of their school and most are very happy to belong to the student body.

Before the Cultural Revolution, their sense of pride and contentment was justified for reasons quite unrelated to the school's environment and facilities. Kaochung's students were an elite who were being trained at central government expense for administrative jobs in official organizations, industries, and businesses. The school's three-year program, while including some academic subjects, led to a terminal or final degree in practical studies which did not prepare students for the college entrance examinations. However, the lack of opportunity to attend college or university was more than compensated for by the certainty of a responsible job appointment immediately after graduation. The students knew also that they would escape assignment to the countryside for farm work, the fate of most young people in China who fail to enter college. Dai Hsiao-ai and his classmates were grateful for their opportunities and keenly aware that they had been admitted to this charmed circle of youth with a secure future from among a very large number of applicants.

I thought that the entrance examination was extremely difficult. I also knew that I would have to wait at least a month before hearing about my acceptance. I grew more worried as the deadline approached.

When I received my acceptance, my whole family was overjoyed. We had a party. Even so, it wasn't until I received notification to report for a medical examination along with a transportation voucher for Canton that I actually believed my good fortune. Later, I heard that only about thirty of my sixty fellow lower middle school graduates had been accepted for further education. I was the only one of a large number of applicants who had been accepted at Kao-chung. I was terribly lucky.

On the day of my departure, some friends came by to give me a tea party. I tried not to show how badly I felt for them by playing down the importance of schooling. We would all make an equal contribution to the revolution. They pretended to agree, but we were all very sad.

On the eve of the Cultural Revolution, Kaochung's students were happy and content. All seemed to be satisfied with their society and were deeply committed to serving it. Their satisfaction was reflected in the harmony and co-operation of their daily lives and by a remarkable absence of tension. If the demands of being both "red and expert" were high, such high standards were essential, they felt, to building a socialist nation. Because virtually all were happy to make this effort, the system worked.

Yet, within months, this closely knit and smoothly functioning unit was to be torn apart by the conflict of forces whose very existence would have been denied before the Cultural Revolution. The process of this disintegration forms a major part of Dai Hsiao-ai's story. Similarly, Kaochung provided the backdrop and organizational framework for most of Dai's subsequent activities. Since it will enhance the understanding of later events, it is appropriate to begin with a discussion of the school itself. The general reader, however, may prefer to move directly to Chapter One with its description of Dai's first impressions of the events which were to alter his life so thoroughly.

ORIGINS OF THE STUDENT BODY

Admission to Kaochung was determined according to a formula which sought to balance within the school academic excellence with political reliability. Before the storm of the Cultural Revolution broke, there were approximately 750 students ranging in age from seventeen to twenty-three; about 225, or 30 per cent of these, were females. Although students from rural areas may have constituted a slight majority, nearly every major city and every county of the province was represented among the student body.

The students' social class background also constituted a wide and representative mixture. Dai recalled that of the 750 students enrolled, approximately 30 per cent were drawn from the so-called "revolutionary classes," children of workers, poor peasants, lower-middle peasants, revolutionary martyrs, revolutionary cadres, or revolutionary soldiers. Another 10 per cent, at the opposite end of the spectrum, were selected from the "backward classes," children of landlords, rich peasants, capitalists, rightists, and "bad elements" (criminals, petty thieves, former convicts, unemployed loafers, etc.). Most of Kaochung's "backward class" students were children of landlords and rich peasants. The remaining 60 per cent of the students belonged to a middle group whom the leadership judged to have revolutionary potential because they accepted the leadership and program of the Party. Neither "revolutionary" nor "backward," these were children of doctors, shop clerks, teachers, technicians, and middle peasants.

In the later stages of the Cultural Revolution, the policies and the system of recruitment which produced a student body of this composition were to be condemned in the most vitriolic terms. However, on the eve of the movement, Dai and most of his classmates regarded it with both approval and satisfaction.

STUDENT RELATIONS AND STUDENT FACTIONS

Dai recalled that class origin was not a particularly potent influence upon student relationships. What conflict did exist was directed solely against students from the "backward classes" and seemed always to be spontaneous and rapidly dissipated.

In practice, there was no substantial difference between the positions of students of the "good classes" and those drawn from the middle group. All of the latter were eligible to stand for election to school or academic class offices and to apply for membership in the Young Communist League. Probably as many office-bearers and YCL members were drawn from this group as from the "revolutionary" strata.

Students from the "backward classes" had a slightly more difficult time. They were also eligible to hold office and to participate in all activities. However, on the infrequent occasions when they actually did apply, they were subjected to such careful scrutiny that they were seldom admitted. Thus, they almost never applied for anything. Most took the safest course and studied hard to earn good grades. This made it difficult to get at them even if someone wanted to. It was difficult to criticize a student whose grades were better than yours and who participated just enough to avoid criticism on political grounds. Apart from that, most of these people were really very good and deeply interested in their work. All of us fraternized together and generally got on well.

However, there was a subtle discrimination which is very difficult to define. "Backward" students lived under a cloud, and any mistake, whether related to politics or not, was certain to be interpreted in terms of their social class standing. For example, a foul committed on the basketball court might become "another manifestation of the rich peasant mentality" or something like that. Occasionally, tempers might flare and someone would be called a "landlord son of a bitch" or a "Kuomintang bastard." These occasions embarrassed us all. But the student who did the name calling was more apt to be criticized than the one who made him angry in the beginning. We all felt that these people had to be educated and we tried to win them over. Nobody held a grudge for very long, but it must have been difficult for them at times.

Students tended to cross class lines and to identify themselves on the basis of their linguistic and regional background. Dai identified five groups, consisting of students from Canton City, Shant'ou (Swatow), T'aishan, Hainan Island, and of Hakkas respectively, as the major factions within the student body.[1]

Frequently the members within these cohesive although informal groups would unite to defend a member who had been accused of some error irrespective of his class background; this was particularly so when the alleged offense was politically neutral. However, regional loyalties also prevailed in matters of political criticism, and an offender's home-town colleagues would assume responsibility for playing a leading role in either proving or disproving charges.

Most positions of leadership were in the hands of Hakkas and students from Shant'ou, since they were farthest away from home and consequently most willing to devote time to school activities.

> Students from Canton and T'aishan could go home frequently and nearly all of them did at least once each week. The distance and the expense made it difficult for the others. Those who remained behind invested their whole lives in the school and gradually assumed positions of leadership. It seemed natural; nobody felt any resentment about this.

THE FACULTY

Dai was hard pressed to recall details of faculty life and activities outside the classroom. He did note, however, that Kaochung's forty-five faculty members were divided into two groups on the basis of geographic origin, age, and experience. The smaller of the two included the then principal, the vice-principal, the heads of the school's five administrative departments, and five or six senior teachers. All were northerners whose association with the Communist Party had begun with the civil war of 1946–49.

A gap of nearly twenty years separated them from the majority of teachers, whose average age was around thirty-five. Nearly all of the younger teachers were natives of Kwangtung who had been in college themselves at the time of the Communist accession in 1949. Dai recalled that student relations with the senior group were formal and strained but that the younger teachers more than compensated for this by their friendliness and accessibility. On the whole, students and faculty formed a cohesive unit.

ADMINISTRATIVE ORGANIZATION

Before the Cultural Revolution, the principal and the vice-principal directed school affairs through a system of five administrative departments, the Student Association, the Young Communist League branches, and the Party branches. All authority was unified in the school's Party committee, of which the principal and vice-principal were secretary and deputy secretary respectively.

Administrative responsibility was divided functionally among five departments to cover every area of Kaochung's operation. The Teaching Research Department (*chiao-yen k'o*) concerned itself with planning the curriculum, evaluating teaching methods, writing course syllabuses, and selecting textbooks. Dai thought that a large proportion of the department's time was also spent in preparing reports for presentation to the higher levels of the educational bureaucracy. The department thus served as a link between the school and the provincial and central education authorities.

Because this department was far removed from the normal routine of student life, neither Dai nor any of his colleagues had much contact with it. Indeed, Dai could only guess that the number of its members lay between five and seven. He did know that the department chief was an older man from the north and that at least three members were full-time administrators. Beyond that, the department and its personnel remained a mystery.

In stark contrast, the Student Department (*hsueh-sheng k'o*) was an obvious, vigorous influence on student life. The department chief, a former army officer in his early thirties, was widely regarded as the best of the school's administrators. He and his five-man staff were responsible for political education, personal counseling, physical education, and relations with the People's Liberation Army, all of which brought them into direct contact with every student at least once each term.

Most political education was conducted outside the classroom in the form of individual study of important texts, seminars, and lectures and discussions; all such activities were led by students.

The physical education curriculum was organized in the same way. Since the Student Department supervised the students who led the political and physical education programs, its presence was felt throughout the school.

However, the greatest source of the department's influence was derived from its responsibility for personal counseling. Dai recalled that this term was interpreted in its widest sense to include discussion of everything from poor sportsmanship to poor grades. Failure to measure up in any area was sufficient to bring the student to the attention of the department chief. Usually, a class leader would present a report to the department outlining the problem and recommending a course of action. The chief would interview the student and either solve the problem on the spot or refer the offender back to his class or Young Communist League branch with suggestions for remedial action. Dai recalled that the most common form of therapy consisted of discussion of the origins of the problem. If the student was particularly recalcitrant, such sessions might become quite intense, but usually they were deliberately kept at a low key. When in the opinion of the students, the difficulty had been resolved, the department chief was called in for a final evaluation.

The close relationship between the Student Department and organization leaders ensured that no problem would go unnoticed for long, since every student participated in some form of organizational life. Also, the record of every student was reviewed at least once each year. By these devices, the school leadership was able to maintain a precise check upon the pulse of student life. It is not surprising that Dai and his classmates regarded the Student Department as a central force in their lives.

The Educational Affairs Department (*chiao-wu k'o*), comprising five senior teachers, worked very closely with the Teaching Research Department. The department exercised control of Kaochung's training program. Dai felt that in practice, the Educational Affairs Department also arranged the schedule of classes, established the teaching load for each instructor, composed examinations, and recorded its evaluation of each teacher's performance. Because these records were used to determine promotions, salary increases, course assignments, and other matters related to basic livelihood, every member of the faculty was concerned about his relations with the department chief.

The Educational Affairs Department, in co-operation with the Student Department, enforced academic discipline. Usually, its five members played the passive role of simply notifying a student of his low academic status and advising him to contact the Student Department for assistance. However, if special assistance or outside tutoring was deemed necessary, the department would assign a teacher to help him. Dai felt that because of its close association with class leaders and its control of the faculty, the Educational Affairs Department held second place after the Student Department as a direct force in student life.

Dai's recollection of the structure and duties of the two remaining departments was vague. The Labor Department (*laotung k'o*) was the smallest of the five with just three members, all of whom were teachers. Students spent the last month of every school term engaged in either farm or factory labor. The last two months of each student's last term before graduation were also spent in practical on-the-job training in one of the many government organs, factories, banks, or stores. The Labor Department assigned students to these different work posts, arranged for their transportation and housing, and forwarded reports of their performance to the Educational Affairs Department, where they were entered into the student's permanent record. Dai thought that the department met only infrequently, during the middle of each term just before the assignments were made. For the remainder of the time, it seemed to him, its members went about their regular teaching duties.

The School Affairs Department (*hsiao-wu k'o*), according to Dai's recollection, had seven members, making it the largest. However, he doubted that any of its members were teachers since it was concerned with such matters as school finances, paying salaries, buying food for the dining halls, and general maintenance of the physical plant. The department was located in the administrative wing, where students seldom had any reason to visit. Dai's knowledge of its operation came mainly from conversations with the seven members of the caretaker's staff, who were under its immediate supervision. He felt that its most vital function was to serve as a kind of secretariat which typed and mimeographed notices, examinations, and reports of various kinds for other departments. In practice, the students had no direct contact with this department.

Dai thought that, with the possible exception of the Labor Department, each administrative organ held a staff meeting at least once each week. Reports of these meetings were forwarded to the principal through the vice-principal and at times one or both of these men actually sat in on the meetings. Dai did not know whether or not they were ex officio members, but it is difficult to imagine that the heads of the school's Party organization faced any opposition to their presence at any meeting.

STUDENT ORGANIZATION

Student organization at Kaochung was complex and thorough. All 750 students automatically became members of the Kaochung Upper Middle School Student Association (hsueh-sheng hui) as soon as they enrolled. In the first days of each term, the Student Association met in general session to elect officers from among a list of candidates proposed by the officeholders of the previous year and approved by the Party committee. By indicating their approval or disapproval in a secret ballot, the general session elected a chairman (chu-hsi), two vice-chairmen (fu chu-hsi), and five general members (wei-yuan) who held office for one academic year. Each of the general members held special responsibility for a certain aspect of student activity; thus, there was a study member (hsueh-hsi wei-yuan), a labor member (lao-tung wei-yuan), a physical education member (t'i-yü wei-yuan), a culture and recreation member (wen-yü wei-yuan), and a student life member (sheng-huo wei-yuan). Dai recounted his election as an officer of the Student Association with some detachment. However, his description of the duties of the leading members of the Association reflected his appreciation of their importance and the respect with which they were regarded.

Elections for officers of the Student Association were not at all democratic. The outgoing members usually nominated those who already held office and then had the list approved by the Party committee. At the first general meeting early in the term, each student received a ballot with the names of seven candidates. If we approved, we placed a mark over the name; if we disapproved, we were to leave the space blank. There was also a space for write-ins but these, like "no" votes, were few in number. The list always included one first-year student who was chosen by the Party committee on the basis of the recommendation of the principal of his lower middle school. That is how I was chosen in my first year.

As soon as a candidate received majority approval, he was declared elected. We seven then organized ourselves according to the suggestions of the head of the Student Department, who would tell us that the Party committee thought that X would make a good chairman, Y might be a good labor member, and that Z was just right for assistant chairman. We always followed the suggestions.

The Student Association was an unwieldy body which only met two or three times each term. However, the officers met as an executive committee at least once every ten days. Since we influenced every area of student life, we were called school cadres (*hsueh-hsiao kan-pu*) and treated with respect.

As study member, I had three main jobs. First, I had to find out what students thought about their curriculum and their teachers. Second, I had to keep tabs on students who were in academic difficulty. Finally, I was in charge of the school's wall newspaper. I tried to include news of national interest as well as school news so that every student could keep informed of important events.

The labor member spent most of his time arranging work assignments, either for our on-the-job training, for our regular stint of labor participation at the end of the term, or for

our school vegetable patches. Perhaps too much of his effort
went into ordering, distributing, and keeping track of tools.
Of course, he also had to keep himself informed of student
attitudes toward labor participation and offer criticisms and
encouragement. When we were sent out to farms and factories,
he and the staff of the Labor Department arranged our living
accommodations, saw that we were fed, and reported on which
of the classes was doing the best job.

The physical education member worked as closely with the
head of the Student Department as I did. He decided who
would lead morning calisthenics, arranged intramural competitions, and assigned recreation space and equipment to different
classes. Frequently, he and the physical education instructors
arranged athletic meets with teams from other schools, banks,
factories, stores, and at times with the military.

The culture and recreation member seemed to spend most of
his time arranging songfests. In upper middle school, we
had no courses in music and many of us missed the chance to
sing revolutionary songs. The member would lead us in song
at all Student Association meetings and sometimes just for
fun in the evenings. More important were the opera and dance
shows he arranged. He saw that each class took its turn and
that its performance was up to standard. Since he used a
system of awards and prizes, his job was easier. Frequently,
we exchanged performances with other schools and, best of all,
with military units. The member spent quite some time arranging these programs.

The student life member had the most thankless job of all.
It couldn't have been much fun for him to have to listen
to endless complaints about the quantity and quality of the
food. He also tried to enforce a schedule of dormitory, classroom, and grounds cleaning for each class. It is hard to
think of scrubbing floors as "making revolution," and there
was some shirking. Besides all of that, he was always being
bothered with reports about broken windows and requests
for light bulbs. He seldom lost his temper even when his
efforts to sample student suggestions for improvements
prompted responses like "shoot the cook."

In our group meetings each of us tried to offer ideas to

the other so that all could have a good idea of what was going on. Almost every recommendation was actually a joint recommendation by all the members even though the member in charge of a particular area would actually present the report to the department concerned by himself and then follow up to see that it was implemented properly. I will say that the Party committee was very good about replying to our requests and recommendations as rapidly as possible. It seldom took more than two or three days to get an answer.

Students were also divided according to their year in the school and were generally referred to as first-, second-, or third-year students. Each year was divided into five classes (*pan*) with about fifty students in each. In all, the approximately 750 students were organized into fifteen semi-independent units whose members had classes, study halls, and recreation periods together.

Each class elected a leader (*pan chang*), an assistant leader (*fu pan chang*), and five general members who corresponded in title and function to the general members of the Student Association. Hence, each class had its study member, labor member, physical education member, culture and recreation member, and student life member elected by secret ballot, and with the approval of the Party committee, from among its members. Students were assigned to different classes at random.

Each class was further divided at random into five small groups (*pan hsiao-tsu*), each with ten members. The small groups elected a chairman (*hsiao-tsu chang*) and an assistant chairman (*fu hsiao-tsu chang*); again, all students were eligible for nomination and election to office.

In discussing the duties of the class officers, Dai emphasized their close relationship to the officers of the Student Association. The class officers were the lowest-level links in the chain joining students, faculty, and administration.

Because gathering information on student attitudes and opinions required so much time, we Student Association officers relied heavily upon the academic class organization, our counterparts at the class level. The class leader would open the weekly meeting with general announcements and then turn the chair over to each of the officers, who would call for comments and criticisms in their areas of concern. It was often difficult to get information, for students were afraid to say something that might cause them to be criticized. Also, there frequently wasn't very much to say. When the silence became overpowering, the officers would pose specific questions to specific individuals in the hope that something would develop. Later, the Student Association officers would meet with their counterparts at the class level to hear reports.

Such liaison meetings, however, were no substitute for actually getting out and talking to our fellow students. In my capacity as assistant leader of my class, I made a special point of talking with each of my classmates as often as possible. Whenever I came upon a problem, I could then mention it to the proper class officer or to an officer of the Student Association. Even though we were specialists, each of us tried to help the other. Communication was really very good at and among all levels.

I suppose one could say that the class officers were agents of information and that we Student Association officers received that information, evaluated it, and took such action as we deemed necessary. If a matter was serious, we reported it to the administrative department concerned and worked out a plan of remedial action which drew in the department head, ourselves, the class, and the small-group leaders. Less serious things were simply referred back to the class for action with the appropriate executive officer taking responsibility to see that the problem in question was solved.

There were two weak points in the system. The first and most important was the small groups. The leader and his assistant were too close to the members and so involved with them that they simply could not evaluate problems objectively. Many small-group leaders wanted to give up their jobs because of the strain their position imposed upon their relations with the other group members. Also, if the small group did not achieve a good record, it reflected upon them personally. I could see why they didn't like the job. I suppose that such tension was inevitable. The meetings, held three times each week, always involved criticism and self-criticism on such topics as record in study, participation in labor, and interpersonal relations. Since such problems were always related to political standpoint, and since having a good standpoint was so important, the tension was heightened. Individual members became angry with each other and not infrequently the whole group would get mad at the leader. People became edgy and lost confidence; performance was frequently bad. It was only our commitment to the higher goals of the Revolution which enabled us to put the bad feeling aside and strive for improvement.

The other problem was that the system made excessive demands upon our time. I probably spent an average of one and one half hours each day attending meetings. Look at the list. There were meetings of the officers of the Student Association, meetings of the class, meetings between class officers and officers of the Student Association, special meetings between me and all of the class-level study members, and, of course, my own small-group meetings three times each week. Finally, I had my weekly Young Communist League meetings to attend. I had to give up all of my evening study halls, and this, plus sheer exhaustion, caused my studies to suffer. Yet I had to do all of these things if the system was to work. I thought of it as my responsibility, as did all of my fellow officers. Sometimes we became so busy that we simply had to let things slide. When that happened, everybody co-operated by not mentioning the matter. We were all in the same boat.

On balance, it must be said that the student organizations had no real power. But we could and did exert influence by virtue of our administrative responsibilities. The Party committee would always back us up because, in effect, we were simply administering their decisions. They had to support us. As a result, our position was really something special. The absence of real power didn't bother us that much anyway. We were young and all of us recognized that we needed training in the techniques and principles of collective leadership. We thought of the student organizations as a training ground. Personally, I was glad to have the chance to develop my skills in this way.

THE CLASS SUPERVISORS

The direct contact between students and administrators was supervised and aided by the class supervisors (*pan chu-jen*). Each class was under the nominal supervision of such an official. Dai thought they were appointed by the Educational Affairs Department with the approval of the Party committee. Usually they were teachers of the more general subjects such as Chinese or mathematics, which helped them in making contact with students. Surprisingly, Dai recalled that political activism did not seem to be a factor in appointing class supervisors.

Their major responsibilities included keeping abreast of each student's over-all academic performance and making weekly examinations of the diaries each student was required to keep in order to anticipate individual deviations from generally accepted political thought. When either academic or political problems came to light, the supervisors reported them to the appropriate class officer and/or to the head of the Student Department if they felt them to be sufficiently serious.

In keeping with the Kaochung philosophy of allowing students to solve their own problems, the supervisors existed more to aid student communication with the administrative departments than to direct it. Usually, they played the passive roles of merely notifying the upper levels of problems and of attending class meetings, while the students themselves dealt with the business at hand. Dai recalled that the supervisors would always be asked to speak and to offer ideas and suggestions, but that they frequently declined the offer, saying that they would prefer not to influence the students too much.

Dai noted that Kaochung's class supervisors had definitely minor functions when compared to their counterparts at the lower middle school level and, for that matter, at other upper middle schools. This he ascribed to the high degree of development of student organization and the extremely active Young Communist League program. Since few of the supervisors were political activists, they served as a relatively neutral sounding board for student complaints and opinions. Dai recalled that all were liked and respected and that their relations with students were generally warm and close.

YOUNG COMMUNIST LEAGUE ORGANIZATION

The second most powerful organization in the school was the Young Communist League. All of Kaochung's YCL members were organized into a general branch (*tsung chih-pu*) which, like the Student Association, met only two or three times each term. The general branch elected a Young Communist League committee (*t'uan-wei*) from a list of candidates provided by the Party committee. The election procedure was identical to that of the Student Association, with the Party committee appointing candidates who had received the approval of a majority of the YCL membership. Dai recalled that the committee had seven members, a secretary, two vice-secretaries, an organization member, a propaganda member, a study member, and a student life member.

The League secretary was a teacher in his late twenties who had been seconded to the school from the army. Significantly, for purposes of Party control, he was also a Party member. The first assistant secretary was a teacher in his early twenties who Dai thought was probably an applicant for Party membership. The second assistant secretary and all of the committee members were older students whose ages probably averaged about twenty.

Since most of Dai's leadership activities were confined to the Student Association and his class organization, he was not well informed about the operation of the YCL committee. This curious lack of information, when coupled with his high degree of activism, indicates that the upper levels of Kaochung's organization tended to work in separate compartments with little or no exchange of information.

Dai thought that, as mentioned above, the League committee met about as often as did the executive officers of the Student Association and that on the whole, similar topics were discussed.

The general members of the League committee had the same functions as their counterparts in the Student Association except that they were concerned exclusively with YCL members. The obvious exceptions were, of course, the organization member, who supervised the mechanics of enforcing League discipline, induction of new members, and the transfer of membership to units outside the school, and the propaganda member, who prepared the texts used in YCL political study sessions. These, Dai reported, consisted largely of studying the history of China's youth movement, League history, the YCL constitution, and methods of leading the masses in all areas of activity.

Directly subordinate to the committee were the Young Communist League branches (*t'uan chih-pu*), which corresponded to the school's fifteen academic classes. Each branch was further divided into three or four small groups (*t'uan hsiao-tsu*) with between seven and eight members each. Dai recalled that twenty-three of the fifty students in his class were YCL members and thought the same conditions obtained throughout the school. Thus, just less than half of the student body were League members.

All officers of the Student Association were members of the Young Communist League, as were almost all of the class officers and class small-group leaders. Youth League organization, therefore, penetrated into every nook and cranny of the school and accordingly simplified significantly the processes of student mobilization and control.

> We League members were the most active students who played a leading role in all activities. Everyone expected us to set an example in deportment, study, and political activism; all of us were proud of our membership. We had hopes of entering the Party as soon as possible and knew that this would depend upon the record we made while in the Young Communist League.
>
> Once a week we participated in League Life (*t'uan sheng-huo*) meetings, where we discussed the texts chosen by the propaganda member of the YCL committee. These were part of a regular curriculum for all YCL members. Usually we

met in our YCL small groups with branch meetings coming second. The general branch met only for such matters as approving new members, hearing directives, and discussions of the League constitution. Since almost every school cadre was also a League member, our League Life meetings proved a good way of keeping up with events in the school.

Sometimes we would have special general branch sessions where events of unusual importance would be announced. I first heard about the Cultural Revolution in this way when the principal told us about a report on Lo Jui-ch'ing.* We had many privileges of this sort but our responsibilities were also greater. We received criticisms not only from our ordinary classmates but also from our fellow League members. This made our jobs twice as difficult, but most of us felt it to be worth the price.

PARTY ORGANIZATION

Kaochung's administrative departments, its student organizations, and its Young Communist League organization were unified, ordered, and directed by the local unit of the Chinese Communist Party. Considering that Dai was a school cadre, who frequently associated with Party representatives, he was relatively uninformed about Party organization and operation. (He was not included at highly secret Party meetings.)

He thought that fifteen of the school's forty-five teachers and two former servicemen who had been pensioned off as members of Kaochung's janitorial staff were members of the Party. These seventeen members were organized into a Party general branch (*tang tsung chih-pu*) which, like the Student Association and the Youth League general branch, was largely a formal organization without real power. The general branch elected the seven-man Party committee, which was the seat of ultimate authority.

* Lo Jui-ch'ing was chief of staff of the People's Liberation Army, secretary to the secretariat of the Party Central Committee, and vice-premier of the State Council. His purge became known in May 1966. The report mentioned by Dai was an advance notice of the purge.

Dai did not know how these elections were held or how individual members were assigned to different committee positions. He recalled that Kaochung's principal, a northerner named Chen, served as the committee's secretary (shu-chi) and that the vice-principal was the assistant secretary (fu shu-chi). The five remaining members were the chiefs of the administrative departments, an arrangement which guaranteed absolute Party control and rendered the principal, as Party secretary, the final authority on all questions. Administrative decisions in effect acquired the force of Party policy and were therefore beyond question, except by higher-level Party authorities.

His dealings with Kaochung's Party personnel led Dai to deduce that the committee had an organization member, a propaganda member, and a Youth League member, and probably some others.[2]

The students thought that the Party committee met formally twice each week and, more important, talked together every day. Since the Student Department chief made a large number of on-the-spot decisions, Dai reasoned that each member had a certain leeway in running the day-to-day affairs of his department.

Party members were organized into branches and small groups. Every Wednesday evening from seven to nine-thirty, Party members would hold Party Life (tang sheng-huo) meetings in the administrative wing or in the teachers' residence quarters. But students seldom, if ever, ventured into these places. The Party remained an elite organization whose operations were not publicized.

Despite their lack of specific knowledge, however, the students were keenly aware of the Party's presence and power. The heads of the administrative departments were members of the Party committee, which fact made the committee's control automatic and all-encompassing. The secretary of the Young Communist League was a Party member who reported directly to the Party committee. The Student Association and its subordinate organs were linked with the Party committee through the head of the Student Department. As secretary of the Party committee, Principal Chen supervised every aspect of his school's operation from curriculum development to academic discipline to student recreation. His word was, by definition, final.

It is meaningless to talk of any relationship between students and the Party. We had no relations with the Party. We all thought of it as a powerful but secret organization. I knew that certain teachers were Party members but I had no idea of what went on in meetings or how the Party worked. If some of the students were members, it might have been different for the rest of us, but this was not the case.

Party members, of course, had great prestige throughout the school. In fact, this led to friction among the teachers. Many teachers who had had good training and experience but who were not Party members were not promoted, while Party members were. The teachers who were not Party members resented this. When these tensions came out during the Cultural Revolution, I was amazed that they were so deep.

Nearly every teacher who was a Party member thought of himself as something special. Because I sensed this, I tried to avoid them. There were some exceptions, like the head of the Student Department and one or two others, but even in these cases, the distance between us was too great. They issued orders and we obeyed.

Mr. Chen, the principal and secretary of the Party committee, was a good example. When I first met him, I liked him and thought he was efficient. Later I discovered that his methods were very bad. He yelled at people, issued orders, and was very authoritarian. He used what he thought were military methods, but I knew that the military was not supposed to be that way. Actually, I thought that he was lazy in that he tried to get other people to do his work. He had his favorites among the teachers and always gave the Party members special treatment. Most of us students didn't think that this was fair. But he was the Party secretary and none of us would dare to question him in anything. I never realized how much he was disliked until the Cultural Revolution started. It was mainly because of him that I had this mixed attitude toward the Party.

THE DAILY ROUTINE

Dai's life moved with almost monotonous regularity within this organizational framework. The schedule seldom varied from day to day except when the students were engaged in labor or out of the school for on-the-job training. A typical day began and progressed as follows:

6:00 A.M.– 6:30 A.M.	Arise, wash, dress, organize notes for the day
6:30 A.M.– 7:00 A.M.	Calisthenics
7:00 A.M.– 8:00 A.M.	Individual study of the Works of Mao Tse-tung
8:00 A.M.– 9:00 A.M.	Breakfast
9:00 A.M.–12:30 P.M.	Classes
12:30 P.M.– 2:30 P.M.	Lunch and free time
2:30 P.M.– 5:30 P.M.	Classes
5:30 P.M.– 6:00 P.M.	Organized recreation
6:00 P.M.– 6:30 P.M.	Dinner
6:30 P.M.– 8:00 P.M.	Organized recreation
8:00 P.M.– 9:30 P.M.	Study Hall
9:30 P.M.–10:00 P.M.	Free time and bed

On Saturday, Dai's school day ended with the dismissal of classes at twelve-thirty. After luncheon, the students fulfilled their labor obligations by cleaning the school buildings and grounds, tidying their rooms, washing their clothes, and working in the school vegetable gardens according to a fixed schedule. Saturday evenings were given over to such recreational programs as operas, dance shows, or perhaps an exchange visit with the local PLA (People's Liberation Army) unit.

Sunday was the one day of the week Dai could call his own. Although he frequently used the day to attend to his myriad duties as a school cadre, he occasionally found the chance to slip away into Canton, where he saw a movie and sometimes dined at a restaurant.

CURRICULUM, GRADING, AND POLITICAL STUDY

Dai's courses reflected Kaochung's emphasis on training in administration and management. He also studied Chinese literature, Chinese and world history, mathematics up to and including solid geometry, and of course general politics. Each class period lasted for forty-five minutes, with a ten-minute break between classes. With the exception of general politics, there was at least one period of instruction in each subject each day. Instruction in general politics was given just four times each week, but since political instruction was also given in class, small-group, and Young Communist League meetings, the total time spent in political education was probably equal to nearly two periods per day.

In one sense, politics was at the core of our curriculum. A bad grade in general politics could mean expulsion. A bad attitude toward participation in political study at the class and small-group level was certain to bring trouble. In general politics we studied different kinds of social systems and their historical development. We learned about different kinds of exploitation in the capitalist system and how to analyze different classes. We also studied international relations and learned to interpret the actions of different countries in light of their social systems.

Much of the time was spent discussing the theoretical reasons for having this kind of study. You must understand that we were aware that many Western observers, particularly Americans, expected that my generation of Chinese would be less revolutionary than the earlier generation and that we would become like the Russians, whom we thought had lost the spirit of communism. This was the major justification for our spending so much time in political study. Actually, we thought that this attitude of the Americans was stupid and naïve. We frequently joked about it.

General politics was supposed to provide a guideline for other kinds of political training. Those exercises were so varied that we enjoyed them more than our classroom study.

Each morning every student and every teacher had to spend at least one hour in study of the writings of Mao Tse-tung. This was an inflexible rule and was never broken whether we were in the school or out in the farms and factories. We were supposed to continue the practice even when we were home on vacation. We all thought that this was important since it was the best way to learn the content of these works.

In addition to this, seminars were held at least once each month, sometimes at the class level and sometimes for the whole school, in which students and teachers who had made a good record in studying Mao's works would speak. Usually they talked about a specific problem that they had faced and then told us how they had applied Chairman Mao's thought to solve it. The Party committee decided who would speak and whether a particular seminar would be held for the whole school or for separate classes. I didn't particularly care for these seminars since they were time-consuming and frequently the speakers chose problems so personal that they were not of great use to the rest of us.

Also, about once per month the whole school would be called upon to participate in "Remember Bitterness and Think of Sweetness" (*yi k'u szu t'ien*) meetings. A student or a teacher or sometimes even a worker from a nearby factory would contrast the hard times he had suffered under the Kuomintang with present conditions. Sometimes these accounts were very moving; I almost always came away with a feeling that I owed a great deal to the Party and to Chairman Mao for making things so much better for me. It was really a good way of building loyalty for it seemed that my own difficulties were minor when compared with the things that the older generation had suffered.

We also participated in practical programs designed to ensure that we maintained our political activeness. For example, we spent one month of each term on farms where we lived and worked with poor and lower-middle peasants. We were supposed to learn how they thought so that we could emulate them in our own work. We did everything from carrying water to tending babies. It was fun for the first few days each time and a welcome change from the routine of classes.

But after a while we always grew to dislike it. The peasants were so backward and conditions were so difficult that it was hard to work. Even the most active students usually were ready to leave after a week or so.

All students and teachers received militia training. The PLA would send instructors to each school in turn and give basic instruction in the firing of rifles, machine guns, and small mortars. We also learned bayonet drill as well as some elementary maneuvers. I really enjoyed this aspect of our training since it made me feel that I was really a part of the army and that I had a real function to perform. We all felt that way, even the girls.

We spent a lot of time with the PLA. Between militia lessons, exchange visits, joint athletic meets, and joint recreation parties, we got to know many of the soldiers very well. An air force unit was stationed nearby, making such exchanges quite convenient. We would mingle with the troops, ask them questions, and try to emulate them. We all had great respect for the PLA.

We were constantly evaluated and criticized on our performance in all of these activities as well as in our regular studies. Part of this was done through the structure of our student organizations but the main force came through competition to be selected as a "Four-Good Class" (*szu-hao pan*) or a "Five-Good Student" (*wu-hao hsueh-sheng*).[8] The competition was very keen, for members of such classes and especially Five-Good Students could look forward to the best work assignments after graduation. Toward the end of the year, the officers of each class met and drafted a report on its performance. The officers of the Student Association examined the reports and recommended certain classes for the Four-Good designation. The Student Association then met in general session and voted on the recommendations. As soon as the Party committee approved, the designation was made official by Principal Chen at an all-school awards ceremony. Five-Good Students were chosen in much the same way. The small-group leaders would recommend one or two members each, we class officers would make a selection, and then the class would vote its approval or disapproval. The Party

committee of course made the final decision, which was also
announced at the awards meeting. Once we held a "red pairs"
(*i tui hung*) movement, which was a great success. We got
the idea from the PLA, which had the same custom. Each
of the students in a class would be paired and would constantly criticize and check each other on the requirements
for being selected as a Five-Good Student. If both students
were so designated, they became known as a "red pair." Such
competitions were extremely effective, first because the large
majority of us really wanted to excel in politics, and second
because we all knew that our future advancement would be
affected. We all tried our best and any student who slacked
off was subjected to great pressure to do better.

Dai could not recall even one day during which each student
did not participate in some form of political training. Militia training was generally integrated within the physical education curriculum, while other activities of a political nature were scheduled
either for the evening during periods that were otherwise reserved
for study hall or during recreation periods.

Including formal classroom study, each student spent about
three hours every day in some form of political training.
If these activities cut into our study time, we had to make
it up. This meant that we would bolt our meals or stay up
after lights out. Sometimes classes were canceled but such
time was usually set aside and planned for when the curriculum
was set up. Our regular classes were seldom interrupted. Because I was an officer both of my class and of the Student
Association, I spent about four and one half hours each day
in these activities. The pace was killing but somehow I managed. It seemed to be my responsibility.

Dai's teachers followed the traditional method of lecturing and
assigning outside work. Students were expected to prepare lessons
and turn their notebooks over to the teachers for inspection. Weekly
examinations were given more as a means of encouraging students
to maintain their preparation than as a means of grading. Dai was,

however, subjected to the usual mid-term and end-term examinations; it was performance on these that determined a student's grade.

A student needed an average grade of 60 per cent out of a possible 100 per cent to qualify for promotion or graduation. Naturally, those with the highest averages and the best political recommendations received the best jobs. This was a powerful incentive for good performance. Curiously, few students failed to receive promotion or to graduate. A few less able students were occasionally held back for one or two years but all ultimately finished the course. Failure was virtually unknown and even students who had not attained the required average were usually promoted with the understanding that their deficiencies would be compensated for by extra work.

It was unthinkable that anyone would reach his third year and yet not graduate. Any student who had difficulty with his studies was noticed immediately and given all the help he needed. The Student Association and class organization saw to that. The teachers also knew that some of us were more talented than others; if a student was less than bright, they would simply give him the minimum grade for passing, provided that he did his part and worked hard. They were under pressure to provide a certain number of graduates every year and a large number of failures might reflect upon them in a bad way.

If a student was simply lazy and didn't work, he ran into trouble. He was surrounded by people who constantly criticized his behavior and probably forced him into studying even if he didn't want to. In extreme cases, we might cut him off entirely and he would soon leave the school. This hardly ever happened since the pressure of the small groups and the YCL was too intense. Students always worked hard. To fail would have been counterrevolutionary.

In one sense, grades really didn't matter, although high grades were essential to being sent to a good first work post. Because our training was practical, performance on the job was what really counted in determining our future advancement. There was an adequate number of jobs for all. Demand

was so great that we knew we would be assigned somewhere
even if our grades weren't too good. Even so, this did not
cause us to relax. We thought that it was our duty to do well,
and most of us tried our very best.

It was the prevalence of such a spirit that in Dai's view distinguished Kaochung from thousands of other middle schools around
the country. He felt that the high political enthusiasm there enabled
the students to move forward through the morass of nagging tensions
arising from ceaseless criticism, the pressure of meetings, a heavy class
schedule, and the frustration of dealing with the domineering Principal Chen. Dai and his classmates found strength in perceiving
themselves as unique.

It wasn't only the special program that made us different
from every other school in Canton. In fact, our school's
organization and structure were probably not terribly unlike
all of the others'. Our uniqueness came from within. It made
us possibly the most revolutionary and politically aware student body in all of Canton.

First, even to consider applying for admission, one had to
have a strong desire to engage in practical work. Very few
students ever thought of using Kaochung as a crutch in case
they were refused admission at a more academic school.
We all wanted to get down to work as quickly as possible.
None of us were theoreticians. All we cared about was implementation and results.

Second, we were all deeply committed to building the
country and to completing the revolution as quickly as possible.
I don't know why, maybe it was because of all the political
indoctrination we had received. It was impossible to deny that
we had it. Naturally, other students had it too, but perhaps
because they thought they could make a more significant
contribution, they preferred to go to college, where they almost
always seemed to become flabby and somehow lose their resolu-
tion.

Kaochung gave us our chance. We were doing exactly what
we wanted to do, and at the expense of the nation. On

the one hand, this made us grateful, while on the other, it caused us to develop a sense of obligation. Ultimately, it had the effect of reinforcing our dedication and caused us to work even harder. In situations where other students lost hope, we kept moving forward. We thought of ourselves as the ones who would actually keep China moving. Because we were thankful for our opportunities, including the material comfort, we felt a greater sense of responsibility. We always strived to set the best example possible. Students from other schools noticed this and usually treated us with a certain special respect. When we noticed it, it inspired us to new heights of enthusiasm. Just before the Cultural Revolution, I felt that there was nothing we could not accomplish if we tried. We all felt this way. We were ready for anything.

The following chapters relate how this revolutionary spirit gradually shed the shackles of organized authority and how, as each link was cast off, the young revolutionaries displayed increasing independence. As the organization of the Kaochung Upper Middle School slowly collapsed, Dai and his classmates turned their attention more and more away from the school compound and out into the world beyond. However, each of their actions was to bear the unmistakable mark of the cohesiveness, the high sense of purpose, and the capacity for meticulous attention to organizational detail which characterized Kaochung and its students on the eve of the Cultural Revolution.

CHAPTER ONE

The Cultural Revolution Comes to Kaochung Middle School

From November 1965 until May 1966, China's literary and artistic circles were caught up in a debate over proper methods of interpreting history. It was essentially an allegorical debate, for the issues transcended matters of literary interpretation and touched primarily basic questions of China's political, economic, and social organization. By May 1966 the conflict had been largely settled in favor of the radical followers of Mao Tse-tung. The Maoists immediately accused certain Party officials at all levels of opposing the Party chairman's educational, economic, and political policies. Thus the Cultural Revolution began. Dai Hsiao-ai at first participated wholeheartedly but in July became convinced that the movement had been recaptured by the anti-Maoist segment of the Party and degenerated into a sham. He therefore challenged Kaochung's Party organization, an action which hastened its destruction, and earned for himself a leading position in the school's movement.

NOVEMBER 1965–MAY 1966: ORIGINS OF THE STRUGGLE

In mid-November 1965 Dai Hsiao-ai and his schoolmates were preparing for their end-term examinations. Before them lay the prospect of winter vacation, reunion with their families, and a well-earned rest. As Dai clipped items for his school's wall newspaper, he became increasingly aware of the existence of a debate within literary and artistic circles in Peking and Shanghai. At the time, it seemed just another bit of "politics at the center" to be duly noted, studied, and discussed. He did not regard it with particular interest.

> We had been hearing things about a revolution in culture and art since 1964. We sometimes discussed this in our spare moments. It seemed to be a dispute among experts that did not concern us directly.

Unknown to Dai, this debate reflected disagreements within the highest levels of China's leadership which were soon to emerge full-blown into the Great Proletarian Cultural Revolution. The issues must be at least briefly sketched so that events in the Kaochung Middle School can be interpreted in proper perspective.

It began on November 15, 1965, when Yao Wen-yuan, a protégé of Chiang Ch'ing (Mrs. Mao Tse-tung), published his "Criticism of the Revised Historical Play *Hai Jui Dismissed from Office*," by Wu Han, in the Shanghai newspaper *Wen Hui Pao*.[1]

Yao charged Wu Han, a scholar and at that time deputy mayor of Peking, with being a dangerous class enemy who deliberately misinterpreted history to blunt the development of class consciousness and recognition of the need for class struggle among China's people. This statement can be viewed with validity as the essence of what came to be known as the radical position that spawned the revolution.

Other commentators held that Wu Han had made serious mistakes in his interpretation of historical data but that he should

not be considered a class enemy. Still others jumped to his defense
in a more aggressive manner and completely exonerated him of any
fault. These views came to represent the conservative position.

Both sides argued in the national press through December 1965
and into February 1966, when the issue came before the central
authorities for adjudication. On February 3, 1966, the so-called
Group of Five in Charge of the Cultural Revolution met under the
leadership of P'eng Chen, then mayor of Peking and secretary of the
Peking Municipal Party Committee. In all, eleven major Party
leaders were reported to have been in attendance. The group's report
was approved by the Party Central Committee on February 12,
1966.[2]

Although the "February Outline," or the "February Report"
as it came to be known, condemned Wu Han for his bourgeois world
outlook, it bore an unmistakably conservative stamp. The dispute,
it said, was to be resolved, not by discussion of the political viewpoint of individual authors like Wu Han, but by improving the
general level of professional competence of China's historians. Wu
Han's political mistakes were seen as the direct result of his misin-
terpretation of historical data; similar mistakes could be avoided if
historians were more thorough in collecting information and cultivated a deeper understanding of historical materialism. A series of
draft "model articles" was to be published to provide the necessary
guidelines. The conservatives, headed by P'eng Chen and his supporters in the Peking Municipal Party organization and the Party
Central Committee, had thus carried the day by turning the focus of
debate away from questions of political viewpoint and toward
methods of raising the general level of historical research and
criticism.

However, the Report met with opposition by the Chiang
Ch'ing group within the central leadership. Throughout March and
into April they marshaled their forces for the counterattack which
clearly had to be launched against the Peking Party authorities. On
April 16, 1966, they struck. *Peking Daily* (*pei-ching jih-pao*) and
Front Line (*ch'ien hsien*) *Magazine*, both official publications of
the Peking Municipal Party Committee, published criticisms of a
series of articles written in 1961 and 1962 by Wu Han, Teng T'o,

and Liao Mo-sha and known under the general title of *The Three-Family Village* (*san chia ts'un*). Also criticized was Teng T'o's *Evening Chats at Yen Shan* (*yen-shan yeh hua*).[3] All three writers had powerful connections with the Peking Municipal Party Committee and the Peking municipal government. That they should be criticized by the voice of the very organizations in which their power was based revealed that the entire complex of Peking's governmental and Party organs was under attack. The counteroffensive of the Maoist radicals had begun to bear fruit.

THE FIRST THREE WEEKS OF MAY: EARLIEST REVOLUTIONARY ACTIVITIES AT KAOCHUNG

Acting upon their newly gained initiative, the radicals immediately began to pressure local Party committees into concrete action. It was in the first week of May 1966, when Principal Chen called a meeting of all school cadres and Young Communist League members, that Dai first realized that he had underestimated the significance of the debate which he had been covering so casually for Kaochung's wall newspaper.

At the end of April, it seemed to us that all literary, art, and some university circles were in the midst of repudiating Wu Han and *The Three-Family Village*. The newspapers were full of it. We simply assumed that the two-year stream of criticism had reached a peak. We speculated that the conflict might turn into a movement involving students at our level, but it was only an idea. The meeting came as a complete surprise. Such things were rare, especially on such short notice. When the principal told us that our school was about to begin participation in the Cultural Revolution by launching a movement to repudiate Wu Han and *The Three-Family Village*, I was amazed. It was completely unexpected. Although Chen did not cite any specific directive, we all realized that he must have had some sort of authorization from higher levels. He would never have dared to mobilize us on his own. We likewise assumed that other schools would be doing the same thing.

That first meeting was very brief. Chen reminded us that our special positions as school cadres and YCL members carried a special responsibility to provide active leadership. He also announced that an all-school meeting would be held on the next day to lay the groundwork. We were very much in the dark, but still in an excited frame of mind. Within a very short time, the whole school was buzzing.

On the next day, Dai recalled, the principal convened an extraordinary meeting of the entire school. Here he presented a report which answered many of the questions that had been raised in his meeting with the activists on the night before. He outlined a wide-ranging, but rigid, plan of activities which allowed for very little student initiative. This tight control and the inability of the students to personalize the distant and virtually unknown phenomena of Wu Han and *The Three-Family Village* were, in Dai's opinion, responsible for the formalism and early decline of the first stage of the movement.

The principal first called our attention to the numerous accounts of the criticisms of *The Three-Family Village*. He accused Wu, Teng, and Liao of using their positions to attack the Party and of seeking the restoration of capitalism. He cited the high tide of criticism to show that conditions were excellent for a counterattack against this bourgeois line and emphasized our responsibility to unite, criticize, and defend the Party and the nation.

Each of us was to write big-character posters (*ta tzu pao*) containing accusations and denunciations of revisionists. We were also supposed to write analyses of the present situation stating our opinions on its causes and how it could best be rectified. Finally, we were to write essays summarizing our experiences and what we had learned.

All afternoon classes were suspended and the time given over to writing, while in the evenings we were to meet with our class small groups to discuss and to criticize the materials we had written. It was all scheduled in advance. Yet, even though we had no say in the matter, we were all very excited and eager to begin.

Dai and the other class and small-group leaders spent the remainder of the day discussing the principal's report, while ordinary
students waited for the activities to begin.

On the afternoon of the third day, we turned our classrooms
into meeting halls and all wrote big-character posters. Most
of us simply copied things from the *People's Daily* and other
newspapers. Since I had been in charge of the wall newspaper
and was better informed than most students, I faced an endless
barrage of questions. The school had a large supply of paint,
ink, and paper, which made our job very easy. Each small-
group leader had to make certain that his students had a
constant supply.

Dai and his schoolmates spent two full days and evenings on
this work. The students had decided that it might be best to write
all of the posters and essays first and then discuss them together;
apparently there was no objection from above to this change of
schedule.

When the writing had been completed, the students began discussion sessions. Dai reported that the time was more or less equally
divided between discussion of essays and posters written by the
students and the convening of condemnation meetings (*sheng-t'ao
hui*) where Teng, Wu, and Liao were struggled against and threatened with immediate and violent extinction.* Usually discussions of
posters and essays were conducted within the small-group structure

---

* The term "struggle" has a very special meaning in the context of Maoist political behavior, different from the understanding of "struggle" in the limited sense
of conflict, difficulty, or strife. In China, "struggle" is a formally defined process
in which the target, usually a political offender, is subjected to charge after
charge with ever increasing emotional intensity until he admits his guilt.
Yet the purpose of the struggle process is more than just punitive. Rather it is
intended to provide the target with a starting point from which to begin actual
political and ideological remolding. Similarly, those who attack are also expected
to learn as they do so and thereby to improve their own political and ideological
competence. Struggle in this almost autistic sense of acting upon a person or the
environment in order to effect a basic change and realize a specific objective is a
basic element of Maoist political style. Thus, for example, one encounters such
terms as "the struggle to increase coal production," "the struggle between the
enemy and ourselves," and "the struggle for Party rectification." Throughout this
book, we use the term "struggle" in this wider Maoist sense.

of each class with occasional sessions of the entire class. Condemnation meetings were always convened by class officers, although two or more classes frequently joined together. After the first two days of such activity, the students implemented the original schedule of writing in the afternoon and meeting in the evening.

The high tide (*kao ch'ao*) lasted for four days. Shortly afterward, Dai noted that student enthusiasm and morale had begun to fail.

> At first, big-character posters were fun. We would write our individual posters together and exchange ideas about the best kinds of criticisms. There was a kind of competition to see who could write the best one. However, we knew nothing about Teng, Wu, or Liao; they seemed distant and few of us had even read their essays. All of our information came from the newspapers. We just copied phrases and accusations from them and incorporated them into our posters. Discussions of our essays were the same. We read the newspapers, saw what lessons we were expected to learn, and got ideas of how the case should be treated. We then wrote these ideas into our own essays. There was nothing else that we could do. All we knew was what appeared in the news and we could only say that something was good or bad. We wanted to criticize in a deep way but could not do so.
>
> The condemnation meetings also suffered from this fault. Most of the time we just shouted slogans like "Teng T'o, surrender or be destroyed," "Destroy *The Three-Family Village*," "Wu Han, you are a son of a bitch," and "If you were here, we would exterminate you." After ten days of this, even the most active among us grew tired. We began to tell jokes in our meetings. Some people stopped attending entirely and dozed instead. We continued for about eight more days but nobody was deeply involved any more. We thought that the end was in sight.

Dai was perplexed when, after expressing this feeling to an older teacher, the man smiled and told him that this was just the calm before the storm. Dai knew of the teacher's past experiences and began to wonder. He did not have long to wait, for events in

Peking soon forced a qualitative change in the direction of the movement in the school and elsewhere.

While Dai Hsiao-ai and his classmates were attacking *The Three-Family Village* and pondering the meaning of the lull in events, the radicals in Peking had maintained the pace of their activities. Having gained the initiative by agitation at the local level, they now pressed the attack against P'eng Chen with renewed vigor. On May 16, 1966, the Party Central Committee issued a Circular which was published in the *People's Daily* on the following day.[4]

The May 16 Circular repudiated the February Report and dissolved the Group of Five. P'eng Chen himself was indicted for taking a rightist line, attempting to obscure class lines, and for subverting the class struggle then taking place. The Maoists further consolidated their position by establishing a new Central Cultural Revolution Group directly supervised by the Standing Committee of the Party's Politburo. Rejecting the notion that the debate over *The Three-Family Village*, as Wu Han, Teng T'o, and Liao Mo-sha had come to be known, was an "academic problem," the Circular set the issues at hand squarely within the framework of class struggle:

> The present struggle centers around the issue of implementation of or resistance to Comrade Mao Tse-tung's line on the Cultural Revolution. . . . Comrade Mao Tse-tung opened up the way for the proletariat on the cultural and ideological front long ago. . . . Yet the Outline maintains that Mao Tse-tung's thought has not yet opened up the way for us and that the way has to be opened up anew. Using the banner of "under the guidance of Mao Tse-tung's thought" as a cover, the Outline actually attempts to open up a way opposed to Mao Tse-tung's thought, that is the way of modern revisionism, the way for the restoration of capitalism. . . . It is necessary at the same time to criticize and repudiate those representatives of the bourgeoisie who have sneaked into the Party, the government, the army, and all spheres of culture, to clear them

out or transfer them to other poistions. Above all, we must
not entrust these people with the work of leading the Cultural Revolution.[5]

The masses were called upon to take up the challenge, attack
those whom the center defined as "monsters and ghosts," and deprive
them of power. Attacks on distant, unknown, and depersonalized
figures like Teng, Liao, and Wu were to be replaced by face-to-face
struggle against well-known individuals in all areas of Chinese life.

Dai's evaluation of the principal's response to the new central
directive is significant in that it culminated in outright defiance of
Chen's orders. Dai felt that, because the principal lacked a clear
notion of the meaning of the term "monster and ghost," and because
he was fearful that he himself might be denounced, Chen chose the
relatively safe course of targeting individuals with records of past
mistakes. Thus, he called his Party committee into session and
selected for attack an older teacher in his forties who had been
denounced in the anti-rightist campaign of 1957, and a young teacher
of literature in her twenties whose "bad" family background placed
her under suspicion. These were to be Kaochung's "monsters and
ghosts." Later in June, Dai felt that the principal's fear, having
turned into overt panic, prompted him to assume even tighter control of the movement. And this ultimately sparked the first student
challenge to Principal Chen's authority.

Unfortunately, it is impossible either to confirm or to refute
Dai's interpretation of Chen's motivation. However, Chen's actions
were consistent with what was known about Party behavior at the
time. It must be remembered that the principal's authoritarianism
was resented by Dai and a large proportion of his fellow students.
In addition, other local Party leaders were being subjected to identical charges at the same time. Thus, the students may have been
doubly inspired by their long-standing hostility to Chen as the
Kaochung Party leader to challenge his authority. Dai vehemently
denied this and, to be sure, a significant number of his fellow
students agreed with his evaluation. On the other hand, the principal
may indeed have been dominating the movement in order to protect
himself. Certainly his position was precarious, and the charge of

using one's position to insulate oneself from criticism had been frequently leveled against persons in authority during past movements. Whatever the truth of the matter, the fact remains that Dai and his colleagues felt strongly enough about the situation and Chen specifically to make an active and public challenge; more important, as will be seen, the provincial Party authorities backed them to the limit.

In any event, at the time of the publication of the May 16 Circular during the last week of May, Dai recalled that the movement had virtually petered out. However, the denunciation of the two teachers by the school Party committee immediately, albeit briefly, restored student spirit and enthusiasm.

> Everything changed with the denunciation of the two teachers. We became more active than before. Since we were all about eleven or twelve during the anti-rightist campaign in 1957, we had never before had the opportunity to participate personally in a political movement. We were therefore very eager and full of enthusiasm.
>
> On the day after the principal denounced the teachers at an all-school meeting, every wall of the school was covered with big-character posters. This time, we were not as indifferent as we had been when the target was Wu Han and *The Three-Family Village.* Each of us wrote at least ten posters on that day.

Dai reported that in contrast with the content of the posters of the first stage of the movement, the content of these reflected the students' firsthand knowledge of the behavior of the two teachers.

They accused the older man of not having completely repudiated his bourgeois ideas. Ever since his denunciation in 1957, he had eschewed even the slightest participation in politics, a sure sign, in the eyes of the students, that he retained his old thoughts. In attacking the woman, the students concentrated upon her preference for pretty dresses. Examples of the teachers' conduct were cited as proof of their bad attitudes and then followed by a demand for reform. The posters differed only in the examples chosen.

The teachers almost immediately became virtual prisoners. They could not leave the school grounds without the permission of the Party committee. Dai recalled that they were expected to spend their time reading the highly critical posters and composing replies. The students then judged them on their progress toward reform. This resulted in new accusations and new replies in the form of self-criticism by the teachers in a seemingly endless cycle.

Dai much preferred the medium of the struggle meeting (*tou-cheng hui*) to the reading of confessions as a means of keeping abreast of the latest developments in the school movement. Every three to four days, the principal would call a general school meeting where selected students and teachers would summarize developments that had occurred since the last meeting, evaluate the self-criticisms made by each of the teachers, and make new accusations based upon the shortcomings revealed in the documents. Such meetings, Dai reasoned, enabled all students to remain in touch with the movement's evolution, provided each with some idea of the themes to be incorporated into subsequent criticism, and enabled the principal and his Party committee to exercise direction and control.

Using these guidelines, the students would continue to confront the teachers in face-to-face struggle.

> The struggle was always very intense. We forced the teachers to wear caps and collars which stated things like "I am a monster." Each class confronted and reviled them in turn with slogans, accusations, and injunctions to reform their ways. We made them clean out the toilets, smeared them with black paint, and organized "control monster teams" (*kuan niu-kui tui*) to see that it was done properly. We would charge them with specific mistakes and not relent until they admitted they were true. It took nearly a week of constant struggle to make the man admit he had said "Mao was wrong" in conversation with one of his fellow teachers. They had little rest and were forced to sleep apart from their fellow teachers. We would join into informal groups, raid their quarters, and begin to work on them again. They could not escape us.

After about two weeks, we were afraid that the literature teacher would kill herself. We kept her under constant surveillance and even wrote a poster and attached it to the mosquito net over her bed reminding her that she was being watched and could not succeed in committing suicide.

Dai recalled that he and other students experienced remarkably little remorse over the teachers' treatment. They were surprised at how quickly their former respect for them was replaced with a new feeling of intense hatred.

Most of us felt that these two teachers were good in their work and were extremely surprised when they were accused of their crimes. We found it difficult to believe that they could have done such things; I was disillusioned.

However, we never once doubted their guilt. We trusted the Party and did not feel it could have made a mistake. While we respected them before, our feelings changed to hatred as soon as they were denounced as "monsters and ghosts." We felt that this was our duty and we showed them no mercy.

In the beginning, I had mixed emotions. I was particularly close to the literature teacher and had always thought that she was a good person and an excellent teacher. At first I was unwilling to criticize or to struggle against her, but my classmates accused me of being sentimental and warned me that I was becoming like her. They even told me that I was headed for trouble. I gradually realized that they were right. The Party could not be wrong and it was my duty to join in the struggle. I did so and eventually with enthusiasm.

Although Dai and his schoolmates continued to attend classes in the morning, afternoons and evenings were thoroughly taken up by the movement. After lunch, the small groups met, as before, for poster writing and struggle. Evenings were used in much the same way with the students conducting struggle sessions, evaluating the teachers' self-criticisms, writing more posters, and, at least once each week, writing essays on the movement's contribution to their own political education. These were read aloud in small-group meetings and criticized; occasionally the better ones were posted on the wall newspaper. This pattern of activity began during the last week in May and continued until the second week of June. Yet it was in the first week of June that events in Peking prompted actions in the school which led to the collapse of Principal Chen and his Party committee.

JUNE 1966: THE CHALLENGE TO THE PARTY COMMITTEE

The Maoists now turned their attention to a thorough reorganization of the Peking political scene. On June 1, 1966, the *People's Daily* published an editorial entitled "Sweep Out All Monsters and Ghosts" which compared a "proletarian" cultural revolution with a "bourgeois" cultural revolution. Naturally, the call was for the implementation of the former. On the next day, the paper published a big-character poster written by Nieh Yuan-tzu, a lecturer in philosophy, and six students of Peking University's Philosophy Department under the title of "Sung Shih, Lu P'ing, P'eng P'ei-yun, What Are You Up To in the Cultural Revolution?", along with favorable editorial comment. The three Peking University and Party officials were accused of placing obstacles in the way of mass criticism and of trying to direct and contain mass criticism for their own ends. In short, they were accused of behaving like "monsters and ghosts."[6]

Public tension increased when on June 4, 1966, *People's Daily*, in line with the call of the May 16 Circular to "criticize and repudiate those representatives of the bourgeoisie who have sneaked into the Party, the government, the army . . ." etc., announced both the dismissal of P'eng Chen as secretary of the Peking Party Committee and a thorough reorganization of that prestigious organization.

Dai recalled that these events wrought a marked change in the principal's behavior. The message of the Peking editorial barrages was unmistakable: "Monsters and ghosts" in local units were now and in the future to be denounced by name. Principal Chen, afraid, in Dai's opinion, that he might be next, called another meeting of his Party committee to denounce seven more teachers, three as rightists and four as "bad elements" who had committed serious mistakes in the past. Dai felt that Principal Chen had by now panicked and hoped to use the seven teachers to insulate himself from criticism.

The regular pattern of denunciation and struggle against the new targets occupied the students through the third week of June. However, the actions of the principal and the Party committee came gradually, and for the first time, to be regarded with skepticism, suspicion, and even outright hostility.

Dai and a large number of his activist colleagues were mystified by the denunciation of the additional seven teachers, since all were popular and enjoyed a reputation for competence, dedication, and fair play. That now a total of nine of Kaochung's most esteemed teachers should emerge as "monsters and ghosts" strained the students' heretofore willing acceptance of Party omniscience. The strain intensified when students returning from weekly visits home reported evidence of widespread activity in other quarters of the city, particularly in other schools. At Kaochung, all targets had been selected by the principal and the Party committee, but at other schools, the students themselves had played an active role in this critically important aspect of the movement. Dai also noticed that the teachers who were most frequently selected to speak in struggle sessions all were either members of the Party committee or known to have close connections with the school's power center. Ultimately, he concluded with even greater conviction than before that Principal Chen and a group of approximately twelve favored teachers were cleverly dominating the movement to protect themselves from being denounced as "monsters and ghosts" and from being dismissed in the manner of their high-ranking colleagues in Peking and Shanghai.

We knew that the movement was spontaneous and dynamic in other schools; yet our own school seemed controlled and dreary in comparison. We realized that we had no course other than to run blindly after these teachers and to do what we were told. They made the accusations and we merely echoed their words. Our only opportunity for spontaneous activity was in the evening when a group of us might raid the teachers under attack in their quarters and even then we followed the line set down by the leaders in the formal meetings. Once we realized this, we began to develop doubts about them and the Party organization in our school.

During the latter half of June, the character of Dai's participation changed. Along with virtually all of the students, he continued to attend meetings, make accusations, and "to run blindly after these teachers" as ordered. However, after the seizure of the seven popular instructors, he and a fluid group of about twenty other students began independent action; their dormitory, dining hall, and the student lounge were transformed into forums for "big debate" over their dissatisfaction with the movement and what they themselves could do to alter it. Like Dai, all were frustrated at not being able to exert greater influence upon the movement, and all were deeply committed to effecting a basic change in the direction of its development.

As an assistant class leader, Dai joined with seven of these activists, six of whom were members of the Young Communist League, one a class study member, and one a class labor member, in accepting special leadership responsibility. They felt someone had to provide direction and unity for what was essentially a formless association. Thus, they led and summarized the small discussion sessions, answered questions on Party or Young Communist League policy, and gradually emerged as a group of hard-core activist leaders within the larger group of twenty. However, the group remained quite informal, both in terms of meeting schedule and attendance. Often, Dai would arrive late, having been busy elsewhere writing big-character posters or simply taking a rest after dinner, and would ask to be briefed on what had occurred. Significantly, he and his cohorts did not include the class leader, a young woman of twenty-two, in their discussions, since they felt that her age and her close association with the school's Party and Young Communist League leadership rendered her inaccessible. Of equal interest is the fact that Dai and his comrades felt little need to shroud their special conduct in secrecy.

We were not terribly afraid of what might happen if the principal and the teachers found out what we were doing. We were all the children of workers or peasants and we knew that we could always claim that we were only interested in improving the movement. While we did not publicize our meetings, and while the presence of elements allied with the principal and the Party committee might have hampered our discussions, we saw no reason to keep them secret.

At first the group attempted to find a means of improving the movement within the framework established by the regular school organization. They discussed forming teams to visit other schools, study the conduct of the movement there, and then report back to the entire student body in the hope of demonstrating the relative backwardness of their school. This they reasoned might force the principal and the Party committee to increase the scale and intensity of student participation in the movement.

Ultimately, however, Dai and his fellow hard-core activists, in focusing upon the example of the teachers who had been arrested, concluded that the principal was committed to a course from which he could not be swayed by ordinary means. They felt that their only recourse would be to appeal to higher authority, the Kwangtung Provincial Party Committee.

Dai was disappointed when this suggestion produced a split in the ranks of the larger group of twenty, although he understood the fears of the dissenters. It was, after all, impossible to foresee future events, and the group might conceivably be severely reprimanded and even formally disciplined if the Provincial Party Committee upheld the principal and the school committee. He recognized that the students who expressed such fears were for the most part neither members of the Young Communist League nor those with well-established reputations for activism; they thus stood to lose a great deal if events turned against them. Thus, he acquiesced when twelve of the twenty stated their intention of continuing to render moral support to the group but at the same time to eschew any further direct involvement. Dai was, however, encouraged by the continued support for independent action given by the hard-core group and remained firm in his decision to join in risking an appeal to the Provincial Party Committee.

I did not know how we would be received and I was concerned. However, I felt confident that the Committee would hear our demands and that they would take action to remove the principal. I truly felt that he was in the wrong and that he would be criticized. Also, the newspapers were full of the student movement and we were all children of working-class families. Therefore, I felt that any criticism that we received would not be too harsh. We stood to lose very little.

Having evaluated the possible repercussions of their imminent action, Dai and his friends decided it would be best to approach the Provincial Committee with a specific recommendation for action. Requesting that a work team be sent to take over leadership of the movement in their school was the obvious choice since the Provincial Committee had already adopted this course elsewhere. Choosing to make a relatively safe suggestion, however, did not completely prevent a feeling of nervousness at departure time.

The next morning, we boarded a bus for the forty-minute trip across the city to the Committee office. I grew increasingly concerned as we neared our destination, for although I was certain that we would be heard, I did not know what the reaction would be. I also feared that we might fail to convince them of our sincerity.

When we reached the building, we paused on the steps for a final consultation. We then realized that we had not elected a spokesman; naturally, we felt foolish. We immediately elected the class labor member, who hesitantly led the seven of us into the building.

As we entered, we came upon a man seated at a reception desk. He rose and asked us to state our business. He was extremely polite and made us feel that he wanted to be helpful. I suspect that this was because he recognized us as students and knew that all of Canton was at that time in the midst of a large-scale student movement. We began to feel more at ease.

Our spokesman stated that we had come to discuss the
circumstances and conditions of the movement in our school
and to acquaint the Party with certain things we felt to be
wrong. The man showed immediate interest and took us to a
large room down the hall. He asked us to be seated and
entered a smaller office directly adjacent to the meeting room
where we could see a man working at a desk. We then realized
that we had been brought to the reception room of a kind
of public liaison department.

When our guide explained our presence to the man inside,
he rose and came to meet us. He assured us that we had
been correct in approaching the Party, called for tea, and
asked us to tell our story. We spent more than an hour with
this man, who appeared to be in charge of the department.

Our spokesman simply described the conduct of the movement in our school and stressed the things that we considered
to be incorrect. The department head gave no indication of
agreement or disagreement but rather seemed most interested
in collecting facts. He asked detailed questions about the
principal, our Party committee, and about the teachers who
had been seized; he also took careful notes of points that
seemed to be of particular interest to him.

At the close of the interview, he again congratulated us
for having shown initiative by approaching the Party. He
spent a great deal of time explaining the Party's interest in
learning the problems of the masses and assured us that all
of our information and our request for a work team would
be forwarded to a higher level without delay. Finally, he
admonished us to continue our study of the thought of Chairman Mao and to play an active role in the movement.

We felt quite relieved and very happy as we left the building
and returned to school. We knew that we had accomplished
our purpose and that a work team would be sent to the
school before too long. Our earlier fears of an unfriendly
welcome had proven groundless and we were deeply impressed
by the willingness of the Committee to hear our request. We
felt that the situation would soon be resolved and were proud
of the fact that we had been able to play such an important
role.

Four days later, after much second thought and not a little fear, Dai and his schoolmates felt themselves vindicated. Their faith in the Party had been restored; a work team presented itself at the Kaochung School's main gate and assumed complete control of every aspect of the movement.

CHAPTER TWO

The Party Enters
Student Politics

The work team's entrance into Kaochung Middle School in early
July 1966 for a month-long stay gave the flagging movement a bold
push forward. With the "rebels" free at last and even less activist
students seeing new opportunities to join in the Cultural Revolution,
a fresh spirit of enthusiasm infused the whole school.[1] Principal
Chen Hsiao-chang and his faculty allies, compelled now to "stand
aside" while the work team assumed "all authority," could no
longer restrain student and teacher activists from criticizing whom
and what they pleased.

The former power holders, soon construed to include all eight
members of the school Party committee but none of the Youth
League leadership, were by no means allowed to "stand aside"
passively. The students demanded that they too read wall posters
and write self-examinations, as well as join in class study and

criticism meetings. Evenings brought little relief for them since the
entire faculty lived inside the school compound along with their
families. Not until early September, after most students had left
Canton to travel about the country, were these eight individuals
able to return to their rural homes, badly in need of a chance to
recuperate.

Dai was not sure about the backgrounds of all the work team
members. All together there were sixteen, averaging slightly over
thirty years of age. The youngest was in his early twenties, while
the team leader and deputy team leader were both government
cadres (*chi-kuan kan-pu*) in their mid-forties. Two others had been
transferred from "Four Cleanups Campaign" work teams then
operating in the countryside, nine were so-called "ordinary cadres"
(low ranking within their own units), and three were workers.
All were either Party or League members, and unlike those at other
schools Dai had heard about, none were soldiers. After observing
them in action for a few days, Dai judged most of them to be
quite capable and experienced in their commissar-like tasks. One
notable exception, however, was the worker contingent.

> They were too funny for words. They couldn't even speak
> properly! At first they followed the example of their fellow
> team members in giving short lectures at class meetings about
> the team leader's recent instructions. But after students began
> to laugh at them for saying silly and inappropriate things,
> they withdrew in obvious embarrassment to a more limited
> role of simply convening meetings and then relinquishing the
> chair to student leaders.

As far as Dai was aware, the work team had no over-all plan of
action. (Thus when they were forced to depart in August the students did not criticize them for having failed to accomplish their
mission.) Soon after setting up a modest headquarters in a classroom, the team leader and his deputy began their work by interviewing the Party committeemen to hear their interpretation of past
and present events.

To complement this version with the views of ordinary faculty and students, one team member was assigned to each class to practice the "three togethers"—living, eating, and studying together with the class members. After three days the work team members were satisfied that they knew the local situation well enough to call a "mobilization meeting" to be attended by the entire faculty and student body (including the power holders). The leader first summed up his work team's findings, and then transmitted an instruction from Provincial Party Secretary Chao Tzu-yang to the effect that the targets of the movement would henceforth be the power holders in the school rather than the group of teachers who had unfairly been attacked earlier as "monsters and ghosts." Dai later learned that some of Mao's colleagues on the Central Cultural Revolution Group (CCRG) had by this time criticized the June 1 *People's Daily* editorial, "Sweep Out All Monsters and Ghosts." Chao's instruction (given originally to a meeting of all Canton work team leaders in late June or early July) thus seemed to him to be consistent with the line currently dominant in Peking. The team leader concluded with a plea for everyone to fearlessly write big-character posters denouncing the principal and other Party leaders: "Teachers and students of the whole school, do not be timid! Speak out what you know and feel, so as to help the old cadres undertake revolution!"

Dai recalled that the atmosphere in the school now became quite lively. He noted not only that big-character posters were flourishing in greater numbers than before, but also that their subject matter was broader in scope and their quality much higher. Principal Chen and the other power holders, alert to the changes, responded by writing self-effacing posters with titles like "We Welcome Criticism and Repudiation from Our Fellow Students." Most active of all in Kaochung School at this time were those teachers who had been slighted or persecuted by Chen's clique in the past. They doubtless found it highly gratifying to strike back at the leaders who had excluded or harmed them. Since they had been privy to more faculty maneuverings than had the students, Dai thought their poster articles were probably most effective, and in reality least welcome to Principal Chen. By contrast, among those teachers most favored by Chen there was great reluctance to criticize him meaningfully. This group, which included a number of students, was consequently condemned with the epithet "royalist."

Although Dai was quick to point out the revolutionary significance of their criticism activity, he also admitted to enjoying the sheer cruel fun of humiliating Kaochung's power holders, particularly the principal. On one occasion, for example, he devoted an entire day to the co-operative manufacture of an enormous cardboard replica of a cow's head, intended as symbolic of an appropriate crown for Principal Chen.

After achieving an initial impact by overthrowing the school Party committee, the work team, in the second half of July, was less effective at influencing student visions and interests, even though as the supreme authority in the school, it continued to supervise students' activities. Dai recalled that he and his fellow students grew more restive under its leadership, which they felt increasingly resembled the domination they had experienced under the old Party committee. Thus, at the end of the month, the team turned its attention to effecting the election of a "preparatory Cultural Revolution small group" (*ko ch'ou hsiao-tsu*) for each class and a corresponding committee for the entire school.

Dai noted that the procedure for electing each small group was established by the work team. Its essential feature was the plan to reach a limited form of consensus before balloting without actually proposing a list of nominees, a method less open to manipulation and thus charges of fraud than the pre-Cultural Revolution practice of publicly designating a single slate of nominees and then allowing only yes or no votes to be indicated by secret ballot. Dai Hsiao-ai's class of fifty broke up into six small groups (according to already existing class organization) to discuss the merits of various potential committee members. After three hours or so, secret balloting was employed to màke the final selections. Each class member wrote his five preferences on a ballot, which were then opened one by one before the class. The first time an individual's name was proposed, his name was written on the blackboard and the first stroke of the five-stroke ideograph *cheng* ("upright") drawn under-

neath. Each succeeding time his name was proposed another stroke
was added. To be elected one needed to win an absolute majority
(in this case five *chengs* plus one stroke) and to place among the
five highest vote getters. If necessary, the process was repeated in
the class until both conditions were met.

By this time, class leadership still consisted of one work team
member, a Youth League committee, and a class committee. It was
therefore no great surprise that four out of five of those elected to the
small group in Dai's class were Youth League members, two of them
League cadres (the class secretary and Dai himself), and two class
cadres. The fifth was neither a League member nor a class cadre,
but a superactive student who had earned a reputation as Kaochung's
best writer of big-character posters.

Once the "preparatory Cultural Revolution small group" was
chosen, Dai and his fellow committeemen held a meeting chaired
by the class work team member to elect from among their number a
representative to the all-school committee. In the case of Dai's
small group, the student chosen turned out to be the League
secretary. The schoolwide committee comprised six students and two
teachers, selected by each of the class representatives from among
their own number. This Preparatory Committee, with the addition of
one liaison member left behind by the work team after it withdrew,
remained the nominal chief authority in the school until it was
openly called to task for its "mistakes" in November. During this
period, Dai described the general authority structure in the school
in order as follows:

1. Provincial Committee
2. Work team liaison member
3. All-school Preparatory Committee
4. Class preparatory small groups

This arrangement, he noted, enhanced student feeling of enjoying
a direct link with the Provincial Party Committee.

Contrasting sharply with the Peking students' open challenges
to the work teams, resulting in the so-called "fifty days of white
terror" in the capital, opposition in Canton apparently assumed the

more passive form of subdued grumbling while the teams were still in residence. Dai's main complaint concerned the way in which the team stifled student initiative. Continued criticism of the school's power holders began to seem passé and boring after a while; yet when some students proposed convening full-fledged "struggle sessions," the team leader forbade it because of insufficient evidence. The task of selecting preparatory groups could not sustain student imagination either, especially since the chosen participants collectively constituted only a slightly shuffled version of the old student political elite. Dai often discussed with his friends what possible purpose the movement might have from Mao's standpoint, although never with much success.

> We were unable to follow the working of Mao's thought in terms of current politics. We thought we understood a little about the purges in journalism, literature, and the arts that had been going on since summer 1964, but the spring purges of Lo Jui-ch'ing and P'eng Chen were both deep mysteries. Principal Chen kept us up-to-date. For instance, in May he illegally read to some members of our Youth League a portion of the Inner Party document announcing Lo Jui-ch'ing's purge, and again in late May he revealed to us, before the *People's Daily* made it public on June 4, that P'eng Chen was to be considered the "backstage boss of Teng T'o." But we didn't know enough to identify trends or predict probable future happenings.

Since the students could not deduce what Mao's goals were for the over-all movement, and since their work team's vision was far too narrow for them, they searched for new sources of inspiration. The student movement in Peking became one object of their attention. Another was the progress of the Cultural Revolution in other sectors of Canton society.

On this subject, Dai and his friends became particularly concerned over the reported difficulties early activists encountered among Canton factory workers. Most workers, in "creatively applying" the *People's Daily*'s incitement to criticize "bourgeois academic authorities," had stepped forward in late May and early June to write big-character posters attacking technicians and engineers who paid too little attention to the study of Mao's writings. Technicians were also accused of being too respectful of bookish rules and foreign stereotypes, demanding that workers obey them without question, and looking down upon workers generally. Criticism of management personnel who tolerated such situations was also unmistakably implied. Some early activists had also criticized fellow workers whose "political manifestation" was passive, who did not work hard, or who thought only of their own welfare. It was often the case that these early activists had failed to win much support in their own shops and had consequently drawn quickly the counter-criticism of the confident factory leadership. Dai first heard about such episodes by word of mouth, either from a sympathetic mathematics teacher whose brother worked in a factory, or from schoolmates with relatives who were workers.

Many times before, during the regular academic year, Dai had gone, for different periods of time, to "labor" at various workshops in and about Canton. Because of this, he had already acquired some knowledge of the political life of the workers. He was particularly struck by the realization that a majority of workers were old enough to have had personal experience in the notorious anti-rightist campaign in 1957–58.

In that period the Communist Party had agitated the masses to "bloom and contend on a big scale" and to make known their critical ideas to the Party organization. But afterward, the Party turned around and criticized them. The ones who had been most active in writing big-character posters and making known their ideas had even been struggled against and labeled as "rightists opposed to the Party and to socialism." Thus, now they were very wary of expressing their true opinions through posters. Many workers felt the best approach to political demands was responding to a minimal degree just to get by. (Unlike students, workers had little to gain from being active. At the same time they had much to lose. If they wrote posters later found to be in error they could bring heavy criticism down upon their heads.) In addition, a considerable number of workers were nearly illiterate. Others thought first of their families, fearing that their political mistakes might react unfavorably upon their sons' and daughters' future lives. Consequently, when the authorities in industrial and commercial establishments opposed worker activism on grounds that it would represent a grave danger to production, all but a few decided not to take the risk.

After hearing several stories about the brutal suppression of politically progressive workers who had decided the risk was worthwhile, Dai and other activists at Kaochung began to talk about making contact with some workers to investigate these disquieting reports for themselves. However, given the atmosphere of strictly school-oriented movement activities established firmly by the work team, no one thought seriously of openly proposing such a program.

Yet as soon as the work team's grip was released, student attention quickly wandered from its singular focus on Kaochung to scan the citywide scene. At the end of August, Dai and a few other activists held a meeting and came to the following highly charged decision, romantic as it was formalistic:

> We must go to the factories to exchange revolutionary experiences. We must go to factories to ignite a revolutionary fire and fan up a revolutionary wind, and to engage in the propagation of Mao Tse-tung's thought. With great determination, we must get the Great Proletarian Cultural Revolution in the factories under way.

Dai organized between twenty and thirty classmates, about half of them girls, to accompany him in early September to the Tsangku Warehouse, situated about five miles from the school. They had been there just six months before for their regular stint of labor participation. In a temporary wave of enthusiasm, almost every Kaochung student dutifully marched to one nearby factory or other work post and some even went to rural production brigades. Dai recalled that students at several other schools in Canton made similar visits to workers at that time, providing a rare instance of a project conceived locally instead of through "imitating Peking" (*hsueh-hsi pei-ching*). Weaker ideologues among them abandoned the workers after a few days in favor of more inviting activities, like *ch'uan-lien* (properly called *ko-ming ta ch'uan-lien*, or "great exchange of revolutionary experiences") and "destroying the Four Olds." Dai's group, by staying about twenty days with the workers, ranked among the most persevering. They ate and slept at the warehouse, maintaining contact with Kaochung by cycling back every two or three days to spend several hours attending meetings and debates, and comparing observations with schoolmates who had gone to other factories and enterprises.

Interestingly, Dai recognized the risks involved in these "visits" and was careful not to inform the manager of the business he went to candidly of his group's purpose. However, the management did not remain naïve for very long.

> The warehouse leaders slowly realized why we had come. One day they invited us into the office for a conference, where they explained that factories were not like schools in that factories had to fulfill production responsibilities. They insisted that we refrain from any disruptive activity that might endanger their chances of fulfilling their plans. In fact, they thought it best that we leave and not interfere in the movement at Tsangku at all. After this meeting was over, we gathered that the leadership was afraid of us because we might report on unsatisfactory conditions in the warehouse directly, without seeking their approval.

The students nonetheless continued to work side-by-side with warehouse employees, to "strike up good relations" with them, and to have "heart-to-heart talks." Since most workers were unwilling to talk freely and openly, the students could not be sure of the scope of the problems they thought they had discovered. But Dai felt they had definitely acquired some useful information.

> We saw that there were opposition sentiments among a part of the workers. Some were burdened with family difficulties to which the factory leadership had paid no heed. Some had been working in their unit for many years with little adjustment in wages. In other cases, a worker's wife had formerly worked at Tsangku but at some point was "transferred down"

to a rural village; not only did they have to live apart after that, but their standard of living had dropped since only one of them could earn a wage. Still other workers bore a grudge against the warehouse leadership for its bureaucratic style of work, staying always in their office and hardly ever descending into the shops to labor along with the workers.

As a result of their investigations, the students collectively decided that conditions in the warehouse were ripe for carrying out their earlier decision taken at Kaochung to bring the Revolution to the workers. They recruited a few of them to join in collectively signing the first big-character poster; it listed no names of power holders, restricting itself instead to a discussion of mistakes that had been made in production and political leadership. This act drew an immediate favorable response from other workers, and before long a separate group of younger ones defied the warehouse leadership in a poster announcing their support for the students.

Tsangku's leadership took immediate countermeasures. Several shop foremen and Party members together wrote a poster of their own attacking those written by the students and their worker allies. They argued that workers should make their ideas known directly to their leaders instead of writing them on big-character posters.

Now that two competing sides of opinion had emerged in the warehouse, the students felt they had won a victory. Their catalytic mission fulfilled, they now decided that the workers should be able to carry on alone. Furthermore, they interpreted the *People's Daily* editorial of September 7 entitled "Take a Firm Hold of Revolution and Stimulate Production" as reflecting a distinctly unfriendly reaction to their continued presence in the factories. Finally, students eager to take advantage of the chance for cross-country travel in the *ch'uan-lien* movement needed no excuse at all to depart from Tsangku.

We went there because we felt it to be our ideological duty. We thought this line was correct and also a meaningful way to advance the Cultural Revolution in Canton. But it was also hard work, and because of the management's opposition, very bitter at times. Most of the ones in our group were quite happy to go and do something else after fulfilling our initial goal.

The workers' movement thus instigated by the students in September faltered and nearly died out altogether in the later autumn months of 1967. To explain why this happened, Dai emphasized once again the general wariness of the older generation.

The workers mistakenly considered the 1966 Cultural Revolution to be no different than the 1957–58 anti-rightist struggle. In this respect they were just like our teachers. One teacher especially close to us had advised, "Don't be too impulsive, or you will find returning to normal very difficult." There were many family heads among the workers who said similar things to their sons. This all shows clearly the attitude held by workers and older people generally toward the Cultural Revolution. Thus, it was unavoidable that they should come into conflict with "rebellious" young students.

But equally important to help explain the relative failure of the workers' movement, Dai thought, was the tactic adopted by Party leaders in several provinces of playing upon this antipathy toward political activism which had developed among the workers to raise opposition against the rebellious students in general and against those traveling to provincial cities from Peking in particular. This latter group of students from the capital, responding enthusiastically to Mao Tse-tung's August call to "Bombard the Headquarters," provoked local students to attack their own Provincial Party Committee. Provincial authorities, reacting in self-defense, secretly organized workers to demonstrate against these outside agitators. Dai felt the provincial leaders dared not confront the Red Guards directly with an order to leave, traveling as they were with the obvious tacit consent of the Central Cultural Revolution Group; instead they employed the worker "masses" (most of whom Dai thought were union members) as pawns.

He supported his hypothesis about such a subtle, clandestine maneuver on the part of the Kwangtung Provincial Committee by pointing to the suddenness with which large crowds had gathered in the streets of Canton to demonstrate against the Peking students. This tactic was later criticized by Canton students as exhibiting the committee's "exclusivist mentality" (*p'ai wai feng-ch'ao*). Noisiest and most visible of all persons participating in the demonstrations were so-called conservative elements among Canton workers, who thrived in the new atmosphere. These confrontations occasionally erupted into open fighting. Dai remembered in particular meeting in Peking in October a group of students from Hofei (capital of Anhwei Province) who had come to the capital to complain about such actions taken by Li Pao-hua, the Anhwei Provincial Party Committee's first secretary.

> They told us that when they had demanded admission to the Party Committee to see Li Pao-hua in person, Li dared not come out. Instead a group of workers appeared, shouting loudly that they would protect the Party Committee. The Anhwei students alleged that these workers had assaulted them, beating them with Mao-quote signboards (*yü-lu p'ai*). We asked them if they weren't giving us a one-sided version, suggesting that perhaps they had started the fighting themselves. They denied this, though, and removed their shirts to show us their bruises.

The central leadership in Peking took sharp notice of this new trend of union-student antagonism. The *People's Daily* published on September 5 an editorial entitled "Use Struggle by Reasoning, Not Struggle by Force." On September 11, the Central Committee transmitted to all provincial committees a "decision" establishing that "It is not allowed to use any pretext and any means to agitate and organize workers, peasants, and city residents against students." For added punch, Mao's "September 7" directive warning that "To go on like this cannot solve problems" was appended to the message.[2] The *People's Daily* followed this statement up with a series of editorials on worker-student unity. On September 12, for example, it carried a page-one article headlined "5000 Worker Representatives in Canton Take the Initiative in

Resolutely Supporting Revolutionary Actions of Revolutionary Students." Thereafter Dai noticed that open incidents ceased for the
most part, but that the conflict of opinion about how to regard
this student offense and the Party-union defense it engendered
continued to fester not far below the surface. In retrospect, Dai
now identifies this division as one important factor leading to the
appearance of "two big factions" several months later.

Dai Hsiao-ai himself did not again become involved in the
workers' side of the movement. In this decision he stood together
with the majority of the students at Kaochung, who because of
the stiff opposition by unsympathetic enterprise leadership, high
interest in countrywide *ch'uan-lien,* and lack of encouragement from
the CCRG, focused their attention elsewhere instead. In spite of
the difficulties, though, there was still a sizable minority of students
who did insistently maintain their contacts with the "rebel faction"
in various workshops and in violation of the September editorial
continued to join in struggles against factory managers. Dai noted
that this group succeeded in keeping alive friction between students
and rebellious workers on the one hand, and conservative workers
and management on the other. They also served as a continuing
source of news about the fading movement in the factories. Shortly
after leaving Tsangku Warehouse in late September, for example,
Dai heard from a schoolmate who had a friend who worked there
that the nucleus of activists sponsored by Kaochung students had
been severely suppressed by the management, who used as a pretext
the standard (and now highly legitimate) appeal to "fulfill our
production responsibilities." Still, some student pressure on factory
management continued in a variety of forms.

During October and November 1966 in the course of small-
group ideological study directed at repudiating even more thoroughly
the "bourgeois reactionary line," Canton students increasingly con-
cretized the discussion by pointing to the erroneous line's "important
manifestation" among factory managers who refused to allow the
Cultural Revolution to be carried on in their shops. In early November a number of persecuted workers, mostly from Shanghai and
Peking, went in person to seek relief from the CCRG. The central

leaders responded to the petitioners by holding a conference of "representatives" of revolutionary employees and workers in the capital on November 11. Wang Li read to this assembly a draft of a twelve-point directive supporting the rebellious workers:

> The current problem is that the leaders of certain units erroneously put the Cultural Revolution movement in opposition against production. Some use the pretext of grasping the movement to suppress the revolutionaries and protect themselves, neglecting production; others use the pretext of grasping production to boycott the Cultural Revolution movement.[3]

As a countermove to Peking's support for appeals from "rebels," local Party and management officials, hoping to confuse and discredit the entire Cultural Revolution movement, organized other workers to masquerade as rebels and go to Peking themselves. Additional large numbers of workers apparently adopted similar tactics on their own for reasons purely of material welfare.

On December 26 a *People's Daily* editorial entitled "Greet the High Tide of the Cultural Revolution in Industrial and Mining Enterprises" significantly fed the fire of the rebel worker-enterprise leader struggle. The editors exhibited approval both of students coming into factories and of workers going into schools for the purpose of forming joint organizations. Less than a month later, during the January 1967 "seize power" episode, these rebel organizations were destined to develop to a point where they could lend considerable support to student radicals; the perseverance of the small corps of student activists in encouraging rebel workers in the factories was to reap a direct political reward.

STUDY PEKING

This digression into student-worker relations in late 1966 has been allowed to anticipate the further chronological unfolding of Dai's story in order to demonstrate one area of potentially wider student interest that had been effectively contained by the work team back in July. A second important outside focus of student attention at that time was the activities of fellow radical students in Peking. Work teams had been first dispatched to schools in the capital in early June, shortly after the *People's Daily* publicized a student poster attack upon the authorities at Peking University. Dai later heard from Peking rebels visiting Canton how their comrades had been criticized by the work teams as "counterrevolutionaries," a very serious charge in China, and how several had even been mentally persecuted to the point of committing suicide.

Among Canton students, the best-known of the early rebels in Peking was K'uai Ta-fu, who had spearheaded student opposition to the work team sent to Tsinghua University in early June commanded by Yeh Lin, the deputy chairman of the State Economic Commission. With the support of Wang Kuang-mei (Mrs. Liu Shao-ch'i) as the work team's adviser, Yeh responded aggressively by labeling the vexatious K'uai as a counterrevolutionary. In protest, K'uai fasted in hopes that such a tactic would call attention to the serious suppression of revolutionary students going on at Tsinghua under Yeh's heavy hand. When his protest came to the attention of the CCRG, one of its number (Ch'i Pen-yü) was sent to investigate. The report Ch'i submitted favored the students, with the result that Wang and Yeh came under criticism for their actions. Dai pointed out, however, that the chances for similar intervention by the CCRG in faraway Canton were infinitely less likely. (This was an important difference between the two cities from the Canton students' point of view, and it served to affect both their over-all revolutionary strategy and specific tactics.)

Large-scale debates quickly began to break out across the several Peking campuses over the question of the behavior of the work teams. The fact that many central leaders came to the universities to participate in these debates, frequently taking opposing stands, indicated to Dai that before the Central Committee's August plenary session the matter of whose political purposes the work teams had served was not clearly settled, even among the Party elite. He thought that Chiang Ch'ing and her associates on the CCRG opposed the work teams as a rule, while Teng Hsiao-p'ing and others generally supported them. In early August Peking students from both pro- and anti-work team factions began trickling south to support through debate respective points of view; by late August 1966 their volume had grown to the point where serious factionalism was being injected into Canton student politics. Dai went often to their "liaison stations" located on Canton college campuses to listen to debates and obtain mimeographed tabloids from Peking.

One day in early August while the Central Committee's Eleventh Plenum was still in progress, all of Canton's middle school and college students were assembled together (either in the giant Sun Yat-sen Memorial Hall or in the municipal gymnasium) to listen to recorded speeches made at the Plenum by Liu Shao-ch'i, Teng Hsiao-p'ing, and Chou En-lai. Instructions for work teams to withdraw were given in these speeches, but no one was yet assigned responsibility for the teams' errors already committed. The August 8 "Sixteen-Point Decision" criticized the work teams explicitly, and the point was elaborated in the CCRG's journal *Red Flag* (number 10) a few days later. But not until November did Dai encounter posters suggesting that Liu had admitted responsibility for the erroneous work team policy as early as the Eleventh Plenum. That admission was to lead to Liu's downfall when the Cultural Revolution reached its height.

CHAPTER THREE

The Birth
of the Red Guards

August 1966 saw the collapse of the Canton City and Kwangtung Provincial Party apparatus as an effective leadership force. In response to the call of the Eleventh Plenum of the Party Central Committee, students once again directed their efforts toward attacking Party leaders in local units. However, the lack of specific guidelines for conducting the struggle heightened the factional differences which had arisen during the debate over work teams. Even the formation of the Red Guards after August 18 accomplished little more than a temporary glossing over of the conflict. As the students carried the movement out of their schools and into the streets, their disagreements intensified. The resulting chaos prompted a complete loss of student confidence in their city and provincial Party leaders.

EARLY AUGUST: THE BASIS FOR STUDENT FACTIONALISM

Dai recalled that after the explicit criticism of the work teams in the August 8 "Sixteen-Point Decision" and their eventual withdrawal, the question of their orthodoxy ceased to be debated. Accordingly, the issues of student disagreement reverted to the original questions of whether or not to attack local Party officials and if so how the struggle should be organized and led.

The "Decision" and the "Communiqué" of the Party Central Committee's Eleventh Plenum, published on August 14, 1966, intensified disagreement. While both documents called for increased activism among the masses, neither, said Dai, explained how the masses were to be aroused or how they were to be led.

In the absence of specific instructions, students seemed free to act according to their own opinion of the conduct of individual local Party leaders. Most students of revolutionary class background, feeling a debt to the Party that had enabled them to improve their lot, continued to be reluctant to attack it. They became known as conservatives. Their opposite numbers, the progressives, seemed almost too eager to begin. This conservative-progressive split, born in the era of the work teams, was now greatly intensified.

Dai thought that the call of the "Decision" and the "Communiqué" for heightened mass criticism bolstered the position of the progressives. In fact, after the call, conservative strength dropped dramatically. However, the progressives were themselves divided on how to organize and lead the attacks against local Party officials. Some favored immediate action, while others advocated first building enthusiasm among the largest possible number of students and then confronting the local leadership with a storm of criticism from a relatively united front. Thus, in the third week of August 1966, students were divided according to their willingness to attack local Party leaders and according to their ideas of how the attack should be mounted.

To reinforce their respective positions, the students of Peking's colleges and universities continued, as during the work team debate, to organize themselves into numerous fighting corps with such symbolic names as "The Eagles," "Red Flag," and "Revolutionary Rebels." One group at Tsinghua University, soon to attain national and later worldwide reputation, was known as "Red Guards."

Dai was unable even to estimate the number of these organizations in Peking. It seemed to him that each coalesced about a particularly persuasive student who, through a network of liaison stations, extended his influence to colleges and universities in other cities. On the basis of his liaison station contacts, Dai estimated that the smallest of the groups had about ten members while the very largest may have had several hundreds of followers. All the groups were characterized by constant shifts in membership. While the absolute number of students within a group might remain fairly stable, individual members freely changed allegiance. The result for those who, like Dai, were trying to keep abreast of developments was utter confusion.

> I could not begin to estimate the number of these groups in Peking. It is impossible, even now. Because things changed so rapidly, we couldn't keep track of the position of each faction. I would leave a liaison station with the impression that "XXX Corps" took a certain line, only to learn that a schoolmate had heard something entirely different just five minutes before. It was too confusing.
>
> Eventually, we began to categorize the groups into "conservatives" and "rebels." The conservatives were those who hesitated to attack their school Party committees, while the rebels were those who would. I suppose because they were the ones who were most loyal to the Party, students of revolutionary class origin tended to be conservative. I felt the same way at first, but it seemed strange to me that those who had been most committed should be labeled as conservatives. The whole business was too complicated for words. I didn't understand it then and I do not understand it now.

Inevitably, the factional conflict of Peking was reflected in developments in Kaochung. As the students read the *People's Daily*, *Red Flag*, and the bulletins distributed at different liaison stations, they began to identify with the viewpoints of different Peking-based fighting corps. Those who remained loyal to the Party naturally selected Peking's conservative student organizations, while those who favored either immediate action or waiting to build broadly based student enthusiasm before engaging in struggle similarly chose the rebel fighting corps which best expressed their individual ideas and preferences.

> We were in a state of confusion. We developed conservatives and rebels within our own ranks. Fortunately, the movement was at an ebb and so these differences weren't as significant as they might have been. The Circular and the Communiqué told us about official policy, but the great number of factions and opposing points of view regarding how the policy should be implemented confused us terribly. We would debate different points of view and try to reach agreement on which was correct. But it was hopeless. We were in need of direction.

AUGUST 18–AUGUST 20:
THE FIRST ATTEMPT TO FORM RED GUARDS

On August 18, 1966, Mao Tse-tung himself temporarily silenced factional debate and provided the direction for which Dai expressed a need when, at a mass rally in Peking's T'ien An Men (Gate of Heavenly Peace) Square, he accepted the armband insignia of one of the organizations of the middle school affiliated with Tsinghua University. The armband was red with gold characters proclaiming the legend *hung wei ping,* or "Red Guard."

By this symbolic act, Mao proclaimed both the approved form of organization for struggle, the Red Guards, and, by his support for the Tsinghua Red Guards' active offensive against the university's Party authorities, its method and direction. The message was clear: All students throughout the country were to emulate the Red Guards and carry the Great Proletarian Cultural Revolution through to its inevitable victory.

On the morning of August 19, when the news of Mao's act

reached Kaochung, students and teachers responded with excitement and undisguised relief.

> At last we knew what was expected. As soon as Chairman Mao accepted the armband and wore it, it was obvious to us that the Red Guards of Tsinghua were backed by the highest authority of all and that it was up to us to emulate them.
>
> Beneath the picture of Chairman Mao wearing the armband was a caption stating that the Red Guards were young Red soldiers who guarded Chairman Mao. Every student in the school was excited beyond belief, even the non-activists. A few of us clipped the pictures from the paper, festooned them with red ribbon, and posted them throughout the school. We then sat down and wrote out a statement describing the high tide of revolution as evidenced by the formation of the Red Guards in Peking. We demanded that our school form a similar organization to protect our great leader, Chairman Mao, and posted it on the wall newspaper. Nearly every student wrote an essay stating his agreement. The walls were covered. All of this occurred within two hours or so. I had never seen such a rapid response.

Despite his deep emotional involvement with the Red Guards, Dai Hsiao-ai was able to explain their strong appeal in quite objective terms. He attributed the enthusiastic, almost devotional response to the movement to the intense political education he and his classmates had received since childhood.

> It is not an exaggeration to say that politics was the center of our lives. Without achieving a high rating in "redness," distinction in studies was useless. Because the leaders were afraid that we would become soft like the third generation of Soviet youth, they kept us busy studying Mao's writings, following the example of the People's Liberation Army, and learning from model workers, heroes, and soldiers. Our futures depended upon good performance in these activities; it is not surprising that everyone was eager to show his loyalty by joining the Red Guards.
>
> We had all been born and raised in a period of Mao's greatest fame. In some cases, his influence exceeded even that

of our families. We had studied his writings from the time
we learned to read and always tried to implement them.
Now he emerged wearing a Red Guard armband and bearing
the title of Marshal of the Red Guards (*hung wei ping t'ung-
shuai*). We became "Little Red Soldiers" (*hung hsiao-ping*).
We felt deeply honored to be able to protect Chairman Mao.
That was one reason. The second reason is much like the first.
Films depicting the heroism of the PLA and the constant drive
to "learn from the army" had given all of us a very good
impression of soldiers and the military life. We were just
students but they were active front-line heroes. The Red Guards
were presented as the reserve force of the army. Red Guards
wore army uniforms and red armbands. They looked wonderful
to us. Everyone was fascinated and eager to join. We could be
soldiers too. Who would not have joined?

At that time, we knew nothing of the real meaning of the
Cultural Revolution and could not imagine its significance.
Lacking any idea of what was to come, we thought that
Chairman Mao was giving us an opportunity to practice and
to gain revolutionary experience. This was a basic reason, I
think. Had we been aware of the existence of any over-all
plan, or what that plan was to be, perhaps fewer students
would have participated. I realize now that in a way we were
being used, but on the morning of August 19, 1966, such a
thought was inconceivable.

In the high tide of enthusiasm, there was little doubt that
Kaochung would immediately form its own Red Guard corps.
However, the reports of the August 18 rally lacked even the slightest
hint of organizational details. Dai and his schoolmates had no idea
of where or how to begin establishing themselves as Red Guards.

In all of the excitement, it seemed as though the Red
Guards were to sprout like bamboo. However, we soon came
face to face with the reality that we didn't know how to
organize. In the past, we would simply have used the leadership
structure that already existed, but that was now impossible.
We had to decide who was to be eligible to join the Red
Guards, what the specific goals should be, and what its re-

lationship with the Preparatory Committee established by the work team should be. We pored over the newspapers hoping to find the answers. All that we found, however, were reports in praise of the Red Guards. These kept our enthusiasm at a peak but were of no help in solving the main problem.

As the students in their discussions grappled with these difficulties, they gravitated toward the school auditorium, where by 2 P.M. on August 19, Dai estimated that fully 70 per cent of Kaochung's students and teachers were gathered. For the first time, the students were in absolute control. Dai recalled that not a teacher spoke as student after student articulated his ideas about the important, but unanswered, questions. The meeting had no chairman; students simply rose, spoke, and sat down again, usually to the accompaniment of tumultuous applause.

At about 4 P.M., Dai became concerned by the lack of concrete proposals. Each speaker seemed to be stating why, in his opinion, the Red Guards were a good thing, but nothing more.

I was afraid that the meeting was going to degenerate into something like a struggle session. Despite the importance of the questions, all we got were generalities. There was no discussion about the aims of our proposed Red Guard troop, who would be eligible for membership, how it would be led, and what its relationship with the school's Preparatory Committee would be. I thought they would never stop. In fact, I began to get angry.

Dai's concern was apparently shared by other members of the group, for one of the school cadres, a class leader, Dai thought, soon rose and suggested that better results might be obtained if the discussion were turned over to a small body. He suggested the formation of a new organization, the Preparatory Committee for the Organization of Red Guards (*hung wei ping tsu-chih ch'ou-pei kung-tso wei-yuan hui*). As self-appointed chairman, he then exercised his new-found prerogative to suggest the names of several students as potential committee members. The meeting responded with applause and shouts of additional names which, Dai stated, were immediately written down and offered as a slate of candidates to be elected by acclamation. Minutes later, the committee was declared established.

Immediately after dinner, the Preparatory Committee (*hung ch'ou wei*) went into executive session to wrestle with the questions of procedure Dai considered to be so important. The remainder of the students waited for the results of the meeting in a state of extreme agitation.

> No one thought of sleeping. We just walked around and speculated on what was happening in the meeting. Once one of the members left the room and was immediately surrounded by a mob of students all demanding information. Finally, he grew so exasperated that he said to hell with us all and fled to the lavatory. I had never seen such tension in the school before.

At 2 A.M. on the morning of August 20, the committee concluded its deliberations with the announcement of an all-school meeting to be held later in the morning. The storm of protest and demands to receive additional information immediately, Dai recalled, were squelched by a very sensible reminder that everyone was tired and that their new tasks would require maximum effort. It was agreed that the all-school meeting would be much more productive if they all first got some sleep. Slightly mollified, but with occasional rumblings to the effect that making revolution was more important than rest, Kaochung's students lapsed into fitful slumber.

Dai had not participated in the meeting of the Red Guard Preparatory Committee, but like virtually all of his colleagues, he was satisfied with its recommendations. Kaochung's Little Red Soldiers were to be known as the Mao Tse-tung Doctrine Red Guards (*Mao Tse-tung chu-i hung wei ping*) and supervised, in the absence of their Chief Marshal Mao Tse-tung and Vice-Marshal Lin Piao, by the school Cultural Revolution Preparatory Committee established by the work team. All members were to submit themselves to the discipline of the People's Liberation Army in following the policies expressed in the *Selected Works of Mao Tse-tung*, writings in *Red Flag* and the *People's Daily*, and the August 8 Sixteen-Point Decision. Membership in the Doctrine Guards was to be open to all students whose political conduct had been "good," irrespective of their class background. The evaluation of individuals was to be made in class small-group meetings which would nominate Red Guards. Each class would then elect nominees to full membership. The Preparatory Committee for the Organization of Red Guards was to be dissolved.

Late in the afternoon of August 20, the students felt they had done all that could be expected of them. In the absence of clear directives from higher authorities, they had fallen back upon the old skeleton of Kaochung's student leadership structure and transformed it into a Red Guard organization. They expected that adjustments would have to be made in the future, but reasoning that such methods had always received official approval in the past, they were confident that they had established a viable and effective organizational framework of sufficient resilience to withstand whatever shocks were to come.

> All of us greeted the committee's recommendations with enthusiasm. It seemed to me that we had done a remarkable job of organizing in such a short time. In fact, I thought that the higher levels would be pleased, particularly since our only guide had been the extremely general accounts published in the *People's Daily*. I was certain that I would be elected a Red Guard; it seemed to be a workable system which combined old and new. I was very satisfied.

AUGUST 20–AUGUST 22: DISSOLUTION AND REORGANIZATION

Dai's satisfaction was thoroughly undermined, however, on the evening of August 20, with the arrival of Sung Hsueh-min, a Red Guard from Tsinghua University in Peking. Sung had been sent south with the mission of proselytizing the Peking model of Red Guard organization among the students of Canton. Dai recalled that within minutes of his arrival, he was mobbed by students, virtually dragged to the auditorium, and besieged by countless questions. The information-starved students listened intently.

Sung had just arrived from Peking. He was a Red Guard from Tsinghua University. That meant he knew all of the latest news and also that he was entitled to our respect. We wanted to know if our organizational plan was correct. Sung was a man who could tell us. Naturally we gave him our complete attention.

As the dialogue between the eager young students and the slightly condescending Sung unfolded, major differences between the Kaochung Red Guard organization and its Tsinghua counterpart were revealed. One of the major differences concerned the criteria to be used in judging candidates for membership. Sung declared that to admit all students whose political conduct was good was wrong. The Cultural Revolution, he said, was to be led by the Red Guards, who were its vanguard. Hence, only the most revolutionary elements among the student body should be allowed to become Red Guards. He then defined the truly revolutionary elements as comprising the five good classes: children of workers, poor peasants, revolutionary martyrs, revolutionary cadres, and revolutionary soldiers. Students from other social classes were to form separate organizations to be led and trained by the Red Guards. As each individual gave evidence of his revolutionary spirit, he might then be promoted to Red Guard status. The Cultural Revolution, Sung declared, should be led by the Five Kinds of Red (*hung wu lei*).[1]

Naturally, Sung's suggestion was enthusiastically accepted by those students who happened to be of the Five Kinds of Red. Students in the middle group of social classes were less enthusiastic, while students from the so-called "backward" classes felt a sudden sense of fear. Dai reported certain misgivings of his own about the membership policy. Although the son of a worker, he felt that a student's conduct was the only real test of revolutionary spirit. Yet because he found the plan for provision of separate organizations for the other students reassuring, he kept silent.

It would have been useless to protest at that point. All of the Five Red students were so excited that nothing could have stopped them. After all, the idea had been brought to us by a Red Guard from Peking who was knowledgeable on matters about which we were completely ignorant. To have opposed him would have been like opposing Mao himself.

I was concerned about the large majority of students who would not be able to participate. However, on second thought it seemed that they would have a chance through their own organizations. I would have preferred it to have been different, but I was willing to go along under the circumstances.

I should emphasize that, given the great enthusiasm of my Five Red classmates, I really had no choice. Sung's background, experience, and credentials naturally put him in a very strong position. We had to accept his ideas. Without the immediate support of the Five Red students, he might have been rejected. As it was, he had their complete backing; there was nothing for it but to follow and hope for the best.

Immediately, all Five Red students present declared themselves a special committee, revoked the decisions of the Preparatory Committee for the Organization of Red Guards, and set about reorganizing Kaochung's Doctrine Red Guards according to Sung's description of the Peking model. Satisfied that he had fulfilled his responsibilities, Sung departed to apply the wisdom of his Peking-Tsinghua experiences in other quarters. Dai never saw or heard of him again.

Dai recalled that in response to the decisions of the general meeting, the Cultural Revolution Preparatory Committee established by the work team, minus its non-Five Red members, went into evening session. On the morning of the next day, August 21, 1966, their recommendations were announced.

All Five Red students were declared to be Red Guards. Members of the Preparatory Committee went to the office of the Organization Department of the former school Party committee, seized its roster of students, and made a record of the names of all who qualified for membership. The list of new Red Guards was then posted for the edification of the whole school. Significantly, no member of the Party, whether under criticism or not, dared to oppose the students' confiscation of what were virtually secret documents.

All of August 21 was required to check the roster of students and post the names of the new Red Guards. Early in the morning of August 22, the Red Guards of each class met separately to elect leaders. Each class in effect had a Red Guard unit, known as a Red Guard small team (*hung wei ping hsiao tui*), appended to it. Individual team members were known as Red Guard warriors (*hung wei ping chan-shih*). Each team elected a leader and an assistant leader who managed such Cultural Revolution duties as the issuing of identification papers, selection of the team flag and armband, and co-ordination of the team's activities. Dai Hsiao-ai was elected leader of his team.

On the afternoon of August 22, all of the newly constituted Red Guards met to elect their highest authority, the Red Guard Headquarters (*hung wei ping tsung pu*). Significantly, the chairman and vice-chairman of the Cultural Revolution Preparatory Committee were appointed to the leading positions. Nothing was done about organizing groups for non-Five Red students.

After dinner on August 22, the entire student body was called to a general meeting where the creation of Kaochung's Mao Tse-tung Doctrine Red Guards was proclaimed. The program of the new organization embraced the substance of Lin Piao's declaration at the August 18 rally.

> We will energetically eradicate all the old ideas, old culture, old customs, and old habits of the exploiting classes and transform all those parts of the superstructure that do not correspond to the socialist economic base. We will sweep out all the vermin and clear away all obstacles.
> We will make vigorous efforts to establish proletarian authorities and the new ideas, new culture, new customs, and new habits of the proletariat.[2]

The time had come to leave the school compound and take to the streets.

AUGUST 23–MID-SEPTEMBER: "DESTROY THE FOUR OLDS"

On the morning of August 23, 1966, Kaochung's Red Guards set out to destroy the Four Olds (old ideas, old culture, old customs,

and old habits) at their very root: the homes and shops of the
Seven Black elements or members of "backward" classes. The students were in high spirits as they marched behind their flag-bearer
into the city. Dai recalled that they sang revolutionary songs, shouted
slogans, and exchanged words of encouragement as they passed
along the line of march. It was on this first trip into the city that
Dai first realized the enormous scope of the movement in which
he was participating.

> Not until we entered the streets did the news reports of
> the past few days come alive. It seemed as though all of
> Canton was in ferment. Red Guards were everywhere. We had
> heard reports of Red Guard activity in Canton since August
> 20 but we were so involved in making our own preparations,
> I suppose, that we never really appreciated that so many others
> were also involved. By August 23 it seemed as though every
> school in Canton had organized Red Guards and that they
> were all out on the streets. As we passed other teams, we
> congratulated them, asked what they had done, where they
> had been, and where we could find the "class enemies."
> They in turn congratulated us and welcomed us to the ranks
> of Red Guards.

Following the procedure agreed upon back at the school meetings, Dai led his team directly to the nearest police station, where
he and his assistant spoke to the sergeant in charge. Pointing to
a large map of the precinct, they asked the policeman to indicate
the location of streets with high concentrations of Seven Black elements. The sergeant readily complied, even helping Dai to plot
the target areas on his own map.

> The police authorities were very co-operative. They probably
> had been ordered by the provincial Party authorities to assist
> the Red Guards in every way. They kept such records as a
> matter of course; it wasn't difficult to find the targets. The
> man who helped us said that we were not the first group to
> come that day. I felt that he was well prepared and eager to
> help.

Pausing only to get their bearings, Dai and his Red Guards set off again with flags flying. Their work, which lasted for two weeks, was systematic, thorough, and, as Dai recalled, merciless.

> Usually we began at one end of a street and worked our way to the other end. Using the police records as guides, we hung signs on the gates of every house that held a Black element. They were always the same, a black background with white characters proclaiming "XXX, Black Element." We would then go back and search each house individually for old things. Each of us judged for ourselves whether or not the items corresponded to the "socialist base." In practice, we confiscated things like vases and furniture decorated in the traditional way. If they had revolutionary decorations, like pictures of Mao Tse-tung or PLA men, we left them alone. Statues and religious articles were either confiscated or smashed. Usually, we would smash something just for effect and confiscate everything else.
>
> Houses of landlords and overseas Chinese received special attention. In these cases, non-socialist objects became associated with items of material comfort. We took all foreign-made items like blankets and quilts from Hong Kong as well as jewelry, scrolls, and even books which had been published before the liberation in 1949.
>
> Because we were afraid that people would hide things, we searched their houses very thoroughly. Some of us would tear down the walls and look behind the plaster while others seized shovels and picks and tore up the cellars looking for hidden items. I even recall seeing two or three people in my group squeezing a tube of toothpaste in a quest for hidden jewelry. They looked so funny with the stuff all over them that I simply had to laugh.
>
> While we searched each house, we made the occupants stand to one side while a few members of our group shouted that they must confess their counterrevolutionary crimes. If the women had long hair, we cut it. Sometimes we would shave half of the hair on a man's head and defy him to shave the rest of it. Our object was to humiliate these people as much as we could.

Whenever we found someone who had a long record of counterrevolutionary offenses, we dragged him into the street, placed a dunce cap on his head and a plaque around his neck bearing his name and a list of his crimes. All of the other Black elements on the street were made to watch while we struggled against him. Frequently, we would call out people of good class background and encourage them to add to the list of crimes. They always had something to say. We could tell that the other Black elements were very frightened.

Usually, we would leave the school after breakfast, choose the area we wanted to cover, and then march there directly. If it was far away, we would commandeer a bus or one of the school vehicles to take us there. Nobody dared to refuse our requests. By midmorning each day, we were deep in the midst of destroying the Four Olds. Gradually, we learned to work in smaller groups. Three or four of us would concentrate upon one house, search the place, and then decide whether or not the occupants were good candidates for struggle. After an hour or so, we would meet again to chose the best example of a Black element and call a struggle meeting for everyone on the street. At lunchtime, half of our group would go back to the school while the remainder carried on. After an hour or so, the group that had been left would be relieved. In this way, we were able to remain active throughout the day. After dinner we would have meetings to discuss problems and summarize our experiences.

After two or three days, I began to notice changes. By this time, there was hardly an area of the city that had not been visited by Red Guards. The people began to take steps to protect themselves, like covering their gates with the quotations of Chairman Mao. Sometimes we would enter a house only to find that all of the furniture had been plastered with quotations or painted red. Old objects became more difficult to find since people began to destroy them themselves. We could see how frightened they were.

We began to have real problems with the things we collected. Naturally none of us would have dreamed of keeping them for ourselves; we wanted to turn them over to the local street committees for safekeeping. However, we needed transportation and that was difficult to find. We commandeered vehicles of all sorts, even ambulances, to haul the stuff away. It was very common to see a truck loaded with furniture, statues, clothing, and books with singing and chanting Red Guards hanging on in every corner. We felt like victorious soldiers returning from the front with our booty.

Eventually, we received a call at the school from one of the local street committees saying that we had left so much that they didn't know what to do with it. They wanted us to come and collect it ourselves. We told them we were too busy.

By the fourth or fifth day, we had reached the point where nearly every neighborhood had been visited by at least two Red Guard groups. It was difficult to find any evidence of the Four Olds. Even on the streets, tight-fitting jeans, pointed shoes, coats and ties, and long hair had been completely replaced by short hair, cotton jackets and trousers, and cloth shoes. It was difficult to find anything to seize or attack. We began to spend more and more time in public places.

Statues, paintings, and other such objects in public parks, temples, and cemeteries were quickly destroyed. We had no plan on these occasions but simply roamed the streets looking for things. Someone would shout, "Let's go to XXX Temple" and we would all follow. Very often, some other group would have been there first and left nothing but a pile of ashes or a group of statues smeared with paint. At least once a day, we would cart a statue to a large intersection and ceremoniously smash it to pieces. Passers-by would stop and watch us; some would congratulate us but most lowered their heads and hurried by. I could see the fear in their eyes and I knew they were afraid that they might be next.

We systematically closed down all joint state-private stores and restaurants and chased away the hawkers who were selling fruit and vegetables. Food was plentiful at that time and business was good. But whenever we ordered a place closed, the manager obeyed. If he showed any resistance, we attacked him, sometimes physically. After a few attacks, no one else resisted us. The waste of food must have been enormous.

Even though the city was full of Red Guards, there was remarkably little friction between groups. Sometimes we would arrive at a place only to find that another group had arrived before us. We would ask them if they wanted any help and usually be welcomed. Some groups were careless in their work. On several occasions, we found some Black elements who had not even been touched. When that happened, we would go over the street again from top to bottom. Once when we were in the midst of going over a street, some members of the first group came back and challenged us. We yelled that they had been careless, and when they defended themselves, an argument started. We almost came to blows before somebody pointed out that this kind of fighting was just what the Black elements wanted. We stopped immediately.

Changing street names provided the greatest source of friction. One group, starting from the east end of a street, might begin changing all of the gate signs to read "East is Red Road," while another group on the west would be writing "Pioneer Road." When the two groups met in the center, there would be a great debate over which name had the greater revolutionary significance. While some members of each group continued the argument, the rest would sneak off and change the signs that had already been revised by the first group. When this was discovered, one side would accuse the other of trickery. Once we actually had a fist fight, but we usually avoided that kind of confrontation. Victory usually fell to whichever side had the greatest number present or to the side with the greatest patience. There were so many streets that it seemed silly to spend time arguing.

We showed no mercy to anyone during these activities. We had adopted the "Red Terror Forever" slogan of Peking's Red Guards in the most literal sense. Perhaps, in our desire to emulate the movement in Peking, we were excessive, but I don't think so. I was interested only in accomplishing the task at hand. Even though I thought of the Black elements as counterrevolutionaries and class enemies, I had no feeling of personal hatred for them as individuals. In truth, this part of the movement was, in some ways, the most fun of all. We were free to do as we pleased, nobody checked on us, and we controlled ourselves. We felt like adults, really for the first time. I thought that what we were doing was important; therefore, I enjoyed myself fully. It was a great deal of fun!

Despite internal co-ordination within some individual Red Guard groups, the movement for destruction of the Four Olds was essentially spontaneous, undirected, and characterized by duplication of effort. By August 26, 1966, even the most rudimentary attempts at planning and co-ordination had been smothered by the frenzied pace of activity.

By the sixth day, it was apparent to me that we were in some ways beginning to waste time. As I led my group through the city, I saw many other Red Guards doing the same things we had done and in the same places. It seemed to be a waste. It was around this time that I first had the idea of going off to exchange experiences with the workers.* Although I kept it to myself, I thought that our work was nearing its end and I was ready for something else. I knew that we could not go on destroying things forever; I wanted to find some unity and organization for our Red Guards. Others had the same feeling.

AUGUST 31–SEPTEMBER 2: THE ATTEMPT AT UNITY

"Others" did indeed have the same feeling. On August 31 Red Guards of the August 1 Middle School called a meeting of representatives of all of Canton's Red Guard organizations. Dai heard the news, delivered by special messengers to all middle schools in Canton, with great interest.

I felt that such a meeting was necessary. It seemed natural that the August 1 school should call it. It was a school for children of high-ranking military cadres with a long reputation for activism. It was perhaps even more a center of activism than Kaochung. In any case, because of the high connections of its students it was regarded as a center of leadership. I knew that if they had called the meeting, it must have the approval of people in very high places. I was very curious

---

* See Chapter Two.

to see how this first attempt to form a unified organization would turn out. I personally wanted it to succeed, but, because I knew of the large number of Red Guard organizations in every school in the city, I had doubts.

The meeting of nearly five thousand representatives of Canton's Red Guard organizations was convened on the evening of September 1, 1966. The elaborate decorations, the large number of reporters, and the presence of leading officials of the provincial and city Party and government organs confirmed Dai's impression that the meeting had been called with the encouragement and support of high-level local officials.

The leader of the August 1 Middle School Mao Tse-tung Doctrine Red Guards, who chaired the meeting, introduced Chao Tzu-yang, the secretary of the Kwangtung Provincial Party Committee, who congratulated the representatives on their exemplary revolutionary conduct in destroying the Four Olds. Dai, who had expected Chao to set forth the guidelines for the proposed unity organization, was disappointed by his remarks. Representatives of other leading organs followed his example of "saying everything while saying nothing" until, finally, the chairman called upon individual Red Guards to speak. Dai listened with growing concern.

The meeting, like so many I attended during this movement, soon got completely out of hand. We had been called into session to discuss unifying all of Canton's Red Guards. However, all we got were innumerable speeches of self-congratulations. No organizational plans were even offered.

Speakers had all been preselected, a fact which made me very angry. Red Guards from Peking alternated with those from Canton in declaring the supremacy of Red Guards organized on the principle of the Five Kinds of Red. Naturally, this principle could only be upheld by defense of the principles of Family Lineage and Naturally Red. Everybody shouted support for these ideas. It was pointless. Nobody disagreed with the idea at that time although there were many who felt as I did that we ought to begin forming organizations for those who were not of the Five Kinds of Red. I had assumed that to be one of the purposes of the meeting.

It went on like this for about two hours. The themes were all the same: "Only leftists are allowed to rebel"; "We are Naturally Red"; "Our parents won the land by blood, we will protect it with our blood"; and "Long live the Five Kinds of Red."

It was then that I began to realize that I did have a real disagreement with these ideas. I was very much in favor of the Five Reds leading the rebellion, but I also thought that the discrimination of the Red Guards was a violation of the principles of mass activism we had all learned. Later, this issue was to divide us almost to the point of bloodshed, but, at the time, no one dared to raise a voice. All I could do was sit and listen to people scream that anyone who wasn't Naturally Red was automatically a son of a bitch. I found it intolerable. Yet the Party officials seemed pleased by it all. They just sat there and made no attempt to direct the discussion.

Suddenly, a group of ten people burst into the hall. It was obvious that they hadn't been invited. None of us could identify them, but since they were wearing army uniforms without unit identification badges and Red Guard armbands, we took them to be the children of ranking military cadres. It was a bit strange because over the last few months, I had gotten to know the faces of many student leaders. Even if I didn't recognize them, somebody else in the hall should have. But nobody seemed able to establish their identity. Briefly it occurred to me that they had been sent by people opposed to Red Guard unity to cause trouble, but I immediately put that suspicion aside.

They ran to the front of the hall and tried to mount the stage, but the leaders of the meeting stopped them. I thought that a fight was going to break out. Then something happened which left me stunned. The chairman grabbed the microphone and asked that, for their own safety, all Party leaders and other officials leave the room. I couldn't believe my eyes when they all complied without a word. They didn't even try to make peace but simply left. In ordinary times, we wouldn't have dared even to raise our voices to each other before them but now they obeyed what amounted to an order from a student. Now I also realized why they had said nothing in the meeting. They were actually frightened by the Red Guards and powerless before them. It was then that I first realized that school Party committees were not the only casualties of the Cultural Revolution. The movement had also affected the provincial and city Party organs. I was shocked.

The new arrivals demanded the right to speak. Our chairman, who turned the question over to the floor, received boos, hisses, and denunciations in response. Suddenly someone demanded that the intruders be made to show their identification papers. Fortunately, they turned out to be Five Reds; had it been otherwise, I have no doubt that they would have been beaten and driven from the hall.

Finally, they mounted the stage and began an immediate denunciation of the meeting. It was, they declared, illegal since not all Red Guard units had agreed to attend, and the title "Red Guard Conference of the Canton District" was a mockery since not every school had been invited. They demanded that the meeting be rescheduled.

The response from the floor was overwhelmingly negative. People shouted their disagreement and demanded that the intruders be thrown out. Several of them rushed up to the stage and tried to seize the microphone. As the intruders resisted, blows began to fly. Soon, there was a brawl, a real free-for-all.

When I saw this, I became totally disgusted. There was no discipline, just everyone doing exactly as he pleased. I had never seen such a disorderly meeting before. Most of the other representatives shared my feelings. We knew now that, barring the direct intervention of Mao himself, unity could never be achieved. In retrospect, I must admit that such disorder was probably characteristic of most Red Guard convocations. In fact, it was characteristic of the whole Red Guard rebellion.

As Dai bicycled back to Kaochung to report on the meeting to his schoolmates, he pondered the implications of what he had just seen. He was particularly disturbed by the docile reaction of the provincial Party leaders to the disturbance caused by the ten intruders. That evening he and his fellow activists reached a startling conclusion: They were on their own. There was no longer any effective leadership they could count on except from the authorities in Peking.

I could not purge the picture of our Party leaders leaving the room from my mind. My schoolmates were equally fascinated. Those Red Guards intruders were obviously related to high-ranking military cadres. They wore army uniforms and spoke with a northern accent. Thus, they had either come directly from the north or their parents were stationed in Canton. They were so spruce and neat in appearance, that I reasoned they must have come from the north to exchange experiences just as Sung Hsueh-min had done.

Our meeting had been called by the provincial authorities. The intruders had obviously intended to break up the meeting. Thus, they were encouraging us to rebel against the provincial Party leadership just as they themselves had done against the local Party leadership in Peking. Given their high connections, their actions must have had the approval of the central Party leadership in Peking. It became apparent to us that the Kwangtung Party leadership must be under some suspicion.

This conclusion was reinforced by the actions of the leaders themselves. Remember, they had simply left the hall when the chairman of the meeting told them to do so. In short, they were aware of a new current and were afraid to do anything to antagonize the Red Guards. How could we regard them as leaders after such a performance? From that point on, we ceased to look to them for direction. They existed for us only as an object of suspicion and criticism. We relied almost entirely upon news from the center for instructions and guidance. If the Provincial Party Committee issued an instruction, we looked for confirmation from Peking before we obeyed. It had come to that.

Indeed, it had "come to that." Kaochung's Party and administrative organization had long since atrophied. Young Communist League organization and activities had been displaced by the Red

Guard program. Now the city and provincial Party apparatus was under a cloud of suspicion. The only direct force of leadership in the lives of Dai and his fellows was Kaochung's Cultural Revolution Preparatory Committee and the Red Guard Headquarters. Yet the Cultural Revolution Preparatory Committee (even minus the non-Five Red members) was the creation of the work team which had been sent by the Provincial Party Committee; therefore it too was suspect.

Dai was happy to rely upon the directives of the Central Cultural Revolution Group in Peking. Hence, when he heard that students were being encouraged to exchange experiences with workers, he willingly set out for the Tsangku Warehouse, confident that he was doing the right thing. Similarly, it was the call of the Peking leadership which caused him to leave the warehouse and venture north to engage in the "great exchange of revolutionary experiences," or *ch'uan-lien*. All leadership power and authority were now vested in the center, and nearly all of Canton's "Little Red Soldiers" were ready and eager to obey it.

CHAPTER FOUR

Revolutionary Tourism: September–October 1966

Reckoned by a Chinese Communist calendar, 1966 could accurately be called the year of the student. Beginning in August of that year, and tapering off only in December, several million youths from China's colleges, universities, and middle schools took advantage of a new movement to conduct "great exchange of revolutionary experiences" (*ko-ming ta ch'uan-lien*) by embarking upon the first long-distance journeys of their lives.

Like most other aspects of the Cultural Revolution, the *ch'uan-lien* movement was launched by Mao Tse-tung and his supporters in Peking with definite ends in mind, ends that were eventually accomplished after a fashion despite severe organizational problems. During the spring and summer of 1966, Chairman Mao had laid down his challenge to Party members throughout the country with a series of actions culminating in the purge of the Peking Municipal

Party Committee and the bold mass campaign outlined at the Central Committee's Eleventh Plenum in August. By autumn, the lines of political conflict had sharpened, and it soon became apparent that many Party leaders would attempt actively to sabotage the Plenum's revolutionary program. Mao countered by arousing widespread attacks against these opposition chieftains. His tactic was to call for *ch'uan-lien.*

Transporting individuals to study the advanced experiences of faraway units was already a familiar educational method in China. However, it had been used mainly to popularize specific techniques applicable to the solution of particular problems such as flood control and hospital organization, to name just two examples. But this politically oriented exchange created a unique problem. Employing the device on a grand scale appropriate to the Great Proletarian Cultural Revolution and involving the workers themselves, Mao would run the risk of disrupting production and seriously affecting the entire national economy.

Only two major groups, then, could plausibly be used to propagate the new radical wave, soldiers or students. Mao's ultimate decision to rely upon the students was probably based upon their supposed greater ideological enthusiasm, their lack of any responsibility for national defense or the maintenance of public order, and the absence within the student group of a regional or national command structure riddled with anti-Maoist or "conservative" officials. On the other side of the ledger, students were largely inexperienced in the complicated business of carrying on a major revolutionary movement. But Mao may well have wished to kill two birds with one stone by giving his revolutionary successor generation a baptism of fire.

Whatever the intention, no sooner did the new program begin than many people outside the approved group of "revolutionary teachers and students" joined in the *ch'uan-lien.* Workers whose local strikes had been suppressed set out for Peking to lodge direct complaints with the central leaders. Other workers were even encouraged by managers to leave their jobs to travel, one of the many strategies of what was later condemned as "economism." People who had been "capped" as one kind of "element" or another traveled either to their provincial capital or to Peking itself to seek a "reversal of verdict." Other people who found themselves among the targets of criticism in the Cultural Revolution at home or at work took relief in *ch'uan-lien* to remove themselves from an oppressive local environment; not surprisingly, this group was reported to be least willing to return home when *ch'uan-lien* was formally brought to an end.

Ironically, the students themselves contributed to the failure of the goals of the *ch'uan-lien* program. Largely ignorant, as will be seen, of Mao's purpose in sending them forth, they escaped into an exhilarating, constraint-free atmosphere of freedom which made them feel suddenly welcome as full participants "in the important affairs of state." Dai noted that *ch'uan-lien* took temporary precedence over all other activities; hordes of youth who squeezed into bulging, creaking trains were plain and simply caught up in an adventure. Indeed, many of them paid only scant attention to their political responsibilities. As candidly expressed by one Red Guard wall-poster author: "Chairman Mao, thank you for letting us travel all over the country without paying a cent."

Dai Hsiao-ai himself made two trips north, one to Peking directly and one which included stopovers at famous cities along the route. His own account of his travels is anecdotal, humorous, and at times full of irony and sarcasm. Neither he nor his companions had much sense of the purpose of their mission. On the contrary, they regarded it as a lark to be enjoyed. Because his own account captures so well the exuberant spirit of *ch'uan-lien*, we will discard our usual third-person, descriptive approach in this and in the following chapter. Instead, Dai's own essay, freely translated, will speak for itself.

> *Ta ch'uan-lien* was one of the "five great [activities]" of the Cultural Revolution.* In Kwangtung Province, the desig-

* These were "great contending" (*ta ming*), "great blooming" (*ta fang*), "great seizure of power" (*ta to ch'uan*), "great debate" (*ta pien-lun*), and "great exchange of revolutionary experiences." It should be emphasized that *ch'uan-lien* with other nearby students and workers was common enough before the Cultural

nated period of *ch'uan-lien* was from August 18 until November 20, 1966. But many students continued to travel until well after that date. In all, nine million Red Guards passed in review in Peking. Countless numbers of army and administrative personnel were detailed to assist traveling Red Guards, and rail, road, and water transport were all mobilized to carry them around. The very scale of the *ch'uan-lien* movement made it an important aspect of the Cultural Revolution without which, in retrospect, Mao Tse-tung could never have overthrown Liu Shao-ch'i; *ch'uan-lien* was significant therefore as Mao's own strategy.

Because Liu Shao-ch'i had been Head of State since 1959, he had been able to construct a personal system of power. Aided by Teng Hsiao-p'ing with his base in the Party and Ch'en Yun with his base in the economic organizations, Liu had formed a camp that was both strong and pervasive. At all levels in China, leadership in everything is exercised from above, and in the Cultural Revolution there was certainly no exception. But since all channels in the systems mentioned above were controlled by people he wanted to overthrow, Mao could not rely exclusively upon ordinary methods. He therefore decided to mobilize the energies of youth, irrespective of human and material costs, to destroy Liu Shao-ch'i's strongholds by means of the *ta ch'uan-lien.*

When Mao Tse-tung first reviewed the Red Guards on August 18, most of them had come from Peking itself or such nearby places as Tientsin. Later on, we went north to Peking while Red Guards from the capital spread out to other places. Ultimately, the whole country was in confusion.

Mao Tse-tung's two reviews of Red Guards in August greatly influenced the entire country; Kwangtung students excitedly demanded to be allowed to go to Peking. Our Provincial Party Committee's initial plan to send a thousand-man delegation to represent Kwangtung failed when students attacked

---

Revolution. But "great" *ch'uan-lien* was distinguished from the earlier version by the great numbers of people involved and by the great distances they traveled. In effect, it was a new phenomenon.

the idea by demanding that everyone be free to go. Two lines of opinion gradually crystallized in the schools, one favoring the strong demands to travel (mostly rebel students). and the other opposing the journey on the grounds that, if everyone left to *ch'uan-lien*, then the movement in the schools would suffer. This latter group, mostly teachers, did not understand the great significance of *ch'uan-lien*. The debate went on for several days, with both sides basing their arguments upon Mao's quotes as well as editorials in *Red Flag* and the *People's Daily*. The Preparatory Committee at our own school came out against *ch'uan-lien* even though most students supported the idea. Actually, I think the students really wanted simply to embark upon adventurous travels, despite their arguments that "We want to see Chairman Mao in person" or that "We want to go to exchange revolutionary experiences."

Speaking at one of the Red Guard reviews in September, Chou En-lai proposed that all college students should come to Peking in turn, and that one out of every ten middle school students should also be chosen to make the trip. Accordingly, our school (then still under the leadership of the Preparatory Committee) began in early September to elect its representatives. This election was carried out by secret ballot with all teachers and students in the school taking part. But since the prestige of the teachers was very low then, we students easily elected both our own and the faculty representatives. It was decided that at least one teacher delegate should be chosen to represent every twenty teachers. However, the faculty could vote only for their own representatives, not for students. As a result our delegation included over ninety students, three teachers, and one worker (a driver). The Preparatory Committee transmitted the outcome of the election to the Provincial Party Committee, which in turn made arrangements for us to leave for Peking on September 25. We were to attend the October 1 National Day celebrations in the capital.

When we entered Canton East Railway Station on the twenty-fifth, our papers were examined by some Doctrine Guards. Since most of our group were official Red Guards wearing appropriate armbands, we encountered no difficulty.

However, all those who were not Red Guards were stopped and required to report their class status. Fortunately, the few members of our group who were not Five Kinds of Red belonged either to the "middle peasant" or "self-employed" categories; none were Seven Kinds of Black. When they were finally passed through the Doctrine Guards' "examination room" and arrived at our coach, we could tell they were very happy. Yet even as they related their experiences to us, they were obviously still frightened.

The train was so packed that four of us were assigned to every three seats; we struggled to find a place to sit amid quarrels and shouting. The fracas tapered off after the train pulled out of the station, and our spirits were soon restored. There was much singing of revolutionary songs. One fellow said exultantly, "Even when dreaming I never imagined being able to go to Peking without spending a cent!" Another remarked hopefully, "When we get to Peking we can see snow!" Still others expressed their determination to see the famous Yi Ho Garden (renamed "People's Park" early in the Cultural Revolution), whose beautiful scenery they had often read about. A few even had great expectations of sampling Peking's famous cuisine. All conversation went on in this way; I cannot remember anyone proposing that we exchange revolutionary experiences in the capital.

The train moved along at high speed. As night came, many students and Red Guards fell asleep in their seats while others spread newspapers in the aisle and lay down there. The place was really a mess; some students could not even make it through to the lavatory. When we awoke at sunrise, we discovered we had crossed into a new province. Much excitement was aroused by the differences in the people's dress, the houses, and the fields.

Even greater confusion reigned when we pulled into a station. Since stopovers were very brief, our huge mass of Red Guards would scramble off the train like hungry tigers bounding from a cage to find something to eat. In the confusion one usually got a few cakes (*shao ping*) without paying. It was also necessary to steal hot water, and many of us got our hands burned while trying. As soon as the whistle blew everyone would pile back onto the train. There was absolutely no discipline.

When we alighted from the train in Peking after two days and two nights of riding, we were welcomed enthusiastically by Red Guards from the capital. We then had to submit to a second strict examination. I saw a few Canton students taken into custody to be sent back home because it was alleged they were Seven Kinds of Black. Peking was still controlled at this time by the bourgeois reactionary Theory of Family Lineage, so Black students were definitely not welcome. It was pitiable the way young students, said to be Seven Kinds of Black, were surrounded by Peking Red Guards speaking the northern dialect, beaten, and cursed. The victims were as pale-faced as if they were being led off to their executions. They were taken away amid a chorus of curses like "Son of a bitch! Damn your mother! How dare you come to *ch'uan-lien!*" We were lucky not to have any Black students in our ranks, but the middle peasants among us were quite upset. They continually questioned those of us wearing armbands, "Will middle peasants be sent away?" They hoped we would protect them at critical moments. In Canton, we could oppose the Peking Red Guards' excesses by making a show of force. But in the unfamiliar city of Peking, we would have to do our best to stick to the rules, even to the point of abandoning our middle peasant comrades. Besides, we felt some genuine respect for the Peking Red Guards: They had started the movement and had already passed through the test of struggle. Both boys and girls had stern countenances, as befitted people who were sophisticated and experienced in revolution.

Next we were taken by one of the Peking Red Guards to a "Reception Station for Revolutionary Teachers and Students Come to *Ch'uan-lien* from Outside the Capital" (*wai ti ko-ming shih-sheng ch'uan-lien chieh-tai chan*) to arrange a place for us to stay. On the way, our guide's fancy was caught by the Canton-manufactured all-yellow Mao badges we wore on our chests. He asked if we would give him one, but no one would oblige since each of us was issued only one when leaving Canton. He finally managed to exchange one Peking-made Mao souvenir for one of ours; later we discovered we had been cheated, since in Peking one Canton-made souvenir could easily fetch three or four local ones. We had to admit that Canton's Red Guards were not as crafty as Peking's.

In early October *ch'uan-lien* had not yet reached its high tide. No small number of people had come to Peking then, but compared with later months, the city was not especially busy. We quickly concluded formalities at the reception center and were assigned to live at a dormitory belonging to the First Ministry of Machine Building.

I noticed that the buses brought to carry us to the dormitory had come from Tientsin, Tsinan, Harbin, and elsewhere. Peking's own buses were doubtless insufficient to handle the crowds. We were tired after spending two days and nights on the train, but our curiosity and admiration for Peking kept our excitement high. We thought it strange that even though Peking was the capital city, the houses were not as high as those in Canton. There were fewer pedestrians on the street, and the lights were not as bright. The Four Olds were, we thought, probably destroyed more thoroughly here than elsewhere.

When the driver told us we would soon pass through T'ien An Men Square we let out a cheer. We had always seen pictures of both the square and the gate in books and movies and as children we had memorized essays describing these places. Many of us could still recite them. Now for the first time we would really see the sights ourselves. However, when the gate came into view, we were a bit disappointed. It was not nearly as tall and grand as we had imagined. A fellow student even cried out. "This is not the real T'ien An Men! It may be a model!", which started up a silly debate. It all happened because the government had exaggerated freely in propagandizing young kids.

When we arrived at the First Ministry of Machine Building (*i chi pu*) it was already two in the morning and everyone was dog-tired. After going through a few more formalities we followed one of the reception personnel to an office where bamboo mats had been spread out on a bed of straw. We were so tired that no one really cared about the crude arrangements; on the train almost everyone had slept in a sitting position. At last there was a place to lie down and stretch out; nothing could have been better. Unfortunately, however, the rubber shoes we had been wearing for two days produced an acrid aroma, which caused the whole room to smell strongly of rubber shoes. But even that did not keep anybody awake.

When we arose at nine the following morning and went to the dining room for breakfast, we saw that the *I Chi Pu* was housing several groups of Red Guards. One group I met there had come from Hofei Technical College to lodge a complaint against Li Pao-hua (first secretary of the Anhwei Provincial Party Committee) for suppressing the student movement in that province.

Since leaving Kwangtung, we had eaten no white rice at all, just an awful-tasting steamed bread (*wo-wo t'ou*). We all hoped that after arriving at Chairman Mao's side we could eat white rice again. How could anyone foresee that in the capital we would have to go on enduring *wo-wo t'ou?* We felt the standard of living in Peking was considerably low in comparison with that in Canton. After breakfast we were all eager to go out sight-seeing, to find out just what the much-talked-about Peking really looked like.

However, an *I Chi Pu* comrade told us that since on the day after next (October 1) we would be reviewed by Chairman Mao at the T'ien An Men Gate, we had to practice. Our instructor, a worker in the ministry, told us we would form nine rows of fifteen marchers each. Groups of fifteen would practice walking in horizontal lines, carrying Mao quotation books in our hands and shouting "Long live Chairman Mao." A line of fifteen locked arm in arm would alternate with a line holding large signs which together made up a Mao quotation. Our rows were seldom straight during this rehearsal, and we showed little improvement even after hours of work. By afternoon most people had slipped away to wander about the city.

We continued to practice in this halfhearted way until the afternoon of September 30. We then went to sleep early at about five or six o'clock but were awakened that same night at eleven to make final preparations for the review. Each person was provided with a small string bag containing some bread, a few pieces of fruit, and three eggs. These items were

meant to be eaten during the parade itself, but some classmates gobbled the eggs down right away. At midnight we
started out.

The *I Chi Pu* was located in eastern Peking, not far from
T'ien An Men as the crow flies. But since the parade would
move from west to east the entire body of marchers had to
assemble on West Ch'ang-an Street. The eastern end of the
street would be kept empty to enable the marchers to disperse.
The entire area was therefore sealed off by the army, requiring
us to travel a long distance to the western side of the city
by a roundabout route.

Peking's lights were dim at midnight and most residents had
already gone to sleep. But out on the streets there was a
mass of Red Guards running about and shouting beneath a
blanket of red flags. Anyone who paused was immediately
separated from his group and had to run to catch up; when
the ranks ahead halted, we halted too. Some who went off
in the darkness to relieve themselves never did find their
original unit again; they could be heard everywhere, calling
hysterically. Many people lost a shoe when the person behind
stepped on their heel. It was chaotic!

We went on running like this for five hours. When we
finally arrived at our destination, a small street running at
right angles to West Ch'ang-an Street, the sky was still dark.
Many people were so exhausted that they spread newspapers
on the ground and tried to nap, but the Peking worker guides
(one for every fifteen students) warned them it was unwise to
sleep on the cold ground. Even though we kept alert for a
while by singing revolutionary songs, the effect did not last
long. Some of us fell asleep and had to be pulled up by our
neighbors.

At last the sun came up, warming our bodies and turning
the dew on our damp clothes to steam. While we pitiable young
red soldiers had been suffering in the dark, cold street, our
great red commander was tucked away in his warm bed. At
eight o'clock, normally our breakfast time, everyone opened
their sacks and took out the *man-t'ou* (a heavy wheat bread
that provides bulk in the northern Chinese diet). The *man-
t'ou*, which seemed to have been made with low-grade flour,

had turned into a hard lump overnight and one could make a noise striking it with a rock. We rice-eating southerners just couldn't swallow the stuff! One fellow who peeled the skin off his *man-t'ou* and tossed it to the ground received a stern lecture from a Peking worker: "This *man-t'ou* is only for officials; ordinary residents have no way to get any!"

In China queuing up ("forming a long dragon") to buy things was in no way out of the ordinary, but here we had to line up even to use the toilet. Temporary facilities constructed for the huge crowds were very rustic, usually a pit dug beside the road with bamboo mats hung around it. This is what it was like to relieve oneself in the capital of China in the middle of the twentieth century. These little huts with the characteristic pile of fresh earth beside them could be seen on every street in Peking during the period of *ch'uan-lien*. After relieving oneself one threw a little fresh earth into the hole. Adjacent sections for boys and girls were separated by a thin bamboo mat that was not only full of holes but was also of limited height (on the mainland, economy must be practiced in everything, you know). By standing in the right place, with one's back straightened, each side could see the other crystal clear.

Shortly after nine o'clock a helicopter flew back and forth overhead, probably to inspect the parade formation. One student thought, "Chairman Mao might be on that plane." However, most disagreed: "Chairman Mao is probably brushing his teeth at this moment," offered one.

To relieve the boredom several of us got up and walked through a small alley to the next street. It was being used to move vehicles, and with the exception of a single traffic policeman directing a large number of automobiles, it was devoid of people. One Red Guard who had been watching there for a long time claimed he had just seen Lin Piao. As we stood there both foreigners and Chinese went by, and as each car passed we Red Guards applauded. Some foreigners smiled and nodded their heads, or even clapped in response. But no small number of them ignored our applause, or glared at us with angry eyes. Judging from their looks they seemed to hate us

Red Guards. Every time such an incident happened the traffic policeman chided us: "They ignored you. What are you applauding for?" We thought that such foreigners were probably embassy officials or guests from revisionist countries. After that we cursed them, "Stinking revisionists . . ."

At ten o'clock the revolutionary song "East Is Red" blared forth from the loudspeaker, followed by male and female voices shouting together "Chairman Mao has arrived!" The whole crowd shouted loudly, "Long live Chairman Mao!" Since we were not sitting in front of T'ien An Men and could not see the reviewing stand, we concentrated on the loudspeaker. First Ch'en Po-ta announced the opening of the meeting; then Lin Piao spoke, followed by Chou En-lai. Chou's voice was loudest and clearest of all, and his Mandarin most standard and correct. But Lin Piao, Chairman Mao's close comrade in arms and the deputy commander of our Red Guards, was awful. His voice was pitiably weak and hesitant, and his Mandarin was a mess. If his speech had not been published in the next day's paper we never would have known what he said. One rather naïve schoolmate complained carelessly that even a primary school student could speak more eloquently than Lin Piao. Fortunately we shut him up before the Peking worker overheard; otherwise he would have been in trouble. We wondered why the great commander had chosen this kind of successor. Could he really lead the Chinese revolution and the world revolution?

In the Cultural Revolution, the Red Guards seldom observed discipline; even while the central leaders were speaking the snoring of many sleepers sometimes drowned out the sound of the loudspeaker. Some played pranks, played games, or even wandered away.

With the morning sun now blazing down upon the unshaded street, many of us began to feel dizzy. Finally, when the end of the meeting was announced at eleven o'clock, we all got up to begin the parade. Advancing slowly at first, we followed the ranks of marchers ahead of us out into West Ch'ang-an Street, the widest in all Peking, where we joined the human tide. Everyone seemed to have red armbands, red flags, red Mao quotation signboards (*yü-lu pen*), and red

Mao quote cards (*yü-lu p'ai*). The ocean of red was uncomfortable to the eyes. Our ranks resounded with ragged cheers of "Long live Chairman Mao." Before long Ch'ang-an Street was smothered in great clouds of dust.

Each horizontal rank had 135 marchers, organized into 9 groups of 15 each. Since our assembly street was the second one, we were the second closest group to T'ien An Men during the march by. First to come into view were the spectator stands for foreigners on the west side of the gate. It seemed that some had already left, unable to endure the hot sun. The rest gave little evidence of interest in our undisciplined ranks; many had their backs turned to us. However, there was one group wearing headbands with Mao quotations and holding high five single-character signboards which together read "Thought of Mao Tse-tung." They looked quite enthusiastic: I think they were Japanese. In sharp contrast to the western side, the eastern spectator stands were filled with Chinese who shouted together with us.

As we slowly approached T'ien An Men, we could just barely make out the VIPs under the large red lanterns. Long ago, even before entering primary school, I could sing "East Is Red" and knew that "China has given birth to a Mao Tse-tung." The song's words described him as a "savior star" but in my younger days I thought since even ping-pong balls were bigger than stars it was not great enough to compare our leader to a star, especially because I felt at the time our leader was not born an ordinary man. Mao Tse-tung might have been born as a sun god. We even called him the red sun who arose at Shao Shan. The Communist Party was created and developed by him alone; the country's army was brought into being and cultivated by him alone; all success and achievement were his alone, and he never made mistakes. Every word he spoke became a "supreme directive" studied by seven hundred million people. More than ten years' of education could not but strike some response within me. I felt our leader was omnipotent, hence it was with great excitement that I hoped to see him.

As we came closer to the gate, we could make out the personages more clearly. First was Chou En-lai, looking lively,

pointing here and there to describe the parade. Standing high
and appearing very healthy was our leader. Next in line was
Lin Piao, very short and resembling an invalid. White-haired
Liu Shao-ch'i was not interested enough even to wave. Except
for Mao, Liu, and Chou, who all wore cadre clothes, everyone
there was in military uniform. Because of his distinctive
mustache, the easiest one to pick out was Ho Lung; he must
have been unaware of his impending fate since he looked
rather lively too. Actually we caught only glimpses of the
leaders; one schoolmate saw only Chou and mistook him for
Mao, which gave us all a good laugh later on.

As we passed before the reviewing stand, our emotions rose
to a fever pitch. The shouts of "Long live Chairman Mao" were
deafening. I should emphasize that no small number of Red
Guards and youth adored Mao Tse-tung, and tears came to
many eyes the moment they saw him; as a remembrance
everyone later recorded in their book of Mao quotations that
we had passed T'ien An Men at exactly twelve forty-five.

We moved by very quickly. Model Red Guards from Peking
had been posted along every block of the parade route to
help maintain order. Sometimes people tried to force their
way past them, to look at famous sights, like the Golden Water
Bridge. At the west end of the reviewing stand a great number
of Peking Red Guards held high their books of Mao quotations
to symbolize that Chairman Mao was before our eyes. Then
they recited the quotation "Be resolute, fear no sacrifice, and
surmount every difficulty to win victory" and exhorted us to
finish the march at a run. We began a "marathon" run from
the west side of T'ien An Men down the entire remaining
section of West Ch'ang-an Street into another street, altogether
about one third of the route. Had we not kept moving, the
ranks behind would have run us down and broken up our
group. In the confusion, we could no longer hold our red
banners high, but rested them on our shoulders instead.
Residents watched us from the alleyways, and friendly street
activists offered us tea and water. Thirsty as we were, though,
no one dared accept their hospitality for fear of losing the
group. After returning to the dormitory, we discovered a few
schoolmates (mostly girls) had been lost in the rush. It was

the following day before we found them; unable to run any farther they had lain down on the ground, and had been taken in for the night by another Red Guard dormitory in the vicinity. On the night of October 1, we walked back to T'ien An Men Square to watch a fireworks display, but even though the sky was brilliant with exploding colors, many again fell asleep on the ground.

Now that sight-seeing no longer conflicted with parade practice, the streets were filled with jostling Red Guards. One had to wait half an hour just to catch a bus. The first time we went out, we encountered many people who wanted to visit the famous Yi Ho Garden, built by Ch'ing dynasty Empress Dowager Tz'u Hsi with funds originally appropriated for naval construction. Getting an ordinary bus was difficult enough, but catching one to Yi Ho Garden even more so because crowds of people wanting to go there were waiting at every stop. When the bus pulled up to where we were standing everyone swarmed forward; girls in particular had a tough time making it on board. Three of us managed to squeeze our way inside, but the other two in our group watched helplessly as the bus pulled away. Actually we felt quite lucky since the ones left behind were the two big northerners we did not care for at all.

As we walked toward Yi Ho Garden someone, probably a Peking Red Guard, handed us a leaflet filled with invective against Red Guards visiting Peking, ostensibly to learn about revolution, but who actually spent all their time sight-seeing. We threw them on the ground. After all, what did Peking Red Guards do when they came to Canton?

We paid two cents to enter the garden itself. Overall, it was a marvelous place, but the presence of Mao quotations everywhere ruined the natural scenery. To hang the words of Lin Piao from the top of a pagoda seemed especially ridiculous. Perhaps someone thought this would "make the ancient serve the present."

I do not think anyone who has visited Yi Ho Garden can forget the long, long corridors decorated with delicate paintings along which the Emperor and Empress Dowager walked. But now, after the "Destroy the Four Olds" campaign, a new décor of big-character posters had been added. Two of these stood out from the rest because of their imposing size. One proposed changing its name to "Long March Corridor" while the other favored "Oppose Revisionism Corridor." A large crowd had gathered there to debate the issue. The anti-revisionists had the upper hand when I left!

On the nearby lake shore, many Red Guards had lined up to pay twenty cents to a boatwoman to row them about. Those already on the lake were laughing happily. I wondered if all the Red Guards who spoke out against revisionism would themselves let a single opportunity for enjoyment pass.

Following the practice of the ancients who composed couplets to commemorate staying somewhere, Red Guards covered the walls of temples with untidy characters like "XXX of Class 302, Futan University, Shanghai, visited this place September 20, 1966." There were also a few odd scribblings such as one that read, "Damn it all, I oppose writing characters all over these walls!"

The great number of Red Guards in the park demonstrated clearly that sight-seeing was their main interest. After we returned to our dormitory, however, we falsely claimed we had been exchanging revolutionary experiences at schools in Peking. Everyone knew we had been out touring just as they had been, but no one spoke of the matter openly.

The next day while touring on Wang Fu Ching Avenue, we found a Mao badge exchange operating in front of the *People's Daily* editorial offices. A Chinese proverb says, "Things which are few are also expensive." Any sort of Mao badge produced in only small quantities and looking a little different from other ones was immediately recognized as higher in value, so Red Guards who had them would demand higher prices. One such badge could be exchanged for seven or eight, or more, common ones.

The following day we sampled one of Peking's numerous Moslem restaurants (it actually tasted pretty good), and afterward went to the office of the Central Committee of the Young Communist League on West Ch'ang-an Street. Since the gate had been sealed shut by pasting up two paper announcements to that effect in the form of an "X" across the front, we entered through a side door. Inside, the walls were covered with big-character posters, mostly about the YCL leadership but also about P'eng Chen and Wang Wei.[1] As members of the League, the purge of its central leadership and the subsequent disintegration of its organization had come as a surprise to us all. We were therefore curious to read these posters, as were the many other students present.

During the last few days we thought we had better have a look at a few schools. Since our fellow students had elected us to do just that, we feared not having any intelligence to report. Our first visits were made to Peking and Tsinghua universities, where we got the impression that the schools in Peking had been more affected than those in Canton. Not only were their loudspeakers noisy but their big-character posters were extremely large. There were bold characters in great numbers, and of generally high quality. People were criticized mercilessly in these posters with clever, well-drawn cartoons. We were especially struck that even Nieh Yuan-tzu, who enjoyed high prestige throughout the country because Mao Tse-tung had supported her personally, was attacked in many of the posters at Peking University (where she was a member of the Philosophy Department).[2] We discussed at length this revelation of rebellious spirit at the Peking schools, and decided accordingly that after returning home we would act the same. By writing the biggest banners and posters and by drawing the most colorful caricatures, we would dominate the big-character poster board. By seizing control of the school's broadcasting station, we would control propaganda. We planned to make a thunderous noise, kick out the Preparatory Committee, and generally stir up Kaochung Middle School. This is what we learned in Peking!

On the evening of October 4, the Ministry informed us we would have to leave Peking the next day. The number of visitors had grown so large that problems had arisen in supplying the city with fresh vegetables and grain.

Our feelings of regret over having to leave Peking were strongest when we passed T'ien An Men for the last time on the way to the railway station. Where else in the world could one find a chairman or a president comparable to Mao Tse-tung; even communism's Marx and Lenin were not equal to our leader. Since we were young we had heard about Mao Tse-tung, seen pictures of Mao Tse-tung, talked about Mao Tse-tung, sung about Mao Tse-tung, and read about Mao Tse-tung. Today it was also our leader Mao Tse-tung who allowed us to travel about to *ch'uan-lien* without paying a cent. As we were about to leave Peking, I resolved to strive very hard to become a cadre or some kind of model and thereby gain another opportunity to come to see Mao Tse-tung. At that time I was simple-minded and childish.

Peking Station on the afternoon of October 5 was in greater chaos than Canton East Station had been two weeks before. As soon as the gates opened we dashed past a group of slower students in the hope of being first to board. We were quite startled to find the seats already full! The other passengers must have dropped from the sky or burrowed up from the ground! Later we learned they were a cunning group of Peking Red Guards who had entered when the gates were opened for a previous train. We always thought the Peking Red Guards were the toughest, shrewdest, and most experienced in struggle, and most prone to exaggerate. I think this was a reflection of their living constantly at Chairman Mao's side and being superior students of Mao Tse-tung's thought.

There was nothing to do but occupy the aisles of the coach, together with our quilts and our luggage. Sitting in groups on the floor we grew angrier and angrier the more we thought about this. We used Cantonese to curse the Peking Red Guards, and held lengthy discussions about avenging ourselves in Canton.

Peking dialect was commonly used all over the country, so we knew what they said; however, when we spoke in Cantonese the Peking Red Guards could not understand us. When we cursed them they simply smiled. After they discovered we were natives of Kwangtung they asked us many questions about our home province. "Is fruit abundant in Canton? Is there one kind that looks like a football, and must be broken open with an ax before it can be eaten?" They were talking about coconuts. Later they asked us if there was a sea in Kwangtung, if Hong Kong was far from Canton, and whether we had gone out to destroy the Four Olds. Sometimes we gave quite colorful answers: One fellow, for example, frightened them good and proper by describing great varieties of imaginary poisonous snakes that were found in Canton; one had to be on guard constantly, he said, since once bitten no medicine could save you. We were repulsed by the conceit the Peking Red Guards displayed, and thoroughly enjoyed putting them on. When our train stopped briefly at Shao-kuan Station [a few hours from Canton], all alighted to have their first taste of bananas. We graciously showed them how to eat a banana properly, skin and all. As you might imagine, banana peels are not easily swallowed. The more gullible ones finally did succeed in stuffing them all down after nibbling at the fruit for a long time. A few even told us, smiling, "Kwangtung fruit is excellent, really excellent." Others were quite angry.

Since the people who represented our school in Peking were activists in our student movement, the group left behind was essentially without leadership. Many simply returned home in the name of local *ch'uan-lien*, but what was worse, the "monsters and ghosts" had taken advantage of the absence of supervision to return home too. We had to send out students to drag the latter group back to continue washing toilets and sweeping floors.

October in Kwangtung is a critical time in the growing season during which it is necessary to pamper young plants with water and fertilizer. Since no rain had fallen for a while, Chao Tzu-yang (first secretary, Kwangtung Provincial Party Committee) issued a call for all college and middle school students in Canton to go down to the countryside with their teachers to help the peasants save the crop. A notice from our Preparatory Committee was posted shortly after calling a meeting of leaders of all organizations in the school to discuss the matter of going to the countryside to participate in labor. The resulting decision was that everyone would go for two weeks to work in some village the committee would name. Feelings of antagonism among various factions had by this time grown to such a point that organizing work teams on the basis of school classes would have been impossible. It was therefore agreed that the whole school should form a single production brigade, under which production teams would be based upon the Red Guard combat groups. Students belonging to no organization at all should quickly form one, or else temporarily participate in one of the existing combat groups.

By October 10, we had decided to help out a production brigade under Kung-she Commune in nearby Hua County. A small minority of students refused to go to labor and insisted instead upon going home or off to further *ch'uan-lien*. A few others were assigned to remain at the school to keep watch over the "monsters and ghosts," since we felt that to have them wearing their high hats in a rural village would not look good.

When we arrived at the village the farmers welcomed us warmly by providing hot water to drink† and helping us with our luggage; afterward everyone was assigned to production teams as planned, either by combat group or by newly formed voluntary group. We slept with the peasants, from two to four of us to a house. Since the peasants had no spare rooms, we were usually given the main room or the barn. There were no spare beds either, since rural families often had husband and wife, elderly parents, and children all sleeping in the same room, sometimes even in the same bed. The leader of the production team to which I was assigned urged his peasants to improvise beds from house doors by taking them down off their hinges. But doors of rural houses in China have a brass ring in the middle for a guest to sound when he wishes to rouse the occupant and it was very painful to sleep on them.

Our host family were poor peasants (all of those who entertained us were either poor or lower-middle peasants) with only the mother and one son over thirty. I heard he was anxious to find a wife. While we stayed with this production team, he often struck up conversations with our girl classmates, to the great amusement of the boys. He did not seem to mind being teased, though. Judging from the calendar on the wall

† A popular thirst quencher in China.

this family must have had relatives in Hong Kong. The top half featured a very undignified picture of a pretty girl. Her sleeves were quite short so that her arms and shoulders were entirely exposed; her neck and part of her breasts were visible as well. Her fingernails were long, and her hair style very tall and awkward-looking. Since we had never seen this kind of clothing before we got quite worked up over it. If this family had not been "poor peasants" they would have been in trouble. We later discovered that they also continued to make offerings to the shrines of spirits. I felt this was awfully strange: Canton had destroyed the Four Olds in a thoroughgoing fashion, but this place was peaceful as a "secluded valley."[3]

We began our labor the very next day. When we reached the fields we immediately noticed several middle-aged people with black signs hanging on their chests. They were of course members of the Seven Kinds of Black. One peasant boy, who had not yet passed his test to enter higher middle school, told us proudly that he and his schoolmates had made those signs themselves. He cursed the Seven Kinds of Black as enemies who must be suppressed. He also informed me that a youth standing directly ahead carrying a hoe was a Black element's son, and that I should be careful not to go near him. The older peasants, however, got along all right with those wearing the black signs; they all worked together, laughing and talking. This puzzled me too: Our teachers had told us that intense class hatred existed between peasants and land-lords. But these peasants seemed to have forgotten about that.

Our job was to move water from a pool to the fields along a wooden *shui ch'e*,[4] just as it was done in ancient China. Even though our country had built an atomic bomb, our rural villages continued to use such tools as this. Actually four of us together had to stand on the *shui ch'e* and tread very hard before any water at all would move; even then the machine squeaked loudly and only a trickle poured into the field. We seriously doubted that there was much possibility of saving the young plants; sitting there in the cracked earth they looked as if they would soon turn yellow and die. The field was dotted with people moving water as we were; others lifted water from wells by dipping buckets suspended from one extremity of a "T" frame balanced on its opposite end with a heavy rock. It was especially bothersome that even after working well into the night we could not wash. The village well was nearly dry and what little water we could raise was mixed with mud.

The power holders had generally got wise in the course of the Cultural Revolution. The secretary of the production brigade Party committee was certainly no exception; he had learned how to pull a fast one or two while "grasping" the thought of Mao Tse-tung. Even though the irrigation work in the fields was very urgent, for example, he required that some evenings be designated for brigade members to study Mao's works. He employed "intellectual youth" who had returned to the village as instructors. We ourselves criticized these sessions for their low quality. The instructors were not well read, their lectures were awful, and the brigade members consequently learned very little. Instead of listening they snoozed or talked among themselves. Before long, however, it occurred to us to use these lessons in Mao study as rest periods. We didn't mind going after that.

While we labored in the production brigade we were unable to follow the progress of the struggle outside, particularly regarding the status of the great *ch'uan-lien* movement. Our sole contact with the world was the official organ, the *People's Daily*, which carried precious little news about the Red Guards. As the days passed this blackout became more and more unbearable, and we began to think about leaving the commune. Life there was too bitter: The work was hard, we could not get enough to eat, and we could not sleep. This kind of "three togethers" was more than we could take. Also, as the great *ch'uan-lien* gathered momentum, we knew people were able to travel to Shanghai, Harbin, and elsewhere, whereas we ourselves had gone only to Peking. And of course, those students who had not even been picked as representatives for the last Peking trip were even more eager to participate now. All of us were quite worried that *ch'uan-lien* might soon come to an end. After all, in the nearly two months of great *ch'uan-lien*, while trains, boats, and motor vehicles were used to transport several tens of millions of Red Guards around the country, great piles of commodities had accumulated waiting to be shipped; furthermore, numerous government organs suffered such great losses of personnel transferred temporarily to the work of receiving Red Guards that their own work could not be completed. We became preoccupied with our worry that *ch'uan-lien* could not go on much longer. The commune loudspeaker announcement on October 18 that Mao Tse-tung had reviewed Red Guards for the fourth time confirmed our guess that *ch'uan-lien* was still in progress. But we feared it had reached its climax. We planned to move immediately.

CHAPTER FIVE

Non-Revolutionary Tourism: November- December 1966

We had learned when returning to Canton from our first trip to Peking that obtaining tickets at Canton Railway Station was very difficult. So fifteen of us who got along particularly well met together secretly one night late in October to lay a plan. At this meeting two of our number were selected to ask permission from the school's Preparatory Committee to leave the commune. They would manufacture some excuse and then sneak into Canton to get tickets for us all.

When our two agents arrived there, they discovered that around fifty Doctrine Guards were still assigned to the station with the responsibility of distributing tickets; long lines of students, some from Kwangtung, some from other provinces, were lined up to purchase them. Our comrades had to wait in line for one whole day, sleeping that night in an empty bus. Meanwhile, the students laboring on the commune could no longer keep their peace. In the face of repeated student demands to be allowed to leave to *ch'uan-lien,* the Preparatory Committee finally called another meeting of the heads of the various organizations. Since the only ones who advocated continuing to help the peasants were a minority of teachers, a decision was quickly made to have all return to the school.

We were met there by our two comrades, who had successfully secured tickets for all fifteen of us. Other groups, it turned out, had similarly obtained tickets in advance, although the majority still faced this task. We observed that Mao Tsetung had been reviewing Red Guards regularly twice a month, meaning that if the pattern continued we would have to make Peking by the beginning of November in order to participate in the next one.

By this time, late October, members of various well-known organizations from other provinces were freely expressing their opinions about the problems of the movement in Kwangtung; consequently criticism of the Provincial Party Committee's work teams, the Five Kinds of Red, the Theory of Family Lineage, T'an Li-fu's speech, and other manifestations of the bourgeois reactionary line was rising in Canton. Recoiling from the outsiders' threats to "reignite the movement in Kwangtung," the Doctrine Guards at the station no longer dared examine class backgrounds of students. The poor sons of bitches who were denied the chance to *ch'uan-lien* before were now free to go. Thus, the numbers of people involved and the level of confusion were correspondingly greater than the first time.

We were due to board our train at ten o'clock the following morning, but in order to secure seats we decided to spend the night standing in line at the station. In spite of our early move, however, others were already in line when we got there. Since we had a medium-sized party of fifteen people, we were able to make some useful advance preparations for the common good. Half of us, for instance, unburdened with luggage, would run onto the train to seize seats for all, while the others took their time carrying everyone's bags.

Predictably, when the gate was opened in the morning, a mad rush ensued. Some of the first ones to board the train blocked the doors to prevent those behind from entering their coach. When several of those outside tried to climb in through the windows, they were rudely pushed out by those who had first occupied the coach. The pervasive noise, confusion, and cursing made it seem as if the crowd's intention was to tear the train to pieces. Even loudspeaker appeals from the stationmaster had no effect. Then a train carrying a delegation of foreigners approached. When the news of their incipient arrival was transmitted over the loudspeakers, we stopped quarreling almost immediately: it would have been terribly embarrassing for foreigners to witness such chaos. Also, people were afraid of being run down. The order which temporarily descended over the station as the foreigners' train rolled slowly to a halt was really quite amusing. We applauded enthusiastically and waved to them; they responded by smiling and waving back to express their good will. Perhaps they thought we had organized specially to welcome them. But as soon as their train passed out of the station, our struggle began anew.

Our departure was delayed for several hours because of the continued fighting. Clearly *ch'uan-lien* was at a high tide. Eventually it became impossible for anyone else to enter the packed coaches; people, squeezed together in the aisles, could not even find space to sit on the floor. A few individuals climbed up onto the luggage racks. Also, because the cold weather forced us to keep the windows tightly shut, the coach was filled with an unpleasant odor. Only the proletarian spirit of facing up to hardship enabled us to endure such conditions for two whole days and nights.

As our train pulled into Peking Station we observed that the crowds were larger and more disorderly than before; there were Red Guards in every street and lane. The reception center to which we were taken at about ten o'clock in the morning was located in the Workers' Athletic Stadium. The playing field and seats alike were filled with people, some still sleeping on the ground, their clothing damp with dew. They looked as if they had spent the night there.

Before we left Canton each student was advanced one

month's food allowance of twelve yuan.* But since we had very ambitiously framed a plan to travel to as many places as possible before being forced to go home, we wanted to save every penny we could. En route we bought only the cheapest bread available and ate only the minimum amount necessary to stave off hunger pains. When we approached Peking we refrained entirely from buying food. Even though we were very hungry we thought it would be extravagant to do so since once in the city we might receive our meals free.

At the Athletic Stadium, however, we waited and waited for a dormitory assignment, while the sun climbed ever higher. Finally, our hunger became so intense that we had to buy some bread. We wolfed it down as we stood there.

Some of the Red Guards at the Stadium were sleeping, others talking, and others chasing around. One group nearby were dirty enough to make one sick. We could tell at a glance they were from Manchuria. Dressed in fur coats, passed down from generation to generation and saturated with filth, they sat idly under the sun picking fleas. We hastily moved to another place, fearing those northern fleas might jump onto us southerners.

Because of the large number of applicants it was not until after five o'clock that the reception center could finally arrange accommodations. When the buses left, shortly after sunset, one of our comrades, sent to fetch hot water (I should say fight for it), had not yet returned. Unfortunately all attempts we made over the next few days to find him were unproductive. Others like us had posted literally thousands of notices for lost people. No wonder we never found our friend.

This time we were taken to Peking's western suburbs rather than to a centrally located dormitory. Residents of this district were referred to as *pan-nung pan-kung;* that is, members of each family sometimes farmed and sometimes held jobs in the city. Their rustic but tidy dried mud houses were all quite low, possibly to help keep them warm during the cold winter months. Upon our arrival the Street Residents' Committee (*chieh-tao chü-min wei-yuan hui*) assigned us all to different families. Mine was a family of four presided over by an old

---

* U.S. $4.80 at the artificial rate of exchange.

grandfather. His younger son worked in the city, while his older son and daughter-in-law farmed. Since the older brother's wife was an activist on the Street Residents' Committee they treated us very warmly. We were given one of their three rooms (while they themselves squeezed into two beds) and even spare blankets.

After we handed the required ration tickets over to the Street Residents' Committee, the old women responsible for preparing our meals brought us rice and vegetables. That first night, we ate together with an uncouth group of Red Guards from Shantung Province. They grabbed all the bread for themselves, guzzled the rice, and ended by polishing off the bread they had seized. Those wolves were enough to make anybody angry. Thereafter we asked to eat separately. We later overheard the old women poking fun at the Shantung contingent: "Whatever *man-t'ou* they couldn't eat they carried away in their pockets!" By contrast we sometimes helped the residents carry water and look after their children, which caused the old women to say approvingly, "The Kwangtung Red Guards are best."

On this trip we had no responsibility to represent our school. We therefore did not bother to go to a single university, but spent the entire day touring.

As we strolled through T'ien An Men Square in the early afternoon on November 2, propaganda vans driven by Peking Red Guards suddenly appeared everywhere making announcements instructing all Red Guards to return quickly to their place of residence to discuss an important matter. As we all rushed for the buses, teams of workers began drawing lines this way and that on the street. We guessed that Mao Tse-tung would hold his sixth review (not counting National Day) the next day. About the same time, a few foreigners happened to be passing through the square. We noticed that none of them payed any attention to the many big-character posters. Perhaps they were scared.

On November 3 we found ourselves before T'ien An Men once again. But this time we were sitting on the ground instead of marching. Women from the Residents' Committee said that were it not for us and the movement they would never have been able to come. Ordinarily they had no opportunity to visit T'ien An Men, even though the bus fare was only a few dimes. One old woman told us she had not visited the city for ten years.

The fact that PLA soldiers had been assigned to our ranks, not only to keep order but also to lead us in political activity, we interpreted as a sign that the Central Committee was losing confidence in the Red Guards. Whereas in the past such duties had always been assumed by Peking's Model Red Guards, it was now soldiers who constantly jumped up to direct us in singing and reciting. We felt uncomfortable about this straw in the wind because stepping into the limelight was a Red Guard specialty. What was the army needed for?

Since our seats were too far away to have a decent view of the T'ien An Men reviewing stand itself, we tried to move to a spot directly under the gate's tower. To get through the wall of army men lining the edge of West Ch'ang-an Street we lied, saying we were just returning from the lavatory to our proper positions up front. After a brief examination they allowed us to pass. We immediately moved to a place near the guests' section. When another group of army men discovered we did not belong there, they urged some of the student guests to kick us out. But a few of them jumped to our aid and half-jokingly warned the soldiers, "You must not incite the masses to struggle against the masses." (This phrase was commonly used to criticize capitalist roaders during the Cultural Revolution.) We managed to stay.

On National Day we had marched past T'ien An Men very quickly. This time, sitting right beneath the tower, we could gaze upon the central leaders at greater length. Mao Tse-tung stood stolidly, like a heroic, victorious general. Tallest of all present, Chairman Mao strode quickly back and forth across the reviewing stand; younger photographers and reporters could hardly keep pace. He looked less like a human being than like one of the proud emperors of China's past. His comrades in arms, the four reddest personages, Lin Piao, Chou En-lai, T'ao Chu and Ch'en Po-ta, he treated like mere servants. Timidly conscious of their proper order, they walked slowly behind him. None dared to pass another's place in line. Also present were the "degree holders" (*hsiu-ts'ai*)† Wang Li, Kuan Feng, Yao Wen-yuan, and others, as well as numerous military officers including Yang Ch'eng-wu and Fu Ch'ung-pi (both later purged). All seemed lighthearted and beaming with pleasure.

White-haired Liu Shao-ch'i looked more dispirited than he had the first time we saw him. Slogans and banners reading "Down with China's Khrushchev,"‡ "Repudiate the Black Book, On How to Be a Good Communist,"§ and "Repudiate the Bourgeois Reactionary Line Led by Liu Shao-ch'i" were already becoming quite common, even though open attacks against him did not begin until April 1967. As he faced the shouting masses of Red Guards who were clearly so loyal to Mao Tse-tung, he must have known his power had slipped. He stared at the text of his speech and seemed unable to hide his inner suffering. He reminded me of a defeated fighting rooster.

The parade lines were crooked and disorderly, with some coming to a total halt as they reached the spot in front of the reviewing stand. Chou En-lai used a loudspeaker to urge them on; his voice eventually became hoarse. "Students (*t'ung-hsueh men*)! Please go faster! It is growing dark, and there are still many ranks behind!" But most of the crowd continued to ignore him and night fell before the parade was concluded.

Red Guards were supposed to leave Peking immediately after passing in review. Cadres from our Street Residents' Committee came up into the stands to persuade us to leave. Also PLA soldiers "accompanied" us to the station. Many students wanted to stay in Peking because they knew they could eat there without spending any money; many even slipped away after receiving their tickets. The soldiers looking

---

† Dai used this old term from imperial days to describe collectively these writers and editors who had been recruited into positions of leadership in connection with the Cultural Revolution's early emphasis upon criticizing the "bourgeois line" in literature, the arts, and journalism.

‡ I.e. Liu.

§ Written by Liu and used as a standard text in Party courses for twenty-five years.

after our group, however, "accompanied" us right onto the train.

Actually we had scotched our original plan to go farther north to Harbin anyway. A brisk north wind brought a Siberian cold front to Peking and the yellow leaves falling through the cold air onto increasingly deserted streets made us realize we would have to race the weather south.

As our southbound train pulled into the nearby city of Tientsin, six of us decided to stop there. The others disagreed, pointing out that the climate there was no different than in Peking. They insisted on making our next stopover farther south where the weather would be warmer. Since we could not agree, the six of us split off from the group.

Although Tientsin was also quite large, the political atmosphere seemed less tense than in the capital. There were also far fewer Red Guards in Tientsin. We arrived shortly after sunset. The dimly lit streets were quiet with just a few pedestrians. Carting our luggage all the while, we had to make a number of inquiries before we found the reception station. There we were finally assigned to a primary school, which also took a long time to locate. A teacher first led us to a classroom with straw spread out on desks in which a group of Peking Red Guards had already bedded down for the night. However, we were unable to bear it. Poor ventilation had caused the air to become filled with dust from the straw; one fellow almost threw up. We all agreed the next room was much more comfortable, despite having to sleep directly on the cold desks.

Before long, we decided that Tientsin was not so interesting after all. But while coming to the city was easy enough, leaving was another story altogether. The problem was that no passenger trains originated in Tientsin. One could only hope to find space on trains passing through and that was impossible at that time. Unsuspecting Red Guards like us had begun to pile up in Tientsin, and at the Municipal Party Committee's reception center we were told that tickets had already been booked as far in advance as January 1967. We made special appeals to the reception center personnel: We southerners were unaccustomed to the cold weather, important responsibilities awaited us at home, etc. Despite our lengthy and well-reasoned argumentation, they could not promise anything. There were simply too many others in the same fix. Some irritated Peking Red Guards even threatened to beat the center personnel up if their demands were not met, but they got no satisfaction.

We eventually adopted the tactic of returning every day to the reception center to beg politely for tickets. Finally, they gave in. We immediately returned to the primary school, dealt with the departure formalities, and, after presenting an outline of our dire financial situation, received seven catties of baked cakes (*shao-ping*) each to eat en route. For all six of us that amounted to forty-two catties¶; we southerners had little taste for *shao-ping*, but we knew it would be valuable for bargaining with hungry people. Sure enough, in the waiting room at the train station we found a long queue in which some individuals with sleeping bags had been waiting for over three days. The front of the line was occupied by a group of Red Guards from Chih-chou City (Liaoning Province) who had a liking for *shao-ping*. We talked business for a while and finally agreed to hand over all the cakes in exchange for being allowed to move to first place in the queue. The Red Guards further back angrily accused us of having cut the line. Fortunately, the ones from Chih-chou managed to convince them the deal was legitimate.

That same evening when a train arrived at Tientsin on its way from Peking to Hsü-chou (Kiangsu Province), a small number of people at the head of the queue, one hundred at the most, were allowed to pass through the platform gate. Like hungry tigers released from our cages, we dashed out of the waiting room to the platform. One would have thought that a delicious dinner was being served on the train. Those inside, however, prevented us from boarding by closing all the windows and doors; no matter how hard we shouted and beat on the coach they just sat passively behind the glass. One fellow whose emblem identified him as a student

¶ About forty-six pounds.

from the Peking College of Architecture finally stormed forward and with unbelievable strength smashed his fist through the thick plate glass of one coach door, thus making it possible to lift the inside latch. After that, even though the passengers inside packed themselves into the doorway, we were able to push hard enough to force open the door and climb into the end of the coach. We had won at last. As we pushed inside, we quarreled with the occupants and demanded to know why they tried to keep us off the train. Some in our group really wanted to beat them. Frightened at our show of force, they gradually retreated. We could not work our way into the heavily packed coach itself, however; there simply was not room for a single additional body. Thus, we stood shivering in the vestibule over the couplers between the two coaches, chilled by a north wind blowing in through the broken window. We did manage to reduce the wind, if not the cold, by stacking luggage in front of the opening. Many people were huddled together in the small space with their legs crossing in a tangle. Some extremely small students crushed under the pile screamed to be let up. The student from Peking College of Architecture was protecting a girl of about his own age by supporting her with both arms, or more accurately, by holding her. When one of my companions unintentionally jostled against her, the architecture student reacted by protesting as vehemently as if his treasure was being stolen. He frequently asked the girl if she were cold, and even gave her his coat to wear. Seeing how affectionate and warm they had become we suspected their object in coming to *ch'uan-lien* was not pure; we were certain they were head over heels in love with each other.

Later that night we began to fall asleep standing up. We were packed so close that even when the train lurched no one had to worry about keeping his balance. We were just like "roly-poly dolls" (*pu tao weng*). Suddenly in the dim light of the early dawn our train came to a stop. A railroad worker opened the door to tell us that since our coach was overcrowded and could not safely support the weight, some of us would have to move. This news frightened us. Still half asleep, we alighted from the train to walk to a new coach. The cold wind outside soon revived our senses and forced us to pull our collars tightly around our necks. The railroad man first tried to lift us up and stuff us through a coach window farther back, but the people inside the coach pushed us out. Then he climbed in himself and directed a little ideological persuasion at the Red Guard passengers. He must have been forceful because we were soon able to climb in by ourselves. We could tell from the glares of the Red Guards inside the new coach that they did not welcome us, even though their coach was rather less crowded. They were a group of teacher and student country bumpkins from a middle school in Hsü-chou.

This crude, dark-skinned crew from Hsü-chou were very annoying. They isolated us right off, and as we expected, conceded us only a tiny space. We were soon very uncomfortable and decided to try to expand our "territory." One companion climbed up onto the luggage rack above our heads, where like a bird building a nest, he arranged the piles of baggage into a "V" shape and lay down. We took turns sleeping up there. As we climbed all over the heads of the Hsü-chou country bumpkins their pent-up anger finally burst forth in a chorus of curses and oaths. We paid no attention at all to their chiming. Before long they set to arguing among themselves over the fact that a few anti-social types had locked themselves inside the toilet. As the number of people waiting to relieve themselves grew, they began to curse those inside: "You rotten sons of bitches, sitting in there so cozy, get the hell out right away or we'll force our way in!" (*"Ch'ou ni ma-ti, tso tsai ts'e-so li nem-ma shu-fu, ku'ai kun-ch'u-lai, yao-pu-jan lao-tzu la-chin-ch'u-le!"*) Those inside came back strongly. "If you dare, I'll push your face in." (*"Ni kan, k'an wo ta ni!"*) But after all, they were from the same town, so after a while the toilet door opened and all of them came out. More than ten had stuffed themselves into that small toilet.

We were supposed to take this train all the way to Hsü-chou. But the Hsü-chou Red Guards were so hostile that during a stopover at Tsinan** we just hopped out the window. We carried our baggage to the reception center, which arranged space

** The capital of Shantung Province.

for us at the large Shantung Normal College. Most of the school's teachers and students had gone off to *ch'uan-lien* themselves, but there was still a fierce struggle going on between members of the two factions who remained behind. They waged a broadcasting war. When faction A broadcast political propaganda, faction B countered by broadcasting revolutionary songs; likewise, propaganda emanating from the B side would be drowned out by revolutionary songs from the A side. Such conflict went on from before sunrise until well into the evening. Late one night we were jolted awake by a loud blast demanding that all proletarians "strongly resist." One faction, it was charged, had deliberately written a subversive poster. They had substituted the phrase "absence of classes" (*wu chieh-chi*) for "proletarian class" (*wu-ch'an chieh-chi*) by deliberately deleting the character *ch'an* ("property").†† The poster's author was denounced as an "undercover counterrevolutionary element." Conducting unmerciful struggle against people who committed the "one-character mistake" (*i tzu chih ts'o*) was actually quite common, so that the terrified student posted a self-criticism the very next day.

Our pocket money had dwindled to a critical point while in Tsinan, but a Peking Red Guard living in our room helped us out with a very useful suggestion. Whenever he and his schoolmates arrived at a new place they would eat at restaurants, confess to the manager afterward that all their money was gone, and simply sign the check. Furthermore, when it was time to leave a city, they would approach the reception center with an application for a cost-of-living supplement (*sheng-huo pu-chu*). Sometimes they even claimed that their group was larger than it really was, and thereby illegally acquired a tidy extra sum. This Red Guard had "enjoyed *ch'uan-lien* prosperity" (*fa-le ch'uan-lien ts'ai*) enough to buy a bicycle after returning to Peking from his first trip. Wonder

†† Mistakenly omitting characters is a common problem among all writers in Chinese. Dai frequently did so in his essays for this book. During the Cultural Revolution, the consequences of such an accidental mistake were obviously regarded as being more serious than might have been the case in ordinary times or in less intense political movements.

of wonders! While we were penniless and starving this clever Peking Red Guard was eating in restaurants every day!

Since the idea behind *ch'uan-lien* was to learn new experiences we decided to put this suggestion into practice at the earliest opportunity. Sure enough, when we told the staff of Normal College's dining hall the next day that our pockets were empty, they allowed us to sign for our meals. We had to give them our names, addresses, and a set of our fingerprints.

Next we set out for the Tsinan city Party committee's reception station to apply for our cost-of-living supplement. Upon entering we saw ten or so Red Guards confronting two of the staff:

"Rotten egg! Call out the secretary of the Party committee!"

"If we don't obtain money today, you gentlemen will not be permitted to leave!"

"Do you know how you will be punished if you fail to support the activities of the Red Guards?"

One staff member whined: "It's not that I don't give support, it's just that we are in financial difficulty; I offered to lend you one dollar each but you refused to take it."

"Of course we did! I want five dollars!"

"I want ten dollars!"

They continued to quarrel. Luckily the two clerks were meek; otherwise they might have been beaten. Several Red Guards actually did roll up their sleeves and clench their fists. However, they were also smart enough to know that because the staff members were not power holders, there was no point in beating them. Attention promptly shifted away from the two staff members when Red Guards searching from office to office uncovered a division chief (*ch'u chang*), who was a power holder:

"Do you want revolution?" they shouted at him.

"Yes."

"Shouldn't you support the demands of the Red Guards then?"

"Yes."

"Right now we demand money!"

"But now there is hardly any money here."

"Then you are a counterrevolutionary and a capitalist roader!"

At this the division chief lost courage. He signed his name to a loan slip, and money was handed over to the Red Guards by the clerks. Following the same method we stepped forward and borrowed money for ourselves. We used the same technique at every subsequent stop. Collectively such episodes formed the backdrop for the succeeding period of opposition to "economism." Fearful power holders who had succumbed to Red Guard coercion to lend out money illegally were made the chief objects of attack. They were rebuked for using money to corrupt Red Guards and required to pay back any sums improperly disbursed over their signatures.‡‡

Given our new-found prosperity, we decided to add Tsingtao, Nanking, and the city world famous as the largest in China, Shanghai, to our itinerary. It was in Tsingtao, however, that we first heard about the Central Committee-State Council joint Circular of November 16, calling for an end to *ch'uan-lien.* This document read, in part:

> . . . In order to fulfill and overfulfill this year's national economic plan and realize next year's national economic plan better, it is necessary to concentrate all the transport facilities to speed up transportation of supplies this winter and the next spring. At the same time, in order to provide the revolutionary teachers and students with free transportation in more satisfactory and planned ways during the warm days of next spring when they come to exchange revolutionary experiences, it is also necessary to sum up the transportation work for the previous stage and to carry out the necessary overhaul of the passenger cars and ships that have been overused at the previous stage. Therefore, it has been decided that as from November 21, the water and land transport services will be responsible only for free transportation to their localities of the revolutionary teachers

‡‡ It should be mentioned that a far more common interpretation of "economism," derived from reading both official accounts as well as other Red Guard materials, focuses on officials who decided of their own volition to use available funds for the purpose of enticing workers away from radical groups.

and students who have come to Peking or other localities for exchanging revolutionary experiences and for
free transportation to Peking of the revolutionary
teachers and students who have gone to various
localities from Peking. They must board trains and
ships on the strength of free passes and return direct
to their localities without making a stopover.[1]

We had always feared that ch'uan-lien would one day be
brought to an abrupt end; now the worst had come to pass.
The document clearly directed that we take a train straight to
Canton without making any further stops. Anticipating widespread resistance, the document went on to promise that:

> . . . Beginning from April next year there will
> be sufficient time in which those university and mid-
> dle school students who should come but have not
> come to Peking for exchanging revolutionary ex-
> periences will have the opportunity to make a free
> trip to Peking by train, ship, and bus to see our
> most respected and beloved leader Chairman Mao
> and to conduct studies and exchange revolutionary
> experiences.[2]

Most of our group swallowed the whole thing and optimistically
persisted in their beautiful dream of new expeditions in the
spring. I myself thought it must be a trick: Ch'uan-lien had
been so undisciplined and disruptive that the center would be
highly unlikely to start up a new round next year. It would be
wisest to take advantage of the fact that the order was only a
few days old and quickly visit a few more places. Moreover,
Tsingtao began to change after the Circular was released. The
authorities gradually seemed more able to maintain revolutionary order. For example, all Red Guards were required to
walk to the train between two columns of PLA soldiers. As a
result one could no longer even see struggles on the station
platform. We departed very quickly. Once on board the train,
out of reach of the army, we again had to engage in the familiar
tussle for seats. And once more a member of our group was
lost in a melee. Even by passing slips of paper back and forth
through the various coaches we were able to locate him only
after leaving the train at P'u-k'ou.

When we arrived in Shanghai the "An-t'ing Incident" had just occurred.§§ Explanations, protests, slogans, and big-character posters filled the streets. Everyone argued that his side was correct. The noise of shouting filled the city like a driving rain. We ourselves could not distinguish right from wrong in the matter. It was that confusing.

In Shanghai we lived at the East China Textile Industry Institute. One unusual sight there was a group of foreign students. "They have all come from allied Albania," one institute student told us. "All students from revisionist or capitalist countries have already returned home." It was a mystery to me why the Albanians did not leave too, since they could neither study nor participate in the Red Guard movement.

Despite the ferment in Shanghai, we didn't really become involved. Actually we spent a greater amount of time trading Mao Tse-tung souvenir badges. Since Shanghai was an industrial city, a great variety of high-quality Mao badges were manufactured there that differed considerably from those made elsewhere.

We noticed in the course of our travels that every city manufactured its own badges, probably because local power holders wished to express their total loyalty to Mao Tse-tung; thus, it had been possible to distribute one to each visiting student. Shanghai was no exception. But of even greater interest was the wide-scale exchange activity surrounding these souvenirs. Shanghai had two major "Mao badge trading markets" (*Mao-chang chiao-i shih-ch'ang*), one at the famous "Great World"¶¶ and one at Shanghai's North Railway Station. The general bustle and confusion in these two areas would be hard to exaggerate. Our Group found it impossible to stay together in the surging crowd, and always arranged in advance a time

§§ In outline, the incident involved one group of activist workers who had been suppressed by the Municipal Party Committee trying to seize a train to carry a complaint to central leaders in Peking. Other workers supporting the Municipal Committee prostrated themselves on the tracks to prevent the hijacked train from passing. Several people were reportedly killed.
¶¶ Formerly like Tokyo's Ginza or New York's Times Square, it is now called "East Is Red."

and place to meet to go home. Because it constituted a serious
traffic problem, policemen came along every now and then to
stop the trading. Whenever this happened, however, everyone hid their badges and told the police they were merely
"enjoying the crowd." Activity revived after the law left the
scene.

One surviving remnant of Shanghai's history as a commercial
city was its concentration of crafty businessmen. No small
number of people over thirty years of age could be found walking through the markets, puffing out their chests to display all
sorts of strange souvenir badges pinned on their jackets. Obviously they were in search of buyers. When we proposed
trades, however, they just looked at us contemptuously; they
wanted seven or eight of our badges in exchange for just one
of theirs.

It was fashionable during the Cultural Revolution to wear
Mao badges to express total loyalty to the Chairman. The
demand from Red Guard collectors was so great, however
(some people accumulated them like postage stamps), that
workers, peasants, and government cadres were often not able
to secure even one. Production was simply insufficient. Our
friends back in Kwangtung were later willing to pay high
prices for badges we had accumulated, just as they might have
done for black market goods.

I heard that before the Cultural Revolution Shanghai was a
prosperous, thriving city. In the wake of "Destroy the Four
Olds," however, we saw no place at all that was anything
special. Most stores had only ordinary goods displayed, and the
magnificent "Great World" was closed down entirely. Other
than a few theaters playing the revolutionary opera *Red Lan-
tern* or one of a small number of older movies not yet criticized
as "poisonous weeds," Shanghai's movie houses were also not
operating.

Our last outing in Shanghai was to visit the two movie studios
located there. Most of the resident actors and directors had
been denounced as "monsters and ghosts" and spent half of
each day undergoing "labor reform" and the other half in
"ideological reform" activities. In the evening they were locked
up in a "monster and ghost pen" (*niu lan*). There were an

exceptional number of excellent big-character posters at the studios. One director named Hsu Ch'ang-lin, for example, was rebuked for attacking socialism by portraying workers as clowns. Several hundred posters cursed him, promising that if he refused to surrender he would be "struggled against until he toppled and stank." Frightened, he had hastily admitted he was a "monster and ghost" and demonstrated his sincerity by drawing red "X"s over his own name in publications. At the same time angry attacks were posted against such famous personages of the movie world as Hsieh Yin, Chao Tan, Wang Tan-feng, Chang Jui-fang, and Han Fei.

The workers had become the masters of the movie studios. One young worker exultantly told the students come to *ch'uan-lien* that in the past they had worked very hard to build scenery so the directors and actors could film scenes in comfort. Now they had turned the tables and were supervising the intellectuals in labor. In cinema circles, it seemed, the Cultural Revolution was not as mild as among students.

When we finally left Shanghai in mid-December, we had stayed there a greater number of days than in any other city along the *ch'uan-lien* route. Crowds of students from Shanghai, unable to obtain tickets to other places themselves, walked back and forth in front of the train station attempting to trade souvenir badges for tickets to Canton. Others had hopes of climbing over the station wall; still others hoped to sneak into the station unnoticed by mingling with students from other provinces on their way home. One middle school student who had successfully crowded his way into our group appealed to us not to give him away, explaining that his grandmother was Cantonese and that he dearly loved the southern city. We did not believe a word of this, but circumstances being what they were, we nonetheless allowed him to stay. We admired Shanghai students for their polite manner of speech and neat dress. Unfortunately he failed to maneuver himself past the ticket taker.

A railway employee cautioned us to expect considerable delay, since only that morning a train en route to Nanch'ang***

*** In Kiangsi Province.

had been forcibly halted outside the city by a number of Shanghai students lying on the track. After the train came to a stop about one thousand of them tried to swarm on board. A similar incident had occurred the day before. We never learned how either one turned out. Our own train, though departing three hours behind schedule, encountered no difficulty.

When we arrived back at Kaochung in late December, only a few other students were still out on the road. There was no authority at all then, and the "monsters and ghosts" had returned home again. Students who had slept at our school while visiting Canton for ch'uan-lien had left a mess. We figured the place could be put in order again only after considerable effort.

The key point of the movement in general had already begun to turn toward criticizing "economism." The most important figure in the central-south region. T'ao Chu, had been overthrown only a few months after his meteoric rise to prominence at the center as head of the Party's Propaganda Department. And transportation facilities had effectively dried up; students still wishing to travel were now forced to go on foot (t'u-pu ch'uan-lien), romantically termed "long marches" (ch'ang cheng).

CHAPTER SIX

The Red Guards: The Movement Redirected

Dai Hsiao-ai spent nearly half the time between September 1966 and January 1967 away from Canton, either at the Tsangku Warehouse, in the countryside, or in the north exchanging revolutionary experiences. From each vantage point, he watched or participated as the Red Guard movement gradually broadened in scope, changed its focus, and increased in intensity. Many new things happened quickly.

In November, the Five Kinds of Red were discarded as the leading criteria for selection of Red Guard membership. Non-Five Red students joined the ranks in ever increasing numbers. Later in the month, references to "persons in authority who take the capitalist road" indicated that the so-called bourgeois-reactionary

line and its leading exponent, Liu Shao-ch'i had been designated
as the new major target of the movement. Finally, at the end of
December, workers and peasants were called upon to form "revolutionary rebel" organizations that "cut across the line of work."
Students were now to be joined by workers and peasants in conducting the Cultural Revolution.

SEPTEMBER–OCTOBER 1966:
THE FIVE KINDS OF RED DEBATE,
PHASE ONE (CANTON)

In early September, Dai felt himself at a crossroads. His
disappointment with Canton's Red Guards, heightened by the
failure of the September 1 Unity Meeting, gradually intensified
even more as he viewed the consequences of their discriminatory
membership policies. The Red Guards had become an elite constituted of the mere 20 per cent of the students who happened to
be of Five Red background. The vast majority were left with
nothing to do and no organization to join. This situation, plus a
lack of success with the workers at the Tsangku Warehouse,
brought his spirits to a low level. But he decided to give the
movement and revolutionary politics in general one more try. Turning to his colleagues for support, he resolved to challenge Kaochung's
leaders by organizing his own group.

During the first week of September, I became very angry
at our lack of progress. I went to Canton from the warehouse
every other day to catch up on the news and report back to my
friends. The situation was impossible. The Red Guards seemed
to have forgotten everything we had been taught.

The vicious snobs looked down on non-Five Red students
and constantly humiliated them in public. A student might be
stopped on the street and have his papers checked by Red
Guards. If he proved to be something other than a Five Red,
they would start to fight with him, call him a son of a bitch,
and chase him away. It rapidly got to the point where non-
Five Red students were afraid to be seen on the streets without
the company of at least one Red Guard.

I thought, and most of my friends at Tsangku agreed, that the Red Guards had, in fact, turned their back on Chairman Mao's teachings. We had been taught the necessity of "gathering the majority of the masses"; even the Sixteen Points had called upon us to "gather up more than 95 per cent of the activists and masses." But they conveniently ignored that. They just enjoyed being in command.

It wasn't easy to understand the reasons for their conduct. It was complicated and perhaps in some cases justified. It was because of resentment at the treatment they had received in the past.

In 1964, P'eng Chen and the leadership of the Young Communist League had introduced a new policy on YCL membership and education. P'eng felt that the YCL should absorb youths of bourgeois background and even of rich peasant and landlord origin. Of course, workers, poor peasants, etc. (later, the Five Kinds of Red) remained the main membership source of the organization, but children from other classes were to be admitted as well, provided that their conduct was acceptable. As a result, in 1965, the YCL accepted over eight million new members, more than in any year since 1949. In some cases, a good academic record was all that was necessary for admission. Naturally, all of the members of good class background resented these new people. Even I regarded some of them as opportunists.

Resentment increased over the issue of academic promotion. Many of these rich kids had a better background than we did. They all seemed to have more leisure; somehow, it was easier for them to study. Naturally, many of them did better than students from the revolutionary, but poor, classes and were promoted. This really caused trouble. When the revolutionary students were denied admission to university in favor of the people from the non-revolutionary classes they became frustrated and angry. Of course, they couldn't openly attack the policy, but they wanted to. It was frequently a topic of conversation in private.

The criticism of P'eng Chen and his subsequent downfall provided the disgruntled elements at all levels with their chance for revenge. Those in Peking attacked his policy of

emphasizing academic and political performance, while those
at the lower levels supported it. But those in Peking went too
far. Instead of giving performance its due place, they insisted
upon emphasizing family origin to the exclusion of all other
criteria. Hence, children of revolutionary activists joined with
children of workers and peasants and drew up a category of
red classes, the Five Kinds of Red. They were determined to
have their revenge, and because they had become Red Guards
whom nobody dared to oppose, they were successful. Still, the
Principle of Family Lineage was as erroneous as the idea of
emphasis upon performance only. We went from one bad
situation to another. The conflict wasn't so intense in my own
school because we all thought it our duty to work together
and the non-Five Red students were really very good. In most
other schools, though, it was more difficult to manage.

The effect of the "Five Red only" membership policy of
the Red Guards was disastrous. Fully 70 per cent of all students were doomed to a second-class status. Nearly all of them
wanted to participate but they could not. Under the circumstances, they became very depressed and began to voice fears
that they had no place in China's future. Whenever I went
back to Kaochung from the warehouse, I would see them
hanging around the dormitory with nothing to do. They read
books and tinkered with tools and radios but their morale was
very low. Meanwhile, the Red Guards were tearing up the city.
It seemed stupid, even unforgivable, that such conditions
should be allowed to exist. I knew what Kaochung's non-Five
Red types were like and I had confidence in nearly all of them.
I thought they should be given a chance.

Accordingly, Dai and his classmates decided to include the
isolated students by implementing the original Red Guard organization plan which had called for establishing separate groupings of
non-Five Red students around a Red Guard nucleus. Leaving a
skeleton staff at the warehouse, they returned to Kaochung in a
confident frame of mind.

None of us were worried about things turning out wrong. We
had heard reports of opposition to the exclusive membership
policies of Red Guard groups in Peking, Shanghai, and Wuhan

and knew that we weren't alone in our criticisms. Besides, we had picked a safe course. The plan to organize separate groups around a Red Guard nucleus had after all first been suggested by a Peking Red Guard. We were acting under the best possible precedent. Finally, all of us were confident that we had come down on the correct side. It was obvious to anyone who looked that the center could not continue for long to countenance the behavior of the Red Guards. There simply weren't enough of the Five Reds and certainly the center wasn't going to alienate the vast bulk of the masses this way. These considerations, plus the great confusion and breakdown of leadership within the school and city, led us to believe that we could pull it off. If it became a physical battle, we thought that the students who had been excluded from membership would probably unite to defend us from the other Red Guards. In a way, we hoped that this would happen. It would have made our job easier and our victory complete.

The situation did not degenerate into a physical battle and the victory was not complete, but their effort generally was successful. On about September 15, Dai and ten of his friends returned to the school and wrote a big-character poster charging Kaochung's Red Guard leadership with using "exclusivist" membership policies to block the development of mass criticism. They also announced their intention to broaden the base of mass participation by forming a separate fighting corps to include both Five Red and non-Five Red students. Colleagues in other classes were urged to follow their example.

On the next morning Dai's class met and established the Chih-tien Chiang-shan Rebel Headquarters (*chih-tien chiang-shan tsao-fan tsung pu*).[1] The Headquarters was constituted of fifty members, most of whom were drawn from Dai's class. Thirty were not Five Red students. The remaining twenty were all Red Guards who functioned as the Headquarters' leadership core. While only they were privileged to wear the Red Guard armband, non-Red Guard members were identified by a special red armband with the Headquarters' name embossed in black. As soon as the probationers had given evidence of their revolutionary spirit in actual struggle, they were to be admitted as Red Guard members of the Headquarters. When a majority had attained this advanced status, the entire organization was to be known as the Chih-tien Chiang-shan Rebel Headquarters Red Guards (*chih-tien chiang-shan tsao-fan tsung pu hung wei ping*).

Dai ascribed the success of his challenge to the school's leaders to a general spirit of disaffection and outright resentment against the elite Red Guards, who, in overplaying their hand, had alienated the majority of other students.

Of course, I was very happy with our success. However, we shouldn't have brought it off had we not been able to turn the resentment that Red Guard discrimination had produced to our own advantage. In fact, I expected more and stiffer opposition. When it didn't appear, I realized that I had probably overemphasized the strength of the Five Reds. As it was, we outnumbered them. There was really nothing they could do. They wouldn't have dared to go to other schools for help; to do so would have left them open to criticism. In any case, their counterparts in other schools had troubles of their own and couldn't have been of much help. Similarly, they couldn't go to the Party. We had lost track of its leadership. All they could do was stand impotently aside and let us organize. They were on the defensive from that point on.

I was disappointed by the lack of response in other classes. Three or four other groups were formed after it was clear that we had been successful, but these never amounted to very much. They lacked leadership and a sense of purpose; hence, they never got off the ground. We were more systematic. All of us were good friends and we made it a policy to choose only the best students from the middle range of classes. The Seven Black elements we left alone. It would have been dangerous for us to let them in. Besides, the Five Reds could have attacked us on this policy. We might have lost our effectiveness. However, we weren't concerned about the lack of success in other classes. We immediately turned to the task of training our new members. They had to be as revolutionary in their conduct as anyone else. If we failed in this, all might be lost.

The training program began about mid-September 1966, and continued well into November. The Headquarters spent its time out on the streets reviewing past "Destroy the Four Olds" actions for the benefit of the probationary members. Dai recalled that when not busy at the warehouse, he or another Red Guard who had been present would describe the actions involved in struggling against a particular household and ask the trainees for their comments and criticisms. The remaining time was spent in the school criticizing the old Party committee and/or the work teams. Because the Headquarters Red Guards were already convinced of the worthiness of their candidate members, the training was not very rigorous. Also, Dai confessed to being distracted by anticipation of his trip to Peking and his first *ch'uan-lien* adventure. When they left on September 25, the so-called training program virtually ground to a halt.

OCTOBER–EARLY NOVEMBER 1966:
THE FIVE KINDS OF RED DEBATE, PHASE TWO (PEKING)

On the first day of his trip, during a stopover in Wuhan, Dai realized that the Five Kinds of Red debate had at last become an issue of national significance. Not all his time was spent in planning sight-seeing tours of Peking. While buying a basket of fruit, he was given a handful of pamphlets published by the Mao Tse-tung Doctrine Red Guards of Peking Technical University (*pei-ching kung-ye ta-hsueh*). With his first glance, he forgot about the fruit and dashed back to his friends to share the news.

The pamphlets, copies of a speech recently given by T'an Li-fu, vice-chairman of the Cultural Revolution Preparatory Committee of Peking Technical University (PTU), were a defiant defense of Red Guards organized according to the principle of the Five Kinds of Red. PTU's Doctrine Guards were at that time under intense attack by disgruntled non-Five Red elements demanding an equal role in the movement, particularly in criticizing the work teams. In his response, T'an Li-fu declared that only the left had the right to rebel and that all others must stand aside. He admitted that the teams had made certain mistakes but continued to defend them as a sound socialist concept. T'an responded to demands for his resignation and the abolition of exclusively Five Kinds of Red organization with a counterchallenge. "If you sons of bitches want to kick us out, I have only one thing to say. I will keep this office as long as I can. If I have to go, I'll stand tall and straight and go as a proletarian should."

As Dai's train rolled north, posters and chanting Red Guards in each station indicated that T'an's speech had received national distribution. Dai was both heartened and wary.

The news was very exciting. Everybody on the train was talking about it. It was the first time that the issue of the Five Kinds of Red had come to national attention. Since T'an's speech was really a defiant attempt at defense of his own actions, it was clear to us that the Five Reds were really under intense pressure. Before, we had known of opposition to the concept but not that it was so widespread. For example, as far as we knew, ours was the only school in Canton where a challenge had successfully been made. Students in other schools had attempted to form organizations like our Headquarters, but they weren't very vital. Now we heard that the same kind of attack was being launched in Peking. Naturally, we found the news heartening even though we knew that opposition would be more stubborn than it had been in Canton.

What struck us most, however, was the wide distribution of the speech. Despite the thorough organization of the Red Guard liaison stations, it would have been impossible for the PTU Red Guards alone to distribute the speech as widely as they did. They simply didn't have the resources. It could have been done only with the assistance of people within the Party, probably within each provincial Party committee. Since the work teams were creatures of the provincial Party committees and support of T'an could actually be interpreted as a defense of the work teams, we thought that the different provincial Party committees were trying to uphold the teams and thereby their own authority. It was a good deal easier to control a work team than a pack of Red Guards. This incident served to bring the provincial Party authorities under even greater suspicion than before. It was another example of how they differed from the authorities in Peking. We had already lost virtually all allegiance to the Kwangtung committee, but this raised the same feelings toward all the other provincial Party committees. We were slowly coming to grasp the real meaning of the Cultural Revolution.[2]

I think I was worried most about the effect the speech might have upon the Five Kinds of Red debate in other schools. If it was that intense in Peking, it was certain to be at least as bad in other schools. I felt that T'an's speech was a kind of last gasp, but he obviously had the support of members of several provincial Party committees. If they supported the Five Kinds of Red, the situation could reach the stage of open conflict. It was disheartening to think that the movement might fail because of such factional conflict.

Dai's apprehension about the effect of the speech in local units was soon confirmed. While he struggled to digest the unfamiliar steamed bread of Peking and marched in review past T'ien An Men, his colleagues at Kaochung were confronted with increasing pressure from Five Red students who found encouragement in T'an's words and in the implicit support of the Provincial Party Committee. Dai learned later that they openly challenged Kaochung's non-Five Red students to try to depose them and then closed ranks to overwhelm the opposition. Dai also heard that his colleagues were convinced that the Five Reds seemed to be prepared to resort to physical violence in the face of a challenge.

In Peking, he saw abundant evidence of similar conflict in every quarter of the city and again in Canton after his return on about October 8, 1966.

One had only to travel the streets of Peking to see the depth of the conflict. We didn't go to too many universities or schools but those that we visited all had big-character posters proclaiming the supremacy of the Five Kinds of Red. I also saw a large number of identical posters in the public parks and museums that we visited.

When I returned to Kaochung early in October, evidence of the struggle really hit home. The Headquarters had been under

attack for its policy of accepting students from the middle
group of classes. It never came to blows. The Five Reds wrote
big-character posters accusing us of errors and stating their intention to stand behind T'an Li-fu to the end. Sometimes
they shouted at us in the halls, and once or twice they even
tried to reason with us in private discussion. As a result, the
non-Five Reds became very discouraged. Everyone thought
that the Five Reds had the support of the Provincial Party
committee, a fact that gave them some increased standing and
prestige.

In mid-October, when we went to Kung-she Commune to
help the peasants, our students were so split that we couldn't
work together. The Five Red students insisted upon working
separately in their own Red Guard Combat Teams and left
the rest of us to shift for ourselves. Although this probably
helped us to get the work done, it intensified the split in the
ranks.

Strangely enough, I wasn't worried. I remained true to my
original belief that the center would soon take a stand against
the Five Kinds of Red. The situation was so impossible that it
simply could not be permitted to exist for much longer. When
the center finally did come out against the Five Reds and their
elitist doctrines, I wasn't surprised. I was more impressed that
our earlier suspicion of a power struggle in Peking was confirmed. That really opened things up.

Dai and his friends had just returned from the countryside
and were preparing for their second *ch'uan-lien* journey when
they heard the news of the center's denunciation of T'an Li-fu.
A recently acquired Red Guard bulletin (*hsiao-pao*) reported that
Ch'en Po-ta, leader of the Central Cultural Revolution Group
(CCRG) and Mao's secretary, had criticized the Five Kinds of
Red, the Principle of Family Lineage, the concept of Naturally
Red, and T'an Li-fu for proselytizing in such emotional terms.

In his speech, which Dai thought was the first in which a
central leader had criticized a student by name, Ch'en declared
that limiting the right to criticize the work teams to the small
proportion of activists who were Five Reds would lead to the gloss-

ing over of work team errors and allow those responsible to go unpunished. Ch'en rejected the concept of Naturally Red and the Principle of Family Lineage out of hand because he said he felt they inhibited the development of mass criticism and encouraged the emergence of bourgeois tendencies. Dai's earlier analysis had been thus confirmed and T'an Li-fu had been criticized by the voice of the highest authority in the land. Almost overnight, the debate over the Five Kinds of Red ceased to exist. T'an Li-fu himself never again raised his voice in public.[3]

Dai and his companions were elated at the news of Chen's speech. As they traveled north on their second *ch'uan-lien* journey, they took time to discuss its significance.

> The rejection of T'an was no surprise. We took that as a matter of course and immediately turned to a discussion of the future. Obviously the ranks of the Red Guards would immediately expand as a flood of non-Five Red students joined.
> The issues of debate at the center were also more clear. Everybody now knew for certain that the provincial Party committees were being accused of inhibiting criticism of the work teams. The central leadership in Peking had lifted the lid on such criticism and cleared the way for a new high tide. It indicated to us that the struggle in Peking had already been partially resolved in favor of the Central Cultural Revolution Group; all we could do was wait for the next round.
> However, the excitement over our second trip north took the edge off our reaction to Chen's speech. In other circumstances it might have been a cause for celebration; as it was, we simply heard the news, discussed it, and turned our attention to the problems of traveling around the country with very little money in our pockets. Somehow, those problems seemed to be more immediate than T'an Li-fu's fate or the possibility of an overt power struggle.

NOVEMBER 1966: EXPANSION OF THE RED GUARD RANKS
AND CRITICISM OF THE WORK TEAMS

Dai was not a direct participant in the development of events in Canton in November and December 1966. He witnessed neither the immediate expansion of the Red Guard ranks nor the broadening of the movement as the Peking leadership specified its new targets, first the work teams and later the so-called capitalist line instituted by "certain persons in authority"—in other words, by China's president, Liu Shao-ch'i.

Even as Dai and his friends made their way to the station to depart, Kaochung's students were reorganizing to criticize the work teams. All but a few of the most disgruntled Five Red elements welcomed the non-Five Reds, who simply declared themselves to be Red Guards and joined the activities. By November 3, 1966, Kaochung's Red Guard structure had been completely changed.[4]

The original Red Guard structure, which had been based upon the school's academic class structure, was replaced by the new Red Guard Combat Corps (*hung wei ping chan-tou tui*), which tended to follow the lines of pre-Cultural Revolution friendship groups. Geographic and ethnic divisions like those described in the prologue replaced formal administrative lines as the bases for Red Guard organization. Dai's Headquarters, which remained intact, was an exception to this pattern.

The student body was now divided in two ways. First, individual students were distinguished according to their new Red Guard Combat Corps; second, the corps themselves were divided into rebel and conservative factions with the former leading the attack against the work teams and the latter holding back in their criticism.[5] By the first week of November, the Red Guards had changed in character from an elite constituting 30 per cent of the student population to a more broadly based mass organization encompassing about 80 per cent of China's students.

During the second week of November, criticism of the work teams reached a new high tide. The leader of Kaochung's former work team and several of its members were brought back to the school to face the consequences of their past errors. First, the office of the Cultural Revolution Preparatory Committee, the creation of the work team, was raided. Its records were seized, its seal confiscated, and its office barred. The last vestige of unified school leadership had been destroyed.

The students then shifted to attacks upon individual members of the team, using the model of July and August. The work team members had taught their pupils perhaps too well. Students wrote critical big-character posters and forced the team members to compose replies. The process was leavened with almost daily struggle meetings. This pattern of activity lasted through November and December and into January 1967, when the teams were totally repudiated.

MID-NOVEMBER–DECEMBER 1966: FIRST IMPLIED CRITICISMS OF LIU SHAO-CH'I AND THE EXTENSION OF THE MOVEMENT TO OTHER SECTORS OF SOCIETY

Having achieved success in broadening the student base of the revolutionary movement, the Peking leadership decided that the time had come to identify new targets for attack and further to involve workers and peasants in the movement. Accordingly, they began to define a "bourgeois-reactionary line advocated by certain persons in authority" and certain of its "more important manifestations." The veiled references to "certain persons in authority" fooled no one. All knew that the chief exponent of the bourgeois-reactionary line was Liu Shao-ch'i.[6]

Reiterating the September 11 Decision of the Central Committee with its call for worker-student unity and the supporting editorials of the *People's Daily*, the Central Cultural Revolution Group issued on November 17 the draft of a twelve-point directive in support of workers joining with students to oppose factory managers who refused to allow the Cultural Revolution to be carried out in their shops. Later, the December 26 *People's Daily* editorial approved the practice of students and workers joining together to form organizations that "cut across the line of work."

It should be pointed out that Dai at the time did not analyze the significance of these initiatives as neatly as they have been presented here. Rather, it was only after much probing in Hong Kong, and largely at our suggestion, that he was able to evaluate them as he did.

When these directives were promulgated, Dai and his friends were deeply involved in *ch'uan-lien*. His colleagues at Kaochung were similarly involved in various other aspects of the movement. Given their concern with these other activities, neither group clearly read or understood the message of the Peking leadership. As a result, the call to join with workers in criticizing the bourgeois-reactionary line, like so many Cultural Revolution directives, produced confusion and exacerbated student factionalism, both within the school and throughout the country. Events at Kaochung provide a typical example.

In the absence of any leading authority, students were free to interpret the new directive essentially as they pleased. The rebels favored an immediate union with workers, the creation of formal unity organizations, and, if necessary, violent struggle with any and all forces of opposition. The conservatives favored a more moderate approach in which students, through continued liaison with the workers, would slowly convince them of the need to organize and then would work to form unity groups. This division over tactics existed in schools throughout Canton.

However, adherents of both positions were cautious about beginning to translate their factional points of view into concrete action. All were aware that students would soon have to share leadership responsibility with workers, but no one knew what the exact role of the students was to be. As a result, overt manifestation of factional disagreement was confined to the schools, and in the absence of activity in the streets, the movement seemed superficially to lose impetus. Dai noted the changes immediately on his return to Canton late in December.

It was obvious that something had caused a major change while I was away. I had heard of the new directives and what appeared to be new policies during the trip. Schools in nearly every city I visited were divided between rebels and conservatives but I was never in one place long enough really to understand what was going on.

By December 25, Kaochung was really a different kind of place. There was no leadership, since the Cultural Revolution

Preparatory Committee had been removed, and numerous factions and fighting corps were engaged either in contacting the workers in various enterprises in the city or in arguing with each other back in the school. The arguments weren't really very intense at this point; groups of students of one corps or faction would debate with others. In fact, the situation was rather unexciting. There was none of the tension and sense of urgency that had characterized the debates over the Five Kinds of Red.

I think that this was because the students sensed that something was brewing. It was certainly clear that the functions of the Red Guards had changed since the end of the summer. We had already been told to end *ch'uan-lien* and return to our native places to continue to make revolution through the next summer. This was exciting. The unknown in the situation concerned our role vis-à-vis the workers and peasants. We simply didn't know what was going to happen. Therefore, the students weren't willing to take any dramatic action. Even those rebels who went out to the factories, despite their extravagant claims, really did very little in a concrete way. I don't think that even one organization was established.

Apart from occasional trips into the city to gather news or to meet some workers, there was nothing to do. Students began to devote time to their hobbies, read, and talk about going home for the Spring Festival (the Lunar New Year). The last targets, the work team and the Cultural Revolution Preparatory Committee, had been effectively destroyed. There was literally nothing for us to do except wait for something new.

Yet Dai and his colleagues were far from depressed. They had seen the movement expand as the Five Kinds of Red controversy was settled and as the Red Guards became a mass student organization. The identifying of a bourgeois-reactionary line with Liu Shao-ch'i as its leader stimulated their curiosity and whetted their appetites for more information and direction from Peking. By the end of December, they had all concluded that the Cultural Revolution had its roots in a conflict between Mao Tse-tung and his policies and Liu Shao-ch'i and his. Its ultimate purpose continued to elude them, but they were at least better informed of its dynamics.

By the end of December, it was at last clear to me that we were involved in a real power struggle between Mao Tse-tung and Liu Shao-ch'i. The clue was the stream of editorials and comment in the press and in the Red Guard newspapers on the bourgeois-reactionary line. In every case, they referred to the proletarian line led by Chairman Mao as opposed to the bourgeois-reactionary, or capitalist, line instituted by "certain persons in authority." If Liu had stood with Mao, his name would certainly have been included among those who supported Mao's proletarian line.

There was also another new development. Work teams and factory managers who refused to allow the Cultural Revolution to take place in their shops had now been condemned as important manifestations of the bourgeois-reactionary line. Yet work teams had been recognized as a proper means of organization in every movement since the liberation in 1949. Similarly, no movement was supposed to interfere with production. It seemed to me and my friends that Mao had changed his demands and was condemning Liu and a host of lower officials who were doing what they had always done. In fact, they were acting as they thought good Communists should act. Mao had, in effect, changed the definition of a good Communist and these others had failed to keep pace or had opposed him. At least that was our interpretation at the time. As loyal children of the Chairman, we were willing to await the new instructions. We knew that the movement had greatly expanded and that non-students were beginning to play a role. We knew in a general way that we would probably be mobilized for even more intense activities in the future. We were prepared to await the new signals from Peking and in the meantime enjoy reminiscing over our adventures in *ch'uan-lien* and have a rest.

The anticipated signals were not long in coming. Within weeks, Dai was to be deeply involved in the movement's new and ultimately most violent stage, the seizure of power.

CHAPTER SEVEN

The Rebels Seize Power

By New Year's Day, 1967, having returned just recently from countrywide *ch'uan-lien*, Dai felt able to define the ultimate goals of the Cultural Revolution only in the general terms of the conflict between Mao Tse-tung and Liu Shao-ch'i. For him, the specific issues and purpose of the struggle remained a mystery. He felt he and his fellow students throughout China were "making revolution" without benefit of a guiding revolutionary vision of the future. This problem was to be a potent factor in shaping his decision to leave China. From January 1967 until his flight from the mainland in November of the same year, his vantage point was largely limited to the city of Canton, from which he was unable to evaluate larger national trends.

In such confined circumstances, students could only make visceral and intuitive responses to Peking's initiatives. On several occasions, they misinterpreted the goals of the Peking leadership entirely, while on others, their understanding was only partially complete. Confusion over specific goals, plus the introduction of worker and peasant groups into the flow of events, caused the already complicated Red Guards situation to become even more chaotic. Individual student leaders formed, broke, and then reformed alliances in response to their imperfect individual perceptions of shifting national trends. In addition, the focus of power centers within the student movement changed. Previously, middle school students had played a relatively active role. However, with the advent of worker and peasant activism, middle school students found themselves increasingly excluded from the newly evolving centers of decision making. Gradually, university students, with their greater access to communication channels, their broader background, and their generally greater levels of experience, emerged as the primary spokesmen for Canton's student groups. Beginning in January 1967, Dai's involvement came increasingly to be manifested in observation rather than in direct participation in events. Middle school students ceased to be a salient leadership force. Accordingly, much of the substance of the following chapters is derived from Dai's second- or thirdhand observations of events. (Indeed, such direct actions as he and his Rebel Headquarters did undertake at times reveal many of the qualities of comic opera.) Despite this, even because of this, his observations of the "seize power" movement in Canton deserve to be recounted.

Dai recalled his feelings during the first days of 1967.

As we saw it then, our task was "one struggle, two criticisms, and three transformations" (*yi-tou erh-p'i san-kai*).[1] We had heard about proposals to transform the education system advanced by students from several universities in Peking, but similar discussions were not held in Canton until several months later. After *ch'uan-lien* was over most students at Kaochung had nothing to do, and since the Preparatory Committee had been destroyed, there was no authority in our school at all. I was very busy myself, traveling around the city to keep informed about the progress of the movement. But ordinary students just slept late, read novels, and played basketball, and some went home well in advance of Spring Festival, even though they had to go on foot.

Most student activists were loyal soldiers of the Central Cultural Revolution Group in Peking. They did mostly as they were told, and usually sought permission before striking out on any major course of action. Now, as the movement was beginning to cool, the Peking leadership lit new fires, which culminated in the "seize power" struggle.

Following on the late December call for workers and students to join units to conduct the Cultural Revolution, the *People's Daily-Red Flag* joint New Year's editorial offered passing praise to the Red Guards for having "served as the vanguard," and then swung into a discussion of the "objective law" that:

> . . . All Cultural Revolution movements in contemporary Chinese history have begun with student movements and led to the worker and peasant movements, to the integration of revolutionary intellectuals with the worker-peasant masses.

Henceforth workers and peasants were to be "the main force in this revolution" as well.

Details of the center's new emphasis became increasingly evident over the next two weeks. On January 9, the *People's Daily* first introduced the experience of Shanghai's "revolutionary rebels" in opposing "economism." Three days later the same paper reprinted an "Urgent Notice" issued by thirty-two Shanghai "revolutionary rebel" organizations which gave every appearance of a government proclamation. For example:

> Apart from necessary expenditure on production, wages, the Cultural Revolution, office administration, and for other appropriate purposes, the circulating funds of all government offices, organizations, and enterprises should be frozen as from the day of the publication of this document. This should be effected by the financial organizations at the municipal level and at all other

levels under the joint supervision of the revolutionary rebel groups and the revolutionary masses.[2]

A message of greetings from Peking leaders to these Shanghai organizations published the same day congratulated them for bringing into being a "great alliance."[3] The last of the newly introduced concepts for future operations appeared in the CCRG's journal, Red Flag, in its second number for 1967: The distinguishing aspect of the Shanghai movement, and one which should be emulated, was said to be that revolutionary rebels had united to "seize power."[4]

Dai recalled that local response to these initiatives was not long in coming. Ever seeking clues to new trends, Canton's "rebel faction" leaders digested these reports with apparent care. Their task, they felt, was to decide how and when they should implement the Shanghai model locally. Most widely known of these radical leaders, Dai thought, if not the most influential (he had no way to judge), was Wu Ch'uan-p'in, a Chung Shan University (CSU) student from Hunan Province who Dai thought was studying physics.

Wu's claim to leadership was based in part upon his own personal resources.

His fellow rebels proudly called him the "distinguished son of poor peasants." He was tall, very energetic, and always wore a neatly pressed army uniform. Speaking before a crowd he was quite articulate, able to go on for hours without notes, drawing thunderous applause from his audience. He was highly respected by Kwangtung's rebel faction.

Wu's second claim to leadership derived from his early activism at CSU.

When a work team took up residence at CSU, Wu Ch'uan-p'in had been the first to stand up and pull Li Chia-jen down off his horse.[5] On August 31, in Peking, Wu Ch'uan-p'in and his friends participated in Chairman Mao's second review of the Red Guards before T'ien An Men. In memory of this occasion they formed the August 31 Combat Detachment (pa san yi chan-tou ping-t'uan) before they left the capital.

Wu maintained "August 31" as an elite group of deeply committed activists. Qualifications for joining were strict, and membership seldom exceeded one or two hundred. A majority of "August 31" were orphans, free of any fear that their families might suffer retaliation for their activism should their side lose. Members of "August 31" were skilled not only in debate, but also in hand-to-hand fighting. Even the belligerent Canton Doctrine Guards from August First Middle School were scared of them. Their flag uniquely displayed black characters on a field of pink, whereas most other groups fielded yellow on red in imitation of the national banner.

The popularity of "August 31" at CSU led to a flood of applications from fellow students. Wu responded in October by forming a separate, more broadly based organization called Chung Shan University Red Flag Commune (*chung shan ta-hsueh hung-ch'i kung-she*). These two groups referred to each other as "most intimate comrade" and took similar stands on most issues. Outsiders consequently referred to them collectively as CSU Red Flag (*chung ta hung-ch'i*).

Wu Ch'uan-p'in's third claim to leadership, according to Dai, stemmed from his close contact with the CCRG in Peking. CSU Red Flag maintained a permanent liaison station in Peking through which they could funnel complaints about unfavorable actions sponsored by Kwangtung provincial authorities directly to the central leaders.

The "old gentlemen" on the Provincial Party Committee were quite bothered by the influence of "August 31." Chao Tzu-yang had even issued an order that "Every facility should be supplied to famous organizations," including money, motorcycles, bicycles, paper, and other items needed for political activity. He was criticized for this tactic at struggle meetings (beginning in December 1966). Chao was dreaming to think he could get by in this way.

Dai also thought that Wu Ch'uan-p'in's organization at Chung Shan University, unlike the groups at Kaochung, maintained direct contact both with Canton representatives of student groups in other provinces and with the rebel workers' organizations formed in Canton beginning in December 1966. To keep up to date, Dai found it necessary to travel to CSU's campus in south Canton to hear debates, collect newspapers, and talk with members of CSU Red Flag.

For ten days after the *People's Daily* began to publicize the Shanghai "seize power" experience, Dai saw no indication of rebel planning in Canton for a local repeat performance. Isolated from the center of power, he could only surmise that tactical discussions were in progress among the leaders of university student and worker groups.

However, Dai found evidence for the developing alliance between the students and workers in their co-ordinated response on January 18 to an initiative by two conservative groups, the Terrestrial General Headquarters (*ti tsung*) and the Red General Headquarters (*hung tsung*). Notices appeared around Canton to the effect that T'ao Chu[6] would be "dragged" back to Canton to face denuciation on that day, and that "Revolutionary workers may leave their work at ten o'clock to take part in meetings and be paid for in doing so [*sic*]."[7]

Dai was suspicious.

I don't know if T'ao was really brought back to Canton then, but I doubt it. In any case, the rebel faction treated this as just another ploy of economism and reacted with strongly critical posters. One thing we Red Guards were really good at was propaganda. On this occasion we cursed the conservative groups until they stank (*kao ch'ou*). We respected Mao's teaching about the need to "prepare public opinion" before trying to seize political power, and thus, we paid great attention to the problem of propaganda.

Dai identified the following day, January 19, as the turning point. The local "rebel faction" perceived that day's editorial in the *People's Daily* as a clarion call aimed at them directly. (A southern edition is printed in Canton, and can be seen there only a few hours after the first edition appears in the capital.)

The basic question in any revolution is that of state power. The proletarian revolutionaries must take political, economic, and cultural power firmly into their own hands. This is an issue of prime importance affecting the destiny of the proletarian dictatorship in China, the destiny of the socialist economy, and the destiny of the Great Proletarian Cultural Revolution. In brief, it is a matter of great importance concerning whether China will or will not change color.

Dai commented:

Even our small newspaper at Kaochung reprinted in full this paragraph from the *People's Daily*. That evening Wu Ch'uan-p'in received a long-distance phone call from the CSU Red Flag liaison man in Peking. He had just then come from a meeting with Lin Chieh, a member of the CCRG with whom he had frequent contact, and had big news to report. Lin had explicitly told him that CSU Red Flag had the center's permission to seize power up to the provincial level! Only the offices of the Central Committee's Central-South Bureau were to be left alone.

Now an impending seizure of power in Canton was in the wind. I don't know how many people in general knew about this, but most middle school students were aware that the move would be made in two or three days. As events developed, however, we middle school students were never actively included. From the first "seize power" activities on January 21, until we all returned home for Spring Festival, we did little more than go down to CSU to pick up the latest news.

Dai's rendition of the course of "seize power" events was, as has been mentioned, secondhand, and marked by severe chronological vagueness.

Of the various rebel organizations who allied to "seize power," eight, Dai thought, were most important in the leading force.

Workers

1. Swear to Die Defending Chairman Mao Rebellion Corps, Canton Workers' United General Headquarters (Workers' Alliance); *shih-szu pao-wei Mao chu-hsi tsao-*

fan t'uan, kuang-chou kung-jen lien-ho tsung-pu (kung-lien).[8]

2. Red Flag Workers' Red Militia Detachment, Canton General Headquarters (Red Flag Workers); *hung-ch'i kung-jen chih-wei tui, kuang-chou tsung-pu (hung-ch'i kung-jen).*[9]

Office Employees

3. Revolutionary Rebel Liaison Station of Organs Directly Under the Kwangtung Province Party Committee (Provincial Organs Liaison Station); *sheng-wei chih-shu chi-kuan ko-ming tsao-fan lien-lo chan (sheng chih lien chan).*

4. Pearl River Film Studio, East Is Red Commune (Pearl River Film East Is Red); *chu-ying tung-fang hung kung-she (chu-ying tung-fang hung).*

Students

5. Canton Medical College, Red Flag Commune (Canton Medical Red Flag); *kuang-chou yi-hsueh yuan hung-ch'i kung-she (kuang yi hung-ch'i).*

6. Chinan University, East Is Red Commune (Chinan U East Is Red); *chi-nan ta-hsueh tung-fang hung kung-she (chi ta tung-fang hung).*

7. College of Physical Education, Revolutionary Rebel General Headquarters; *t'i-yü-hsueh yuan ko-ming tsao-fan tsung-pu (t'i yuan ko-ming tsao-fan tsung-pu).*

8. Chung Shan University Red Flag Commune (CSU Red Flag); *chung-shan ta-hsueh hung-ch'i kung-she (chung ta hung-ch'i).*

Northern Red Guards also participated in the alliance. Dai identified three groups among them as most prominent.

1. Peking College of Aviation Red Flag (*pei hang hung-ch'i*).[10]
2. Harbin Military Engineering College (*ha chun kung*).[11]
3. Wuhan Third Headquarters (*wu-han san-szu*).

As best as Dai could remember, these three schools maintained between ten and twenty-five liaison men in Canton, only a small fraction of the nearly thousand representatives of non-Kwangtung groups then in the city. Their great and disproportionate influence derived partly from the fact that local university students regarded them as models. Peking Aviation Red Flag, for example, enjoyed a wide reputation among Canton students as "very strong." They were strong because they seized the initiative; they continually made suggestions and prodded and challenged the local leadership. In fact, all three had set up liaison stations on the campus of Chung Shan University. But whatever their ultimate importance as catalysts to the movement, Dai thought the later conservative charge that Kwangtung's seizure of power was dominated by agitators from other provinces was nonsensical.

Dai strained to recall details from the initial "seize power" actions taken on January 21.

The initial tactic was commonly called "three simultaneous roads," which meant dispatching groups to the Provincial Party Committee, to the provincial Public Security Department (*t'ing*), and to the municipal Public Security Bureau (*chü*). Serious resistance was offered only at the last of these. The incident there on January 25, involving actual fighting, may have been the second attack against the city's public authorities.

Obtaining a unit's official seal was always a goal in seizing power, even though it was a symbolic act with little real importance.

A more significant object of the January 21 movement was to secure from Chao Tzu-yang a formal concession of power to the "seize power" alliance. Chao was not present at provincial Party headquarters when the rebels arrived, but they finally located him later in the day at the Agriculture and Forestry Bureau. He was taken to Chung Shan University, where, shortly before midnight, he relinquished all his authority to Wu Ch'uan-p'in and his comrades.

The following day, January 22, the organizers of the seizure of power in Kwangtung formed a new organ called the Kwangtung Province Revolutionary Rebel Allied Committee (*kuang-tung sheng ko-ming tsao-fan lien-ho wei-yuan hui*), or Provincial Revolutionary Alliance (*sheng ko lien*) for short.

Toward Chao Tzu-yang and the other province-level Party secretaries, the PRA adopted a policy of supervised work (*chien-tu kung-tso*). They allowed Chao to live at home, and required that he continue to come to his office each day to fulfill his responsibilities as first secretary, although all his actions were subject to final approval by PRA supervisors. Critics of the PRA fancied this system to be a sham seizure of power, imagining wrongly that PRA leaders had struck a secret bargain with Chao.

The PRA by no means represented a new provincial government; it was simply a loosely structured organization of rebel groups who joined the "seize power" alliance. It had no goal or program, and no apparent purpose beyond the negative political one of denying power to the former authorities. Its headquarters, in the form of a Revolutionary Alliance Service Group (*ko-ming ch'in-wu hsiao-tsu*), was set up in the home of Ou Meng-chueh.[12] Subordinate to this group were three "supervisory groups" (*chien-tu hsiao-tsu*), responsible respectively for the Provincial Party Committee, the provincial Public Security Bureau, and the municipal Public Security Bureau.

Dai stated that the following organizations, some of which joined the PRA only after the initial "seize power" activities, contributed members to the Service Group.

2 *members each*
   1. Workers' Alliance
   2. Red Flag Workers
   3. Mao Tse-tung's Thought Red Peasant Friends (*Mao Tse-tung ssu-hsiang hung nung yu*)[13]

1 *member each*
   4. Old Red Army (*lao hung chün*)[13]
   5. Canton Medical Red Flag
   6. Chinan U East Is Red
   7. College of Physical Education, Revolutionary Rebel General Headquarters
   8. Provincial Organs Liaison Station
   9. CSU Red Flag

Dai also maintained that student leaders continued to dominate the alliance. Workers and peasants, he said, were added only to provide legitimacy in a period when the center was stressing workers as the "main force" for revolution and insisting that intellectuals unite with them.

Throughout the high tide of revolution, lasting until mid-February, the PRA continued to be quite successful in recruiting allies. New groups linked up with the alliance, and more individuals entered affiliate groups. In some organizations, like Dai's Headquarters, membership had been increasing since December. But in others, like the August 1 Combat Detachment, which joined the PRA in mid-February, the main stimulus for membership growth had come from the "seize power" victory itself.[14] Most groups openly encouraged defection through a policy of trying to "win over" (*cheng-ch'ü*) wavering members of opposition factions; the object was to "disintegrate" (*wa-chieh*) the other side's organization.

Dai told us that at Kaochung, the most common manifestation of this tactic was to approach individually those conservative students who showed the greatest promise of responding in a positive way. One or several rebels would endeavor to persuade the target individual to join their group by engaging him in serious "heart-to-heart talks." Hard-core conservatives, on the other hand, were definitely excluded as targets of this policy; rather, the rebels isolated them as objects of vigorous criticism. Those conservatives who were neither wavering nor deeply committed wilted under the barrage of critical propaganda and temporarily dropped out of the conflict.

But while the Provincial Revolutionary Alliance was thus enjoying over-all success, however temporary, its tactics became a matter for sharp debate within the rebel ranks themselves. This internal division produced the first important break in the relatively stable alignment of factions which had so far developed. Beginning the previous summer, there had been a clear rebel position on each emerging issue, so that by knowing a person's stand on one problem, one could usually predict his stand on others. For example, Dai reported that as a rule, the same Kaochung students who opposed

Principal Chen later came to oppose the work team and, after
that, the Preparatory Committee. They also were subsequently reluctant to accept the Family Lineage criterion for selection of Red
Guard membership. Shifts from one camp to the other had previously
occurred primarily among more opportunistic individuals who lacked
firm political commitment. Now, however, the PRA's leaders were
unable to unite Kwangtung's entire rebel faction under their banner.

Rebels who supported the PRA's policy of striking quickly
and then afterward setting out to construct an alliance on
the basis of its success and of CCRG approval were said
to advocate "the time is ripe for action" (*shih chi ch'eng
shu*). Rebels who favored constructing an alliance before seizing
power were said to advocate "the time is not yet ripe for
action" (*shih chi wei ch'eng shu*).

One objection made by the "slow" school concerned the
Provincial Party Committee: "We haven't yet taken the lid
off the struggle against the Committee, its ranks are still
intact, and the attitudes of all its cadres are not yet clear."
Another related to the rebels themselves: "Within our own
ranks we lack strength; there has been too little preparation
of an alliance."

Within our rebel faction at Kaochung, the majority supported the PRA's proposed early seizure of power, even though
we middle school students were excluded from active participation in the operation. Even after the fact, we did not
participate, and never formally joined the PRA. Middle school
students had very little understanding of the seizure of power.

In Canton as a whole, though, this ratio was reversed.
Most rebels were suspicious of the PRA's early move. The
most active advocates of the slow approach were: 1) Third
Headquarters; 2) Chung Shan Medical College East Is Red;
and 3) School of Chinese Traditional Medicine 301.

Dai recalled that the attitude of workers toward the PRA was
somewhat surprising. Generally more conservative than the students, so-called "rebel faction" worker groups withheld their ap-

proval from the January 21 PRA coup. But quite inconsistently, a few conservative worker groups offered their support. Dai noted that this did nothing to allay the suspicions of those critics who believed that the PRA's seizure of power would not be effective in eliminating the influence wielded by the old Party leaders. Rebel leaders who cherished the theory of a conspiracy between Chao Tzu-yang and the PRA clique argued that conservatives would inevitably gain from an incomplete seizure of power; it would merely serve to delay a better organized, more comprehensive one later on, and from the Party committee's point of view, certainly represented the lesser of two political evils.

In the days after January 21, the "seize power" phenomenon was duplicated at lower levels in Kwangtung. County Revolutionary Alliances (*hsien ko lien*) and Town Revolutionary Alliances (*shih ko lien*) soon appeared throughout the province.

Even some production brigades on rural communes experienced a seizure of power. My uncle (a farmer living near Mafan) told us when we visited him at the Spring Festival that at that level the action had often been formalistic and meaningless. In some instances, peasant rebels had satisfied themselves with taking away the brigade's seal and keeping it. Other than denying its use to the existing brigade leadership, this accomplished nothing but inconvenience to other members of the brigade, since some documents, notably ones required for travel, were not likely to be honored if unstamped. I can't tell you much more than that about the peasant rebels. I only know that student leaders were encouraging peasant participation.

At the same time that the PRA was attempting to consolidate its position, a new major participant was entering the movement, the People's Liberation Army. In Kwangtung Province, the PLA's presence had always been represented in many different organizational forms. Most important in the Cultural Revolution, however, was the Canton Military Region command under Huang Yungsheng.[15] This command, one of thirteen into which all China is divided, includes not only Kwangtung but Kwangsi and Hunan provinces as well. Arrayed under the region command are local units of the army, navy, and air force.

Dai had been somewhat baffled by the fact that before January 1967, the PLA had been largely insulated from the Cultural Revolution.[16] Only students in military academies had been allowed to join in the movement as their civilian counterparts had. Beginning with the so-called "four big activities" in May and June 1966,* work teams were later sent to military academies, and cadets were eventually allowed to engage in *ch'uan-lien* with other students. But unlike the experience at Kaochung, the work teams in military schools emphasized to students their "special character" and refused to allow the existing authorities to be overthrown. The minority rebel faction within the military academies was subsequently suppressed and the movement severely limited in comparison to those at civilian schools. The first rumble of disapproval of such actions from Peking was heard on October 5, 1966, when the Military Affairs Committee and other central organs issued a series of highly critical directives. Dai Hsiao-ai remembered one of these to be the first call for the Cultural Revolution to be carried out in the entire PLA:

> Whenever erroneous words and deeds that run counter to Mao Tse-tung's thought and the general and specific policies of the Military Affairs Committee under the Central Committee are encountered—irrespective of who the persons involved are and what posts they are holding, irrespective of at what time and in what place, and irrespective of whether the persons involved are directly led by you or not—all comrades must dare to struggle. . . .[17]

Dai recalled that Liu Chih-chien had been bitterly criticized by Red Guards as early as December 1966 for being personally responsible for having suppressed the Cultural Revolution within the PLA.

> We charged him with fearing that the revolution led by Chairman Mao might disrupt the PLA to the point of com-

---

* Big democracy; big blooming and contending; big-character posters, and big debates.

plete chaos, and with having therefore responded by setting down sundry taboos and commandments (*ch'ing-kui chieh-lü*) to control it tightly. In May and June 1966, the army had joined in the campaigns to criticize *The Three-Family Village*. In fact, commanders themselves sometimes contributed articles. But when the movement descended to individual units the whole situation changed. Under newly issued regulations, soldiers were prohibited from even learning about the Cultural Revolution. Army units were to have no contact with Red Guards. Army men were not to seek information about the movement from members of their families, they were forbidden to listen to radio broadcasts about the Cultural Revolution, and they were not to read big-character posters along the street.

Further instructions strictly prohibited any interference with Red Guard activities. Leaves of absence were also canceled to seal off the troops. Canton in late August was boiling: The city was covered with big-character posters, and students and others were setting about destroying the Four Olds; everywhere people were debating and arguing. But when soldiers came along, they remained purposefully aloof, often not daring to raise their heads to read posters. Some who did read the tabloids dared not express their opinions.

PLA men from an anti-aircraft position near our school who came over once every three weeks or so to watch a movie and mix with the students continued to do so, but they would not read our posters or involve themselves with arguments between the two sides. Some of these soldiers talked with Principal Chen. When we criticized them on the spot for mixing with capitalist roaders they were dumfounded, and appeared not to understand what capitalist roaders were.

On January 11, 1967, a newly constituted Cultural Revolution group in the PLA was announced with Chiang Ch'ing (Mrs. Mao Tse-tung) as "adviser." Liu Chih-chien was replaced as head of the group by Hsu Hsiang-ch'ien.[18] On January 23, the center issued a five-point Decision, publicized widely in Canton through wall posters, although never appearing in the newspapers, stating that all previous regulations restricting PLA involvement in the Cultural

Revolution were "null and void." This document also contained another important directive.

> Active support must be rendered to the broad masses of revolutionary leftists in their struggle to seize power. When genuine proletarian leftists ask the army for help, the army should send out troops to support them actively.[19]

The Military Control Committee followed this up on January 28 with a supplementary eight-point Order to bewildered commanders containing slightly more specific guidelines for handling particular problems.

Dai thought it significant that the PLA was given its new "support the left" task just as it began to carry out meaningfully the movement in its own ranks.

> Since local commanders had been told simply to help the true left suppress the right, it was left to them to decide which groups were associated with which category of opinion. They had no experience in sorting out the many views and arguments surrounding issues which had divided rebels (in the eye of the CCRG) and conservatives, and were thus very unsure of themselves.

Some commanders must have personally preferred to aid groups other than the ones they finally deduced were the CCRG's "rebels," but thought it unwise to support the "wrong" side overtly. No good could come from local rebels deluging their friends in Peking with complaints about the rightist behavior of their local commander. High-ranking officers had already been purged in the course of the movement, including Chief of Staff Lo Jui-ch'ing, so few local commanders could have doubted Mao's capacity to effect further removals.

> We students thought that most commanders decided the safest approach was to find out which groups had CCRG backing and support them. This was the case, for example, in Shanghai, Shantung, Heilungkiang, Shansi, and Kweichow. Elsewhere commanders ended up suppressing groups who at-

tacked the military district headquarters. This happened with the Hsiang River Wind and Thunder (*hsiang-chiang feng lei*) in Hunan, the February 7 Commune (*erh ch'i kung she*) in Honan, the Lhasa Revolutionary Rebel General Headquarters (*la-sa ko-ming tsao-fan tsung pu*) in Tibet, and the PRA in Kwangtung.

The January 28 eight-point Order tackled this problem directly:

> The question of assaults on military leadership organs should be dealt with differently according to different cases. Prosecution should be instituted in the case of assaults made in the past by counterrevolutionaries, but action need not be taken if the assaults were made by leftists. Henceforth, no assault shall be permitted.

But Peking's views notwithstanding, conflicts between rebel groups who indulged in such assaults and the defending military district headquarters were seldom resolved.

Dai was unable to explain with any confidence how antagonism between the PRA and Huang Yung-sheng developed in the first place. The January 25 incident at the Canton municipal Public Security Bureau might have been one point of contention, representing as it did a PRA attack on military authority. Several resisting policemen had been captured by the rebels that day, subjected to struggle under the charge that "to oppose the PRA is counter-revolutionary," and later paraded through the streets of the city. Another underlying factor might have been Huang Yung-sheng's failure to give active support to the PRA. Especially in the area of propaganda the Canton regional command had ample opportunity to help out, but they chose instead to remain silent. They apparently neither criticized the PRA nor supported its opponents. In the light of Peking's directive to render "active support" to the revolutionary left, however, Huang's silence clearly implied opposition. Perhaps he calculated that, given sufficient time, those rebels who favored "the time for action is not yet ripe" approach would grow in strength and thus weaken the PRA's internal unity and strength. By failing actively to support the PRA, Huang could both stimulate this development and at the same time win support from more moderate rebels.

Whatever the truth of the matter, on February 7, a number of the PRA's constituent organizations sent members to the region headquarters in Tung Shan district to confront Huang Yung-sheng with their criticisms. This decision was not taken in the name of the Alliance, and some constituent groups were opposed to such a move.

The leaders were Wuhan Third Headquarters Canton Liaison Station, the liaison people from Harbin Military Engineering College, CSU Red Flag, and Pearl River Film Studio East Is Red. The bulk of ordinary participants, about one hundred all together, were from several other organizations. Interestingly enough, one group who joined in this venture were from within the military itself. Called Massive Cudgels (*ch'ien chun pang*), they were all army cultural workers who, like students in military academies, had been able to participate during an earlier stage of the movement. The Massive Cudgels as an organization was formed on January 3, 1967, after Liu Chih-chien had come under intense criticism.

When the group first arrived at the gate of the region's compound, they staged a demonstration and pasted up many posters criticizing Huang Yung-sheng, and then withdrew. Later, however, the more radical leaders (especially the liaison people) persuaded the group to take a further step. They returned to the compound, forced their way in, occupied the command headquarters and the logistics department, cut the telegraph line, stuck up more posters, and arrested a few people. The telegraph was repaired after three or four hours, and someone wired Peking about the attack. Not until the following day was a reply received from the CCRG ordering the students to leave. I can't remember why, but the student leaders refused to obey. Only after someone talked to them personally by long-distance phone did they finally retreat.

This was the first and last instance of confrontation with the military. The fact that Huang chose not to have his troops forcibly expel the small group of rebels shows how gingerly all good children of the CCRG were being treated by local authorities at that time.

The PLA did finally assert itself, however, one or two weeks after this episode, when Kwangtung Province began to implement the center's new "two military" policy. On the one hand, military control committees were introduced at all levels of administration in the province to supplant the PRA's organizations as the highest authority. On the other hand, the instrument of "military training" was employed by these committees to suppress those rebel elements opposed to them. Huang Yung-sheng's attempt over the next two months to break up and discredit the PRA deeply intensified the degree of mistrust and enmity that Kwangtung's rebel faction held for him.

CHAPTER EIGHT

The Military Asserts Itself

The proclamation of military control for Kwangtung Province on March 15, 1967, amounted to official approval of an accomplished fact rather than the launching of a new policy. Military control committees (*chün-shih kuan-chih wei-yuan hui*) for most of Kwangtung's government and business units and corresponding military training platoons (*chün-shih hsün-lien t'uan*) for its schools had already been established. The Kaochung Middle School received its military training platoon (MTP) early in the last week of February. Shortly afterward, on March 1, the Kwangtung Military District Headquarters issued an order banning the Provincial Revolutionary Alliance.[1] Subsequently, its constituent groups were subjected to considerable suppression by the new military authorities.

Worker and professional groups within the PRA were consistently treated more severely than their student affiliates. Dai was not sure how to explain this. Perhaps the soldiers realized that the workers and professionals were less well connected in Peking. Otherwise, it would have been normal for them to direct their heaviest criticism at the PRA leaders (predominantly students) rather than at secondary targets. Worker and professional leaders might have been viewed by the military as a political force in their own right, while the students' influence could have been regarded as wholly dependent upon the strength of Peking leaders who were using them. Another factor influencing the military's behavior, Dai thought, might have been the withdrawal from Canton of "liaison personnel" who represented groups primarily composed of students from other places. Some of the most effective student activists in the city, Dai recalled, had been drawn from this source.[2]

At this time, the most prominent worker groups under the PRA, like Pearl River Film Studio East Is Red, August 1 Combat Detachment, and Chung Shan University Red Flag Workers' Red Militia Detachment, were criticized as counter-revolutionary and forcibly disbanded. Most of their leaders were arrested and imprisoned. CSU's student rebel organizations, however, were allowed to continue because the Military District dared not oppose them too forcefully. The MTP there pursued a policy of "education" toward them which, in fact, was a form of suppression.

Kaochung's MTP consisted of approximately twenty soldiers, one or two assigned to each class. Their treatment of the students, Dai recalled, was not particularly harsh.

I think the leader was a battalion commander (*ying chang*) or commissar (*cheng-wei*), but I couldn't even guess about the others. The MTP itself had a platoon leader (*t'uan chang*) and naturally a commissar as well.[3] The MTP's line was well defined and forcefully presented. Unlike the work team that came last summer, the MTP soldiers did not live with us students to investigate thoroughly the situation. Rather, they kept to themselves during non-working hours.

The platoon's main activities were to hold study meetings and write posters. In the meetings we devoted a great amount

of time to discussing Mao's writings. The bastards frequently
selected passages for study which implied criticism of the PRA's
line. We also discussed materials from the official press. The
rest of the time we spent debating the merits of organizations
in our own school. These study sessions were an important
forum where platoon members, in my opinion, encouraged
the conservatives.

Rebel teachers, on the other hand, were subjected to direct
criticism. Usually, they were attacked in big-character posters, a form
of rebuke which could not be taken lightly, especially since it came
from an official source. To have ignored the publicly displayed and
written criticism would have been equivalent to an admission of guilt.
The teachers had three options: They could have acknowledged the
charges and made a self-criticism, explained why they considered the
charges to be either distorted or incorrect, or repudiated the criticism
entirely. Dai reported that most seemed to adopt the last as a defense. However, Dai could not recall the content of the posters
because, he thought, they did not strike him as being particularly
serious at the time. Neither could he recall any arrests or struggle
sessions involving rebel teachers. In fact, Dai characterized the
MTP-sponsored criticisms as being rather low-key.

Ordinarily about half of each day was devoted to MTP-
supervised activities such as meetings. We spent the remainder
of the time in our own group activities. Usually, we discussed
our studies, wrote posters, or occasionally contacted other
schools in the area. The MTP absolutely forbade other forms
of activity when we were supposed to be following their
program. The ball fields didn't get much use, as a matter
of fact.

Students of Dai Hsiao-ai's persuasion continued to characterize themselves as rebels and the other side as conservatives. The
conservatives, of course, eschewed such designations and referred to
themselves as the "revolutionary faction." However, they conceded
that Dai and the others were "revolutionary too." Dai described the
conservative approach as the less militant of the two, less antagonistic

to existing authority, and less sweeping in the scope of its attacks. In fact, Dai stated that even though neither group had a unified headquarters in the school, MTP members were easily able to distinguish who was who merely by observing and rating everyone's activism.* Canton's conservative circles enjoyed a revival during the March suppression of the rebels. The most prominent citywide conservative alliances were District General Headquarters (*ti tsung*), Red General Headquarters (*hung-tsung*), Red First Headquarters (*hung yi ssu*), and the Doctrine Guards (*chu-yi ping*). Of these, the last two had affiliates at Kaochung.

The new line of criticizing the rebel faction sponsored by MTPs and military control committees brought the conservatives out of the doldrums induced by the earlier rebel attacks on them. The appearance of the new line uniformly throughout the city led Dai to conclude that a general instruction must have been personally issued by Huang Yung-sheng for the purpose of restoring the conservatives' flagging spirits.

We were very upset about the MTP's actions. Before they came the conservative faction was on its deathbed. But now our victory had been lost. The soldiers did not openly encourage the conservatives to revive their organizations and assume leadership of the movement. But the MTP message was not lost. Even outside formal study sessions relations between conservatives and the platoon personnel were close. They began to hold meetings again and also to criticize us.

Student rebel organizations were severely affected by MTP policies. No posters naming students directly were written by the platoon, but their posters criticizing teachers were naturally recognized as applying to all rebels. Dai reported that at Chung Shan University membership in CSU Red Flag dropped sharply from around 1100 to 300. A few defected to conservative groups, but

---

* Activism is manifested by showing enthusiasm, a spirit of initiative, concern over the outcome of projects, and willingness to encourage, criticize, and set an example for laggard comrades. In movements like the Cultural Revolution participation in meetings, far-reaching self-criticism, and energetic poster writing also count as activism.

more adopted what Dai described as a new "neutral" stance (*chung-li ti tzu-t'ai ch'u-hsien*).⁴ This new position involved several different moves which Dai thought were essentially the same. A tiny proportion eschewed all group affiliation. Others formed new groups which remained aloof from either rebel or conservative organizations. Finally, the majority stayed with their old group in name but abandoned rebel interests in fact. More committed students like Dai rebuked the deserters bitterly as "failures" at revolution (*ching-pu-ch'i k'ao-yen ti jen*).

However, some rebel groups made an honest attempt to evaluate their conduct in light of the new "truths" presented by the MTP. Dai's Rebel Headquarters was among these. Surprisingly, Dai cited the students' continued high regard for the PLA as the most potent motivating force for this action.

> When the MTP first made known their criticisms of the rebel faction we were very unsure of ourselves. We entertained seriously the possibility that they might be correct. The army's prestige was very high, and remained so even after several months of receiving the MTP's criticism. In addition, the *People's Daily* had given prominence to an example of Red Guard "rectification" on February 26, just a few days after the MTP had come to our school. We thought that might apply to us too.

The *People's Daily* article referred to was a reprint of a wall poster entitled "Whither Our Lu Hsun Corps?" written by students of the East Is Red Fighting Column of the Lu Hsun Corps of the Revolutionary Rebel Headquarters of the Physical Education Front of Shanghai.⁵ It described a rectification conducted by the group to eliminate deviations appearing in their ranks after their seizure of power. The most serious mistake was nicknamed the "purely military viewpoint," manifested principally by "dragging out so-and-so" (*chiu-ch'ü* X X), "smashing so-and-so" (*tsa-lan* X X), "dismissal of so-and-so from office" (*pa-mien* X X), and "overthrowing so-and-so" (*ta-tao* X X), as though such activity alone would forever ensure China's revolutionary purity. This major deviation was linked with numerous others, including "individualism, liberalism, the 'mountain stronghold mentality,' and the desire to get into the limelight." In a prefatory note applauding both the students' analysis and their prescription for solving the problem through rectification, the editors of the *People's Daily* called attention to these "very important problems which have a universal character" and singled out the Shanghai experience as a "model of creative study and application of Chairman Mao's works."

Dai Hsiao-ai read this article carefully and discussed it with the other leaders of the Rebel Headquarters.

> After four or five days we decided to stage a similar rectification within our own group. We notified most members of Chih-tien Chiang-shan one evening, and then, on the next day, posted notices informing the whole school of our intention.

> > *"Special Notice*
> > Our Chih-tien Chiang-shan Rebel General Headquarters has decided that, beginning tomorrow, we will undertake three days of rectification. We desire that all fighters in our headquarters comply."

> Ours was the first such poster to appear at Kaochung, and many people came to read it. All fifty or so members of our group participated in all three days of meetings, even though they had no hand in the decision to call them. The schedule was as follows

> | First day: | Morning: study the article written by the Lu Hsun Corps |
> | | Afternoon: discuss the article |
> | Second day: | Morning: members propose criticisms of the Chih-tien Chiang-shan leadership |
> | | Afternoon: members propose criticisms of the group's line |
> | Third day: | Morning: self-criticism by leaders |
> | | Afternoon: discuss and decide upon future policy directions for the group |

> Criticisms raised against the leadership the second morning were that we took "subjective decisions" with regard to the

work of the Headquarters, that we failed to seek out the
opinions of the broad masses, that we were guilty of not
carrying out the mass line,[6] and that we were sometimes
divided among ourselves. This last comment referred to our
inclination to retain our individual points of view instead of
taking the trouble to resolve points of disagreement through
discussion.

Criticisms raised that afternoon against the policy of Chih-
tien Chiang-shan were that it betrayed the "purely military
viewpoint," that insufficient attention had been given to win-
ning over elements within the conservative camp who were
awakening to the rebel cause, and that organizational discipline
had been allowed to slacken (meaning too many fighters were
spending most of their time at leisure activities).

This rectification, I thought, produced some good results.
However, many problems remained unsolved.

In our desire to imitate the Lu Hsun Corps, we wanted to
stage an "open-door rectification" (k'ai men cheng-feng), in
which people outside our group would be invited to offer
criticism. We had begun with a "closed-door rectification"
(kuan men cheng-feng) expressly to keep conservative representatives out, but now we felt they should be included as
well. Over the next few days all organizations at Kaochung
were invited to send people to criticize us, and as expected,
most of the conservative groups responded. This operation
really had no effect upon us at all. We all sat quietly at
these meetings and took notes on points made by the visiting
critics, but none of their ideas became matters for serious
debate, much less implementation.

As I recall, the new policies we agreed upon the third
afternoon were: "establish links with the PLA, attack the
capitalist roaders, break up conservative organizations, win over
uncommitted students, study Mao's works in a big way, and
firmly grasp the general orientation of the movement." We
wanted to criticize the MTP, but we had to be careful. The
conservatives had put forward the slogan "to criticize the
PLA is counterrevolutionary" and no one had objected. There
was thus a possibility that any criticism of the MTP could
get us into serious trouble. Our first solution to this dilemma

was to try and develop more cordial relations with the MTP so that any specific criticism we directed at them could not be construed as a general attack on the PLA.

Rebel leaders at Kaochung continued to believe that their stance corresponded with the line coming out of Peking. They were optimistic that if only Huang Yung-sheng were convinced of his mistake in suppressing the rebel faction, all would soon be well in Kwangtung once more. Since this end clearly lay beyond their own competence to achieve, their only recourse was to wait patiently until the CCRG leaders learned of their plight, perhaps from the CSU Red Flag liaison personnel in the capital, and then acted to rescue their allies in the south.

But the rebels' optimism soon waned. The March 1 banning of the PRA came at the height of Chih-tien Chiang-shan's rectification. Throughout Canton a massive propaganda campaign got under way criticizing and vilifying both the PRA and Chao Tzu-yang. It was, Dai reported, strongly implied that they had acted in collusion.

> Giant banners crisscrossed department store fronts: "Sentence the PRA to Death! PRA Is a Product of Chao Chih-yang!" His proper name (literally Chao Purple Sun) was often written with alternative ideographs (Chao Paper Sheep) to curse him all the better. Streamers reading "PRA Are Stinking Bastards" (*sheng ko lien hun tan*) were draped on sides of automobiles, and effigies bearing the PRA label hung like corpses along the city streets.

Rebel activists at Kaochung, in addition to being furious with their MTP for reviving conservative organizations that would otherwise have collapsed, were further enraged at their loss of status implied in the anti-PRA campaign.

> After nearly one year of making revolution we were to receive no reward at all, only "re-education." Many adopted tactics of unspoken resistance to the MTP, simply refusing to obey them. When the platoon called meetings they slept soundly in their dormitories. Some of the bolder ones tried

to establish good relations with MTP personnel on the surface, all the while posting highly critical unsigned articles.
The MTP, they said, was a work team in disguise carrying
out the bourgeois-reactionary line. A few hotheads even dared
to argue openly with the soldiers.

Dai was suspicious that conservative students, by putting forward the slogan "To criticize the PLA is counterrevolutionary,"
hoped to open the way for "capping" more audacious rebel students
as counterrevolutionaries.[7]

This period was a low tide for the rebel faction. Individually,
we encountered our severest test. The staunchest ones wrote
slogans like this and posted them around the school:

"We Must Raise Our Heads and Gaze at the North
Star.
In Our Hearts We Must Think of Chairman Mao."

"A Red Heart Faces Peking.
The Revolutionary Side Knows They Are Close to the
Chairman."

"Chairman Mao!
Your Young Red Soldiers Will Be Forever Loyal to
You!"

Some students even broke down and wept when thinking
about the cruel turn events had taken for them.
Through it all we refused to submit. We carefully recorded
all debts we would someday collect from the conservatives.
No one among the rebel groups at Kaochung had a camera
to record photographic evidence, but we did make a point of
copying down all posters and notices emanating from the
MTP. All materials collected by our group we kept in the
classroom which served as our headquarters. I don't think
the MTP knew about our archive, but it was really nothing
special. Copying posters was quite common, since they were
intended as public statements.

Not all rebels were unwavering in their stand during this
time of trial. Almost every student at Kaochung, whether interested

in politics or not, felt compelled to join one group or another. Thus, almost every group had its block of uncommitted members.

It was largely these more casual members that deserted during March and early April. A complete about-face into a conservative organization was made by only a few, I'd say about ten per cent of the former rebel faction at our school. They surrendered because they had no courage and feared being struggled against as counterrevolutionaries. We gave them a name, "capitulationists" (*t'ou-hsiang fen-tzu*), but they were not a threat to us and we spent little time answering their arguments.

Far more dangerous were a group we called the "Trotskyite capitulationists" (*t'o-p'ai*), who comprised roughly half of our rebel faction. They were the ones who defected in reality without defecting in name. They were really bastards. They even wrote posters criticizing actions taken by their own groups and rebel leadership in general. We got the name "Trotskyite" from an article written at Tsinghua University.[8]

Apart from its greater size, Dai felt the "Trotskyite" threat to be worrisome because it came from within. The recently concluded rectification had already introduced the notion that rebel leaders had made mistakes. This factor in combination with the "Trotskyites'" practice of ambiguously retaining their rebel group identification made them a less well-defined opposition. Dai Hsiao-ai and other rebel stalwarts devoted considerable energy to combating their arguments. Indeed, one reason for using the "Trotskyite" label might well have been to distinguish clearly this ambiguous group from genuine rebels.

A third category of defectors was those "neutralists" who retreated from activism altogether instead of changing their stand. Some retained their old organizational affiliation, while others moved into a new group.

The Red Women's Army (*hung-se niang-tzu chün*), a group of girls having little interest in politics, moved as a group into the neutral column. The Myriad Red Mountains (*wan shan hung pien*), newly formed in March, collected individuals recently disengaged from several rebel groups. One new group called Fu Ts'ang Lung[9] had a membership of only three boys with a common interest in radio repair.

This phenomenon of organized non-participation was yet another expression of the general pressure students felt to make at least a pretense of interest in the movement. Dai estimated that no more than three or four per cent of Kaochung students remained unorganized.

Dai also noted that every one of Kaochung's thirty or so teachers participated actively in the movement. Roughly one third were organized into Red Vanguard (*hung chien-ping*) under the Red Flag Commune (after April) on the rebel side. The other two thirds were organized into the August 1 Combat Corps (*pa yi chan-tou tui*) on the conservative side. This two-to-one faculty ratio favoring the conservative side was the reverse of the proportion which Dai thought applied to the students.

Immediately after winding up Chih-tien Chiang-shan's three-day rectification, on March 2 or 3, Dai Hsiao-ai and several other rebel leaders from Kaochung went to visit Wu Ch'uan-p'in at Chung Shan University.[10]

> It was my first chance to meet the famous Wu Ch'uan-p'in personally. He was suffering under the rule of the MTP assigned to Chung Shan University. But he and his colleagues seemed well provided with clothes and daily necessities like cups and toothbrushes. He told our delegation with great determination: "We intend to persevere in our stand! We will not compromise even a little! We are prepared to go to prison if it comes down to that!" We were all struck with admiration for Wu's indomitable revolutionary spirit. His words inspired our fighters to continue their struggle through to final victory.
>
> While at CSU we also paid a visit to the MTP. The officer who received us was quite highhanded and unreasonable: "If the Red Flags do not own up to their mistakes and change for the better they will be suppressed just like the August 1 Combat Detachment."

The fortunes of Canton's rebel faction continued at low ebb throughout most of March. At Kaochung, the tactic of trying to soften the stand of the MTP through limited criticism of their "mistakes" produced no results that Dai could observe.

Toward the end of the month, however, two new opportunities for the rebels presented themselves. First, "little tabloids" (*hsiao-pao*) from Peking-based student groups began to unfold the story of T'an Chen-lin's attempt to "reverse verdicts" upon "veteran cadres" working in the agriculture and forestry departments in Peking.[11] Allegedly part of a large-scale plot to alter Mao's line of severely criticizing Liu Shao-ch'i and Teng Hsiao-p'ing, T'an's activities were collectively tabbed the "February adverse current flowing from top to bottom" (*tzu shang erh hsia ti erh-yueh ni-liu*).

Students in Canton had little feeling for Peking politics, and were unable to judge the "correctness" of political "verdicts" passed on Liu, Teng, and other high-ranking officials at the center. They found immediately relevant, however, those aspects of the case describing how T'an had suppressed the rebel faction within organizations under his jurisdiction. Persecuted groups included East Is Red of Agricultural University, Red Flag of the Institute of Agricultural Science, Red Flag Combat Group in the Ministry of Agriculture and the Central Meteorological Bureau, and Peking Commune in the Eighth Ministry of Machine Building (in charge of farm machinery).

We immediately fanned up a vigorous propaganda campaign against "T'an Chen-lin in Kwangtung" (*kuang T'an*). Given the current atmosphere we dared not mention any names, but everyone knew we were referring implicitly to Huang Yung-sheng and other leaders responsible for suppressing our local rebel faction. In conjunction with groups from other schools we filled the streets with posters about Kuang T'an. In the process we coined a new phrase, the "March black wind" (*san-yueh hei feng*), to describe the February adverse current's particular expression in Canton.

Just as this campaign was gathering steam, a second helpful injection came from Peking in the form of the Chao Yung-fu affair. Chao Yung-fu was a deputy commander of the Tsinghai Provincial Military District and a trusted follower (*ch'in-hsin*) of Ho Lung.† He had squeezed out (*p'ai chi*) the district commander and secretary of its Party committee, and thereafter supported the Tsinghai Red Guard General Headquarters (*ch'ing-hai hung wei ping tsung pu*) in its attacks upon Chiang Ch'ing's favored group, the Tsinghai August 18 Red Guard Combat Detachment General Liaison Station (*ch'ing-hai pa-yi-pa hung-wei chan-tou tui lien-lo tsung chan*). The culmination of his policy was the February 23 tragedy in which more than two hundred persons were killed and over two thousand wounded.

Because this affair had no connection with Peking students, it first became known through a central directive reproduced in the Red Guard "little tabloids." Relevant parts of the document read as follows:

> First, the question within the Tsinghai Provincial Military District is one of counterrevolutionary coup. Deputy Commander Chao Yung-fu has overthrown with conspiratorial means the leadership of Comrade Liu Hsien-ch'uan, secretary to the Party Committee of the Military District, and usurped military power.
>
> Second, after usurping military power, Chao Yung-fu worked in collusion with Chang X X, deputy director of the X X X unit, to carry out ruthless armed suppression against "August 18" and other revolutionary mass organizations of Hsining, killing and wounding more than X X of the revolutionary masses—even opening fire on fifteen- or sixteen-year-old girls—and arresting X X of the revolutionary masses. . . .
>
> The People's Liberation Army is great. The February

† Ho Lung, formerly one of China's marshals, was a vice-chairman of the Central Committee's Military Affairs Commission. Informally he ranked third behind Mao and Lin Piao, and was probably the person really responsible for the MAC's work. By early 1967, he had already been purged as one of the plotters behind an alleged attempt at a *coup d'état* in February 1966.

23 incident was engineered by a handful of those in authority taking the capitalist road, and the broad masses of the army cadres and fighters stationed there are absolved of responsibility. All of the revolutionary masses must closely unite with the PLA units stationed in their place, firmly hit at a handful of those in authority taking the capitalist road, and make a success of the Great Proletarian Cultural Revolution.[12]

Even more than the T'an Chen-lin case, the Chao Yung-fu episode provided the Canton rebel faction with new propaganda materials with locally relevant overtones. Some PLA leaders had made serious mistakes in Tsinghai Province, and of equal importance, these "bad" leaders had been "pulled down" by the PLA itself. But both sets of events, Dai emphasized, stimulated rebel morale in Canton tremendously. Kaochung was no exception.

Rebel posters and tabloids now blossomed in our school pointing in reality at the MTP through a substitute discussion of "people like Kwangtung's T'an Chen-lin" (*kuang-T'an jen-wu*). To criticize the MTP's policy of reviving the nearly defunct conservative groups, we wrote that "The February adverse current has manifested itself in many ways in our school." But just as Huang Yung-sheng and other leaders were never mentioned at large, the MTP and its personnel were never named by us.

Consequently, feeling between the rebel faction and the MTP grew further apart. The conservatives continued to exploit their advantage by currying favor with the MTP (*ta p'ai ma-p'i*), constantly holding discussions and joining with them in recreational activities (*kao wen-yü lien-hsi*). They wanted to be on good terms with the platoon, and to convince them that rebel criticisms were, in fact, "pointing the spearhead at the PLA" and consequently counterrevolutionary. We countered with the line that "Our criticism of the PLA in reality expresses our concern (*ai-hu*) for the PLA. If we were to protect the platoon's mistakes, that would only serve to ruin the reputation of the PLA."

To Dai's satisfaction, March brought a definite change in the PLA's behavior.

> They began to realize their mistakes and shortcomings, and slowly changed their former approach of "intimacy with one faction, aloofness from the other." Some MTP members became more open to contact with rebels, even though good relations between the two were still minimal.

Dai's phraseology aside ("realize their mistakes and shortcomings"), it would seem apparent that the members of the Canton Regional Command were losing confidence in their prediction of ultimate victory for the conservatives, and had thus decided to hedge their bets by no longer supporting that group alone.[13]

Rebel faction liaison stations in Peking were maintained throughout this phase of the struggle, including the one set up by CSU Red Flag. Thus, groups from many places could easily complain to the CCRG directly and continuously about their maltreatment at the hands of local military authorities. Where open confrontations had occurred (Dai cited incidents in Fukien, Nanking, Sinkiang, and Peking), they urged the central leaders to intercede on their behalf.

In mid-April, rebel holdouts in Canton were rewarded with a personal visit by Premier Chou En-lai. Neither the source of the initiative for this move nor responsibility for its arrangement were known to Dai, but he was crystal-clear in his view of its importance: Chou was carrying forward to a new qualitative stage trends set in motion by the rebels themselves in the preceding three weeks.

CHAPTER NINE

Struggle by Force: Summer 1967

Dai Hsiao-ai thought that Premier Chou En-lai might have been invited to Canton by the provincial Military Control Committee itself to help preserve order in the city during the very important Canton Export Commodities Spring Fair, one of only two occasions each year (the other is the Autumn Fair) when great numbers of foreign businessmen enter China to negotiate foreign trade agreements.[1] Before Chou's arrival, Cultural Revolution conflict had already intruded onto the fairground itself. The sign above the entrance to the exhibition hall, identified as the calligraphy of Foreign Minister Ch'en Yi, had been torn down by a crowd of students. Ch'en at that time was under intense criticism by rebels within the foreign affairs system in Peking. The possibility of similar ugly incidents involving Red Guards and foreigners as well during the fair was unthinkable. Chou En-lai's prestige among the students was then very high, while the position of the Military Control Committee had declined markedly in the wake of the T'an Chen-lin and Chao Yung-fu affairs. Hence, the Military Region Command, which was ultimately responsible for the success of the fair, must have felt that only Chou could control Canton's growing factional tension.

Chou's visit lasted from April 14–18. Dai felt certain that the Premier generally understood the Canton political situation before his arrival, but that he urgently needed up-to-the-minute intelligence to make meaningful decisions.

At first Chou engaged only in comprehensive fact finding. He even brought along ten or so correspondents to assist him. These cadres, who I imagine were detached temporarily from various State Council offices in Peking, Chou sent around to investigate conditions in many more units than he would have time to visit in person. No correspondent came to Kaochung but I heard about their interviews at other schools. Thus, I knew they were working hard at collecting information. A few of these correspondents remained behind after Chou departed.

After concluding his brief assessment, Chou summoned representatives of all the Canton factions to a mass meeting in the Chung Shan Memorial Hall, where he announced his findings and decisions. Dai recalled that one ticket for this meeting, distributed by the military control authority, was made available to the factional groups in each unit. At Kaochung, one ticket was given to the rebels and one to the conservatives. The various rebel leaders met together informally and decided to give theirs to Dai, largely because he alone expressed interest in attending.

Since his notes and diary entries on this meeting were left in China, Dai had to rely upon memory alone to produce an account of the proceedings. He did, however, particularly recall his feeling that the large number of empty seats indicated that attendance had been controlled.

Premier Chou told us he was "sent by Chairman Mao," but that was just a ceremonious phrase. He had to say it.

Actually Chou's prestige was so great at that time that Mao may well have been wary of him. Chou first briefly reviewed the international and domestic situation, and commented on the progress of the Cultural Revolution countrywide. Then he made a series of specific points regarding our locality.

First, Chou said in no uncertain terms that the provincial MCC had made mistakes in its work of "supporting the left." Nevertheless, we were to consider these mistakes in light of the MCC's achievements, which were more important.

Second, Chou certified that Kwangtung Technical College Red Flag (*kuang kung hung-ch'i*), CSU Red Flag, and Kwangtung Medical College Red Flag (*kuang yi hung-ch'i*) were all bona fide members of the "revolutionary rebel faction." These three groups Chou called the "three red flags of Canton." He singled out Wu Ch'uan-p'in for special praise in this connection as one "daring to uphold revolutionary truth" and "having political farsightedness."

Third, he said that even though District Headquarters (*ti tsung*) and Red Headquarters (*hung tsung*) were overly conservative (*p'ien pao*), they were still capable of reforming themselves and should not be forcibly closed down.

Fourth, he directed that well-intentioned efforts be made to help and educate "our little brothers and sisters of the Doctine Guards" (*chu-yi ping*).[2]

Fifth, Chou "rehabilitated" (*p'ing-fan*) Pearl River Film Studio East Is Red (*chu ying tung-fang hung*), one of the workers' groups banned by the provincial MCC. He did not name other banned groups, probably because their cases were more complicated. Most notable of those left unmentioned were the August 1 Combat Detachment, the Massive Cudgels, and Chung Shan University Red Flag Workers' Red Guard Detachment. But the membership and activities of the government-employed cinema workers' group were undoubtedly not too complicated.

Sixth, Chou cautioned against the apparent "revival of an adverse current of provincialism" (*ti-fang chu-yi fu-pi ni-liu*) in Kwangtung Province, a recurrent problem there.[3]

In the first two weeks of April, before Premier Chou arrived, it had been difficult to evaluate Canton's political scene. Neither the relative strength of the various contending forces nor the direction of future trends could be known for certain, and the provincial MCC seemed increasingly reluctant to take firm stands. Premier Chou's contribution was to realign power relations in Kwangtung by introducing some definite and specific decisions about rebels and conservatives. In fact, the rebel faction felt that Chou had effectively turned the tables on Huang Yung-sheng's policy of sponsoring a conservative revival by his obviously favorable comments on the rebel position.

Dai's own analysis demonstrated his sensitivity to political factors of prestige and short-run support, even though in expressing himself he often chose to employ the doctrinaire language of "lines" and "mistakes." Dai's sensitivity was essentially limited to narrow notions of who was on whose side. He could not describe Chairman Mao's revolutionary strategy for Canton and Kwangtung, nor could he list the critéria that Chou En-lai might have used to assess people and organizations, such as the nature of their membership, their activities, the quality of their leadership, or their style of work. He was only aware that some cases were "simple" and others relatively "complicated."

Although Chou's visit briefly curtailed factional conflict, the process of factional polarization continued unabated after his departure. Probably to his chagrin, terms used in his speech emerged as generally accepted names for the two opposing sides. Borrowing from Chou's announcement that the "three red flags of Canton" were genuine revolutionaries, the rebel faction elected to call themselves the "Red Flag faction," or more commonly just "flag faction" (ch'i p'ai).[4] The conservative group elected to designate themselves "East Wind," referring to the debate over military control back in March when their slogan had been:

San-yueh tung-feng hao-tang,
Chün kuan ch'eng-chi hui-huang!

"The March east wind is imposing,
The achievements of military control are brilliant!"

This was designed to counter the critical rebel propaganda slogan:

San-yueh hei-feng kun-kun!

"The March black wind is raging!"

As a result of Chou's over-all support for the flag faction, all rebel groups enjoyed a relief from MCC harassment. Dai recalled, for example, that members of the Chung Shan University Red Flag Workers' Red Guard Detachment had been imprisoned when the group was suppressed in March. After Premier Chou's decisions were handed down, the provincial MCC released some of them. However, this action was far too limited for Red Flag tastes, and on May 3 over sixty students proclaimed their intention to fast until every worker was freed.* A large crowd was assembled to express support for the protesters. At first, some soldiers attempted to discourage the students from going through with this potentially explosive move, but they took no strong action when the protesters refused to heed them. The sixty fasting students then resolved before the crowd to abstain from eating until both the provincial Public Security Bureau and the Canton Municipal Garrison Command released the remaining prisoners. After the oaths had been declared, the crowd hoisted the sixty upon their shoulders and paraded them enthusiastically through the streets of the city.

Immediately upon learning of this tactic, the CCRG sent a telegram from Peking asking the rebel students not to continue with it. The message successfully ended the fast, but the aroused students were not to be entirely denied. They subsequently held a conference with the police authorities at which they secured an agreement for the workers' release. Dai was uncertain, though, as to whether or not the entire number were finally set free.

Dai Hsiao-ai characterized the new political situation in late April as one in which the flag faction had "emerged suddenly from a humble station into an honorable position" (*yang mei t'u*

---

* This protest event was held at the Canton Tung-chiao Field, which Dai thought had been used for practicing martial arts in the days of imperial China. Under the Communists it was occasionally the scene of mass rallies because of the large available space on both sides of the road at that point.

ch'i). Not only did they recover the strength they had enjoyed during the January seizure of power, but they even managed to expand their base of support. Opposition East Wind organizations suffered mass defections from their ranks, with the defectors sometimes simply retaining their former name augmented with the preface "new" to indicate their changed allegiance. For example, New First Headquarters (*hsin yi ssu*), New District Headquarters (*hsin ti tsung*), and New Doctrine Guards (*hsin chu-yi ping*) all appeared now for the first time.

At Kaochung, Dai and the other activists who had gone to Chung Shan University to interview Wu Ch'uan-p'in in early March decided collectively to form a new headquarters organ in their school which would link up with a citywide rebel headquarters. The new organization, Kaochung Middle School Red Flag Commune, did not have any more powers or responsibilities than the old, more loosely structured alliance, but simply represented a desire on the part of middle school student leaders to become more meaningfully involved in the activities of the flag faction during its period of revival. After a brief debate, they decided to affiliate with Wu Ch'uan-p'in's Canton Red Headquarters and dispatched a messenger the following day to inform Wu of their desire. Two days later, Wu responded by sending a representative to Kaochung for the purpose of certifying that the Red Flag Commune was, in fact, the school's rebel group. This mission was accomplished with little difficulty or delay. In the months that followed there were no more organizational realignments in Canton, a fact which seems to underline the rigid polarization that more and more came to characterize local politics there.

Dai cited the debates over the Provincial Revolutionary Alliance as the one expression of the Kaochung rebel students' newly found feeling of involvement in the wider Canton movement. At the time these events took place, the rebel faction in the school had expressed its support without really knowing much about what had occurred. Shortly afterward, the coming of the Spring Festival and the imposition of military control had temporarily deflected their collective interest. In late April, they disagreed for the first time over how to evaluate the PRA's actions. All agreed, Dai reported, that the PRA had committed errors; thus, the question which divided them was only that of how seriously its mistakes should be regarded. The PRA's severest critics argued that a "sham seizure of power" (*chia to ch'uan*) had taken place, meaning that PRA leaders had colluded with the existing power structure and merely pretended to seize power for their mutual advantage. On the contrary, PRA's more tolerant critics argued that their effort should be considered a "seizure of sham power" (*to chia ch'uan*), meaning that the Alliance had acted too hastily and thus achieved only a surface-level seizure of power. No consistent line on the PRA evolved from this debate, and the issue was eventually pushed into the background as more pressing problems arose in May. The status of these discussions was never allowed to broaden beyond an "internal debate" within the flag faction itself and Dai and the rebel students steadfastly refused even to listen to East Wind attacks against the PRA.

According to Dai, the issues of conflict between the two factions at Kaochung continued to center around the past behavior of the military training platoon. Curiously, differences were still expressed in terms of allegorical "winds":

> The argument over this question was very important. If the "March black wind" theory were victorious, then the army's policy of propping up the conservatives and suppressing the rebels would be mistaken. If the "east wind" theory were victorious, then the army's policy of opposing the rebels would be correct. The real issue was the effect of the MTP's behavior upon our own welfare. In debating, though, little mention was made of Kwangtung's T'an Chen-lin and no outright naming of Huang Yung-sheng occurred at all.

Dai suggested at one point that the students' reluctance to argue specific charges could be explained by the continued high prestige of the PLA in general, even though some commanders had chosen the wrong road. But the reservoir of support enjoyed by the PLA was waning rapidly, particularly among groups which had been

more vigorously suppressed than middle school students. Dai chose
Chung Shan University as an example.

Sometime in April, I don't recall exactly when in relation
to Chou En-lai's visit, Wu Ch'uan-p'in's elite group CSU
August 31 issued a challenging call for a "Combat Mobilization Meeting to Bombard Huang Yung-sheng!" Outsiders
don't seem to understand how bitter it was to suffer under
the suppression of the military. I read recently [November
1968] that Chou En-lai has strongly criticized Wu Ch'uan-p'in.
That really is unreasonable!

In the student view, the Canton Military Region Command
seemed to have no clear political policy during spring and summer
1967. Hence, it was roundly criticized by both factions. Red Flag
and East Wind alike failed to win the outspoken support of the
hesitant military leaders. At Kaochung, the charge was heard from
both factions that the MTP's "'support the left' banner is indis-
tinct." The Kaochung MTP's political commissar even undertook
a personal "self-examination" (*chien-ch'a*) before the Red Flag students, in which he acknowledged the correctness of Premier
Chou's criticisms and freely admitted the platoon's error in suppressing the rebels in March. In Dai's view, while the platoon members were unwilling to form close relations with the flag faction,
they were equally hesitant about angering them. As a result, they
could no longer approach their work with much enthusiasm. Finally,
in May, Kaochung's MTP, along with those in all other Canton
schools, suddenly withdrew, ostensibly because "the tasks of preparing for war are heavy."

"Preparing for war" usually meant preparing to defend
against military provocations by the Kuomintang. That situation was long-standing. This time they told us they had to
make preparations against the Soviet Union.

However, Dai and his fellow students were not convinced.
They believed that the MTP's real reasons for withdrawing were
its declining prestige and its inability to perform its tasks properly.
Throughout the period of withdrawal, which lasted for four months

until September, members of the platoon continued to come and go, although Dai had no idea what they were doing then. Sometimes they would stay as long as a week.

The provincial Military Control Committee remained on the job and continued to maintain at least a brave façade of military control, even though throughout the summer of 1967, the Military Region Command itself was also an essentially passive force. Dai Hsiao-ai's experiences with the PLA at this time will be taken up in Chapter Ten. In the remainder of this chapter the story of local escalating factionalism will first be carried further. Dai will present in his own words his admittedly biased version of how the antagonistic debates of spring developed inexorably into incidents of bloody violence between June and September.

In 1967, Canton and many other places suffered through nine months of confusion caused by uncountable incidents of struggle by force (*wu tou*). These numerous incidents had a negative influence upon both industrial and agricultural production and interfered with the progress of the Cultural Revolution. There seemed to be no way to solve the problem. Although the CCRG tried a whole range of measures to restrain struggle by force, people still carried shields and spears [i.e. weapons]. If two people belonged to different factions, no matter how close their personal relations had been in the past, they would now face each other as enemies. Correspondingly, people from the same faction would treat each other like brothers, even though they came from different units and had never before met. This change in social relations thus had a political origin.

In a society rent with class struggle like ours, nobody could remain aloof from the movement. After going through the Cultural Revolution, some people were inevitably promoted because they stood staunchly on the side of the revolutionary faction, like Yao Wen-yuan.[5] Others were capped with political hats and subjected to struggle or thought reform. Thus, everyone naturally took the view that one's political standpoint was a matter of life and death. People hotly contested the issues arising in the course of the movement, fervently hoping

that they themselves would end up in the group considered
to be the genuine revolutionary left. Such intense competition
inevitably produced factions which, never successfully controlled, finally indulged in the extreme of physically attacking
each another. Actually, the CCRG itself was largely responsible
for the outbreak of violence. Since its members were inexperienced in struggle [sic], they tended to move indecisively,
like a chess player who had lifted his piece off the board
but could not settle upon a move. As internal unity within
rebel ranks around the country diminished, the CCRG even
more frequently changed its mind. Then Chiang Ch'ing on
her own initiative propagated the slogan "Attack with reasoning, defend with force." All of these considerations were
factors underlying the spread of struggle by force.

In order to understand fully the nature of these violent
struggles, we must first be clear about how factions were
originally formed in Canton.

By December 1966, when the "great exchange of revolutionary experiences" was in the main concluded, the majority
of students had returned to their own schools. They had
absorbed experiences from all over China, and in particular
they had learned about struggles carried on elsewhere. They
turned their spearheads away from their own schools and
toward society generally, and began to rebel against power
holders in Party and government organs. In addition the
workers' movement in factories and other units started up in
December. Since most workers tended toward conservative
thinking, the two new forces appearing in the wider society
at this time created a general conflict situation.

On December 12, students from Wuhan's rebel faction
came south and united with Canton's rebel students to form
the Seal Up *Hung Wei Pao* Action Command Headquarters
(*feng hung wei pao hsing-tung chih-hui pu*).[6] In response,
another organization calling itself Oppose Sealing Up *Hung
Wei Pao* Command Headquarters sprang up. It was dominated by conservative workers and included conservative students. This was the first occasion on which two big factions
in Canton were squared off against one another in a test
of strength. The end result was defeat for the conservatives.

A later announcement, issued by the Central-South Bureau, admitted that mistakes had been made by the paper, and thereafter it was no longer published.

After this incident all revolutionary organizations in the city felt compelled to take a position. The rebel faction predictably grouped themselves under the Seal Up *Hung Wei Pao* Action Command Headquarters. The conservatives threw in their lot with the opposition, and both sides launched a propaganda offensive.

Our school's Chih-tien Chiang-shan Rebel Headquarters immediately declared for the Seal Up *Hung Wei Pao* Action Command Headquarters. We commandeered our school truck, mounted a loudspeaker upon it, and headed for Canton to propagate our views in the urban districts.[7] The banner of our Headquarters unfurled and fluttered in the heart of the city, and the sound of our broadcasts was heard everywhere. Usually we just repeated the following slogans over and over again:

"Sealing up the paper is a revolutionary act."
(*feng pao shih ko-ming hsing-tung*)

"The act of sealing up the paper was very, very good!"
(*feng pao hsing-tung hao-te-hen*)

"Whoever dares oppose the sealing up will be destroyed!"
(*shei kan fan feng chiu chao t'a hui chih*)

The opposition faction was similarly engaged in propagandizing their own slogans. Once we were broadcasting while driving along Chung Shan Road's very crowded Section Five when suddenly we encountered a District Headquarters propaganda van. Since they outnumbered us they jumped down off their truck and surrounded ours, demanding loudly that we climb down for a face-to-face debate. But one look at their angry glances and clenched fists was all we needed to know that we would be beaten up if we complied. They were all workers, while our van had only five students, three boys, and two girls. They would not dare attack us where we were since the crowd's presence meant they could easily be held responsible for such a brazen act. However, if we alighted, then it might appear that they were defending themselves against our attack. We didn't fear real debate; after all, compared to us they were inarticulate. As we outtalked them, their shame would have turned to anger and they would have begun to beat us. We thus refused to budge.

We were trapped now because the crowd of onlookers had also surrounded our van. We used our loudspeaker to explain our propaganda mission, and to accuse District Headquarters people of wanting to beat us. Before long, several truckloads of our own people came along, and since we now constituted a majority, the workers had no choice but to retreat. Considerable friction between the two factions led to numerous similar incidents during this early period, but none were serious enough to warrant being called struggle by force.

When the Central-South Bureau later posted their announcement acknowledging that sealing up *Hung Wei Pao* was a revolutionary act, our entire rebel faction was elated. The conservative headquarters opposed to sealing up the paper was subsequently dissolved, and the prestige and power of both Red General Headquarters and District General Headquarters suffered badly. Conservative organizations were now much less lively than when first formed. Their members became passive and unresponsive even when cursed or criticized. A few groups came close to disbanding altogether.

This situation lasted until the "seize power" phase in January, when the rebels were defeated because they failed to unite internally. Later, under military control, conservative strength was restored, and they were able to suppress and disband rebel groups. When Chou En-lai visited Canton in April, the situation underwent another big change. The Premier pointed out the Military Region's mistakes, recognized the "three red flags of Canton" and their allies as the genuine rebel faction, and criticized Red General Headquarters and District General Headquarters as overly conservative.

The flag faction's prestige increased sharply after Chou's commendations and acts of rehabilitation, but in contrast to the earlier "seize power" phase, the conservatives this time were unwilling to accept their defeat. Their numbers were still relatively large as a result of the Military Region's open support in March, and they continued to express themselves strongly. Having already seen the movement shift twice, they no longer believed that rebel victory was inevitable. The following slogan displayed by the Doctrine Guards illustrated the conservative feeling that their day would come again:

> "February was yours; March was ours;
> April is yours; May will certainly be ours!"

The flag faction counted with the slogan:

> "We will pass through an April of fluttering red flags
> into a May in which even bigger victories are won!"

Actually, the month of May remained fairly calm. The few fights that did occur were minor and propaganda activity generally diminished. We were later to discover, however, that this lull was only the proverbial calm before the storm. We were not aware that the East Wind group was preparing for war. At our own school, for example, we paid no special attention to the Doctrine Guards, even though they spent much time practicing hand-to-hand combat with wooden clubs, jumps to the ground from high places, and knife throwing.[8] We figured they were doing this for recreation, and even laughed at them for engaging in such antics. We made no attempt to interfere with them, nor did we use our propaganda capability to inform the people of Canton of their activities.

Later in May, as the general situation around the country grew more unsettled, the first gunshot was heard from the southwest. A conservative workers' organization in Ch'eng-tu (Szechwan Province) known as the Workers' Production Army (*kung-jen ch'an-yeh chün*) opened fire on student Red Guards from Szechwan University's "August 26" group, killing several. Included among the dead was a Ch'eng-tu liaison man from Peking Geology College East Is Red, Li Ch'uan-hua. This incident shook the whole country. When we heard about it in Canton the atmosphere became quite tense.

Violent struggle finally broke out in Canton itself on June 24 when members of the Chung Shan Medical College East Is Red Commune seized back propaganda vans stolen from them earlier by District General Headquarters. Angry workers from the latter group showed up at the gate of the college demanding a fight. The provincial MCC quickly convened a negotiation meeting to deal with the problem, but before the conferees concluded their talks, District Headquarters called in reinforcements. The new arrivals forced their way into the meeting hall, put out the lights, and under cover of darkness beat up the Red Flag participants. In the resulting confusion, even the MCC's representatives and the liaison personnel left behind by Premier Chou were given beatings. Following this encounter both factions employed the ancient tactic whereby "the shrewd person lodges the first complaint." Each side furiously propagandized its position by posting in every corner of Canton accusations that the other side had provoked the fighting. Following this incident, the first to occur on such a large scale in Canton, the city fell into a state of greater disorder. Both the CCRG and the provincial MCC tried to mediate conflicts in the tense atmosphere, but their efforts to head off violent fighting were in vain.

In Wuhan on July 20, the "One Million Heroes" supported by local commander Ch'en Tsai-tao kidnapped two emissaries sent from Peking to solve local problems, Hsieh Fu-chih and Wang Li.† This incident had a direct effect upon the rest of the country.‡

In Canton, on July 21, the District Headquarters attacked the Overseas Chinese Sugar Refinery and beat Red Flag workers to death.

On July 23, the Canton flag faction slowly marched to Yueh Hsiu Shan Athletic Field carrying wreaths of flowers to convene a memorial service for our fallen comrades. But

† Wang Li was deputy editor in chief of Red Flag and a member of the CCRG. Hsieh Fu-chih was Minister of Public Security and chairman of the Peking Municipal Revolutionary Committee.
‡ This famous incident provided CCRG leaders just the excuse they needed to attempt a broad-ranging attack upon generally conservative military commanders. The CCRG's organ Red Flag introduced a new battle cry, "Drag out the handful of power holders taking the capitalist road within the People's Liberation Army." In the country at large the army was first rendered helpless to act in any way as its prestige fell to an all-time low. Later, in September, a massive campaign to contain this advancing anarchy was launched and several CCRG leaders associated with the anti-army slogan were purged.

as our procession passed the Chung Shan Memorial Hall, Doctrine Guards who had been meeting inside rushed out, blocked our vehicles, and attacked us. In the course of the fighting a vehicle belonging to the South China Agricultural College Red Flag Workers was isolated and surrounded and some of its passengers killed by Doctrine Guards wielding long-handled spears and throwing knives. No sooner did we hear the news than we jumped from our trucks and hurried to their aid. The Doctrine Guards thereupon retreated inside the hall, where they withstood several of our assaults. The last time a few of our number advanced too quickly and were cut off from the main body. Seeing their comrades about to be wiped out, the members of the Chung Shan Medical College August 31 Combat Corps mounted a ferocious charge carrying long knives and holding throwing knives in their teeth.[9] When they broke through and successfully saved their allies the Doctrine Guards fell back. At that moment, a unit of about thirty soldiers appeared. Note that they were nowhere to be seen while we were getting the worst of it, but only showed up after the Doctrine Guards were on the run. When nightfall came, the Doctrine Guards retreated in safety under the protection of the PLA. Our flag faction lost thirty-three killed that day.

On July 25, the Canton flag faction together with rebels from other provinces and members of the Capital Red Guard Congress (*shou-tu hung-tai hui*) convened another memorial service at Tung-chiao Field. On this occasion speeches expressing support for the flag faction and strongly rebuking the Doctrine Guards were contributed by Wuhan Second Steel Headquarters (*wu-han kang erh ssu*), Steel Workers General Headquarters (*kang kung tsung*), and Steel September 13 (*kang chiu yi san*), all three of which had risen to a position of prominence in Hupeh Province after the Ch'en Tsai-tao affair, as well as Peking Aviation Institute Red Flag, Tsinghua University Ching-kang-shan, the group from Harbin Military Engineering College, and others. The conflict was truly nationwide.

Afterward a great demonstration was held to display the

corpses. Over eighty thousand paraders were led by rebel workers from the Canton Fire Department, whose protective clothing shielded them from flying missiles or other weapons. For show they held large knives in their teeth and carried long spears, to communicate to the conservatives their intention of fighting a battle to the death.

On August 13 an armed launch manned by District General Headquarters and Red General Headquarters sank a boat being used to transport flag faction arms. Eighteen rebels were killed by the attackers and their bodies thrown into the water.

Red Flag anger over this incident led directly to the organization of a retaliatory counterattack on August 15 against the headquarters of the Kwangtung Province General Trade Union. This tall building allowed conservative workers to control the streets in the area of Hai Chu Kuang-ch'ang, the site of Canton's biannual export commodity fairs. Every time rebels passed below they would be bombarded with bottles, and sometimes even sprayed with small-arms or machine-gun fire. We posted guards at each nearby intersection to prevent other conservative forces from coming to aid their allies at union headquarters, and then leveled heavy mortar [sic] fire at the union building itself. This job was handled with great skill by the demobilized soldiers of the August 1 Combat Detachment. The District General Headquarters men in the union building were forced to retreat to higher floors, shooting down the stairs as they went. At that moment a cable was received from Chou En-lai in Peking demanding the flag faction give the General Headquarters faction a chance to surrender and withdraw. This was done, but the trade union building, Nan-fang Building, Ai-ch'un Building, and the export commodities hall were all occupied by the Red Flags.

Non-combatant city residents were, of course, frightened to death. They were not so much threatened by Red Guards directly as by criminal elements who were taking advantage of the disorder to commit freely burglaries on residential dwellings. To meet this problem the flag faction organized a special Red Garrison Command to patrol the city streets. Red Guards riding in cars or on motorcycles and armed with pistols or light machine guns cruised through every district.

Taking a turn at this job was always very interesting because it made us feel strong and militant.

Geographically speaking, the fact that Canton factories are concentrated in the suburbs meant that conservative worker strength was greatest there. The workers were much less able to render assistance to their student allies downtown. Now that the flag faction had established hegemony in the urban districts, conservative-minded students consequently found it impossible to stay there. Most withdrew to rural villages, and talked about employing Mao's tactic of "surrounding the cities from the countryside."

Yet another expression of August anarchy was the widespread factional attempts made to attack and occupy suburban schools. At Kaochung we felt it imperative to construct defenses. We used cement to seal off the entrance steps and strung a wire conductor fence around the entire outer wall. Should anyone attempt to force his way into the premises we were ready to connect this fence to an electric power outlet. We also arranged some concrete water pipes of wide circumference on the roof to look like artillery. A poster outside the school warned passers-by:

"If anyone dares encroach upon our school property,
 his wife will be called a widow
 and his filial son will pay homage to a dead father."

(*shei yao ch'in-fan wo hsiao,*
chi chao ni ch'i-tzu shou-kua
erh-tzu tai-hsiao.)

When leaving the school to stick up propaganda posters outside, we always traveled in groups of at least three lest someone try to murder us. The danger was real.

After the *People's Daily* began to popularize the notion of "great alliances" (*ta lien-ho*) in September, the frequency and intensity of violent confrontations between factions began to taper off. One contributing factor was the presence of representatives from various Kwangtung factions in Peking for negotiations sponsored by the central authorities. After a twelve-point agreement was signed by these negotiators (in November) struggle by force nearly terminated altogether.

Readers familiar with the full range of information about the Cultural Revolution in Kwangtung will easily detect the sketchy and one-sided nature of Dai Hsiao-ai's account of factional violence. It is thus pertinent to emphasize again that the sole object of this book is to represent as accurately as possible the way in which the events of the movement were seen and felt by one single active participant.

Ironically, during the very period when factional violence rose to its highest pitch, Kwangtung Province was formally under "military control." Where were the soldiers while open conflict raged in the streets? How did their failure to intervene in the fighting affect relations between the rebels and the PLA? How did the conservative groups fare politically with their military protectors temporarily disarmed? Dai's experiences with the army in summer 1967, the subject of the following chapter, touch upon all three questions.

CHAPTER TEN

The Fall and Rise of the People's Liberation Army: July–October 1967

In Dai's view, the assertiveness of the military authorities in Canton decreased sharply on two separate occasions after the heyday of military control in March 1967. The first followed Chou En-lai's visit to the city in mid-April, the second occurred after the Canton Military Region submitted a self-examination to Chairman Mao on August 20.[1] The aftermath of Premier Chou's April investigations in Canton has already been discussed in Chapter Nine; hence Dai's views on the latter event will constitute the primary focus of the present chapter.

Fully a month before Huang Yung-sheng apologized publicly to Chairman Mao, the general prestige of the PLA had already suffered a sharp setback as a result of the so-called "Wuhan Incident." On July 19, Hsieh Fu-chih and Wang Li, sent to the city five days earlier to attempt to stabilize the situation there, were captured by a conservative mass organization known as the One Million Heroes. The open support given this group by Ch'en Tsai-tao, commander of the Wuhan Military Region (responsible for Honan and Hupeh provinces), increased their strength to such a degree that combined air and naval forces had to be mustered by Peking to force the release of the hostages. This overt challenge to the PLA on the part of a local commander provided a long-awaited opportunity for the CCRG to square accounts with the military leaders around the country who had been suppressing rebels in recent months. Chiang Ch'ing directly challenged the PLA's appointed mission of discouraging all violence in the interest of peacefully constructing "great alliances" among factions.

On July 22, she reportedly instructed that, while it was still correct for mass organizations to "attack with reasoning," they would henceforth be permitted to "defend with force" (*wen kung wu wei*). Barely a week later, on the eve of celebrating the fortieth anniversary of the PLA's founding (August 1, 1927), a new *Red Flag* appeared with an editorial urging revolutionaries to "take the tiny handful of persons in authority taking the capitalist road *within the army* and throw every last one into the trash heap."[2] On its very anniversary, the PLA's prestige had plunged to the lowest point in its history.

> The tiny handful in the army were dragged out everywhere after the Ch'en Tsai-tao incident. Anyone harboring grievances against the PLA could now attack military authorities openly. Because the center had supplied us with a theoretical framework (*yu le chung-yang ti li-lun tso yi-chü*), we felt confident in dragging out "Canton's Ch'en Tsai-tao." This term did not refer to Huang Yung-sheng alone but to a group of leaders holding various responsible positions in the Canton Military Region Command. Both factions now began to raid the military region facilities for weapons.

Also, some Canton groups attempted further to disparage local military authority by purposely fanning up violent incidents between factions. We knew that regional and district commanders were judged in Peking primarily on how well they contained the fighting within their spheres of jurisdiction. Some rebel Red Guards we knew had been personally told as much by either Ch'en Po-ta or Lin Piao. Therefore any incidence of factional conflict would give the appropriate PLA unit a black eye.

Dai was first aware of the regional command's self-examination when a copy of it was posted on the wall at his school. Later, wall posters revealed that a request for "pardon" appearing in the original (the phrase was *hsiang Mao chu-hsi ch'ing tsui*) had been struck out by Chairman Mao when he approved the document for general distribution without comment or signature.[3]

The Canton commanders first detailed their mistakes and accepted full responsibility.

So serious have been our conservative thoughts and so numerous have been the old rules and conventions in our minds that we have had a poor understanding of the new approach, of the Great Proletarian Cultural Revolution, and lacked the stand, viewpoint, and ideas and feelings of proletarian revolutionaries. Hence, after our intervention in the Great Cultural Revolution in the Canton area, we have not been able to take the struggle between the two lines as the key link; we have not identified the left correctly, and thus committed mistakes on the basic question of how to treat the masses correctly. Chairman Mao has taught us: We must trust the masses, rely on them, mobilize them with a free hand, and respect their creative spirit. But we have overconfidence in ourselves as we have always wanted to confine the vigorously developing mass movement to the framework of our own subjective imagination. As a result, not only have we failed to give strong support to the actions of revolutionary rebel groups, but sometimes we have restrained them. We mistakenly restricted or even resorted to dictatorial measures against certain revolutionary rebel groups and mass organizations. In this way, we virtually placed ourselves in a position antagonistic to the masses and departed from Chairman Mao's proletarian revolutionary line.

They then stated that they would do better in the future.

We have the determination to correct thoroughly the mistakes made in the work of supporting the left. We reaffirm: All those revolutionary mass organizations inside and outside the army which we formerly banned and dissolved shall be vindicated and rehabilitated without exception, and all public statements, notices, and "indictments" which we had promulgated in respect to banning and dissolving these revolutionary mass organizations shall be null and void without exception. All people who have been arrested—with the exception of those bad people whose crimes have been proved by evidence and who should be dealt with according to the law as provided by the Central Committee—shall be rehabilitated.

In their self-examination Huang Yung-sheng and the Military Region's Party Committee publicly acknowledged the Red Flags as Canton's genuine "revolutionary rebel faction." However, Dai and his fellow flag faction members were far from satisfied.

No small number of PLA fighters continued to sympathize with the East Winds, telling them privately, "We want to be on your side but the higher-ups won't allow it." Such behavior offered clear evidence that the attitudes of PLA personnel at lower and middle levels departed from the expressed views of their commanders. We therefore adopted the slogan "Your banner is not clear." The East Winds, thrown for a loss by the self-examination, bitterly accused the Region Command of "supporting one faction and suppressing the other" instead of supporting the broad masses of the left as directed.

Most active in supporting the flag faction in Canton were local air force units. I don't mean they gave us weapons. But whereas Huang Yung-sheng's pronouncements and propaganda expressed correct support for our side and left it at that, the air force's propaganda was enthusiastic and sincere.[4]

The promulgation of Huang Yung-sheng's self-examination increased the tendency set in motion after the July fiasco at Wuhan for both big factions to raid PLA installations in a quest for arms. Dai and other rebel students participated in one such expedition against the Anti-Aircraft Searchlight Company near their school. This, incidentally, was the same company that, before the Cultural Revolution, had come to Kaochung periodically to give military training, to watch movies, and to fraternize with the students. Since it was part of the Air Force Ground Services Unit, Dai felt that as Red Flag students they would receive a sympathetic welcome. However, its selection as a military installation to be raided was more heavily influenced by its convenient location, only one and one half miles away. By staying close to home, the Kaochung students would avoid the risk of crossing swords with another Red Guard group or mass organization on "unfriendly" ground.

Because there were unforeseeable dangers we selected twenty boys for this mission. Each of us was armed with a knife. We also had three pistols. All the girls remained in the school. Two of our three guns had been issued to us by Red Headquarters, while the third had been stolen by a member of our group who had participated in an earlier raid on the Public Security Bureau in Foshan city.[5] Even though it was broad daylight, we managed to give the impression of carrying six guns in all by removing the weapons from their holsters and tucking both pistols and holsters under our shirts. That way we had six telltale bulges instead of only three.

When we approached the camp, the startled sentry immediately turned tail and dashed inside to report to his comrades. Then the whole group ran out to welcome us. They offered hot water to drink and then exhibited their enthusiasm by noisily shouting slogans:

"Learn from the revolutionary young generals.
Salute the revolutionary young generals."

(*"hsiang ko-ming hsiao chiang hsueh-hsi;
hsiang ko-ming hsiao chiang chih-ching."*)

We responded pointedly:

"The liberation army must support the revolutionary rebel faction."

Our three leaders met with the commanding officers (one battalion-level political commissar, one company commander, and one platoon leader) and demanded that the company "offer" real support to our revolutionary rebel faction by lending us guns, so we could "attack with reason but defend with force." The officers temporized. This, they said, was impossible since all arms had been withdrawn by order from above. The students outside got the same story: The company stood as one with the revolutionary rebel faction and supported all revolutionary actions; but there were simply no arms in the compound. We suspected that the arms had been hidden away, and when it was apparent that nothing would be achieved by negotiation, we ordered a search. (About a month later our suspicions were confirmed when we noticed that the weapons carried by this company had rusted, the result, no doubt, of having been buried.) We drew our knives, entered the barracks, and proceeded to tear the place apart. The frightened soldiers merely watched even when we overturned their beds. When we threatened them by flashing our knives and demanded that they hand the guns over immediately, they could only stammer: "I . . . , I don't know." It made us laugh! The much-respected People's Liberation Army was in reality a pack of cowards!

We were still burrowing around when a crowd of angry peasants appeared outside. As their numbers increased they spread out and surrounded the installation. A few wilder types even began to throw stones. It appeared they wanted to give us a good beating.

At our request, a call for help was placed to the regional air force commander. He gave strict orders for the company to protect us, and warned further that full responsibility for our safety would rest upon their shoulders. Each of us was then surrounded by three soldiers until the military ambulance, sent by the regional commander, arrived. We then made good our escape. Since we left empty-handed, we had a good fright but got no weapons.

During the last stage of our confrontation with the army men, the peasants had cursed us roundly. It was soon clear that, unable to distinguish factions, they were seeking revenge for an act of outrageous thievery committed against their commune two nights before by another middle school group. That incident, already known to us, involved a group of Doctrine Guards from downtown Canton. After unsuccessfully attempting to steal weapons from the commune's armory, they had walked off with a transmitter belonging to the commune's Postal and Telegraphic Bureau. They also took numerous packages of mail and two wrist watches belonging to the postal employees. They had even tried to force their way into the branch bank but found it impregnable.

In the name of "dragging out the small handful in the military," Red Guards continued to seize arms throughout the month of August. So effective were the Red Guards, Dai reported, that even troops on sentry duty in downtown Canton ceased to carry guns. They knew full well, said Dai, that they would be likely to return to their units without them. Even the sentries on the Pearl River Bridge went unarmed, as did the troops commanded by the Public Security Bureau. Dai cited the following incident as representing the spirit of the times:

> One day in August while walking along Section Five of Chung Shan Road, I saw two PLA officers in a chauffeur-driven jeep being stopped by two East Wind Red Guards who had chased and caught them on a motorcycle. When the Red Guards demanded the jeep in exchange for their motorcycle, the officers pleaded with them: "Please don't force us to exchange vehicles. We have an urgent duty to perform." But the Red Guards replied, "Nothing doing! Your duty may be urgent, but ours is even more urgent."

They took the keys from the chauffeur's pocket and sped off in their newly acquired jeep.

At that moment the owner of the motorcycle arrived on the scene. It turned out the two Red Guards had stolen it from him just minutes before. This gentleman recovered his motorcycle and the dispirited officers continued with their "urgent duty" on foot. This is only a small example of how far the PLA's prestige had dropped during the period of violent struggle.

Finally, in September, the trend toward anarchy was arrested and the few CCRG members most closely associated with the radical line of opposition to the army were purged. Wang Li, Kuan Feng, and Lin Chieh* (Mao's wife Chiang Ch'ing was notably excluded) were charged with promoting a counterrevolutionary line, described as "'left' in form but right in essence." Shortly the old civil war slogan "Support the army, cherish the people," injected into the Cultural Revolution for the first time by Chiang Ch'ing herself in April 1967, now received renewed emphasis. Anti-military activities were further forestalled by announcing a drive to undertake "revolutionary great criticism and repudiation" and the formation of "revolutionary great alliances."† Finally, with unmistakable clarity, revolutionary mass organizations were specifically directed to refrain from "pointing the spearhead" at the PLA, an act now to be poetically equated with "destroying our own Great Wall" (*tzu-hui ch'ang ch'eng*). Clearly the PLA had risen again.

However, revival of the reality of military control inevitably engendered renewed conflict between the Military Control Committee and the Red Flag faction. At Kaochung, the military training

---

* Kuan Feng assisted Ch'en Po-ta on *Red Flag*. Lin Chieh had been standing deputy editor in chief of *Red Flag* and chairman of the journal's Cultural Revolution Group.

† As Dai explained it, the accomplishment of a "great alliance" among factions was prerequisite to establishing a "three-way alliance" among representatives of mass organizations, PLA, and cadres, which in turn was to be the organizational basis for a "revolutionary committee" in each unit. A "great alliance" itself had no organizational expression; various antagonistic mass organizations would merely agree to subordinate their factional differences to the common cause of order and broad-based participation in a "revolutionary committee."

platoon (now in permanent residence once again) and the Kao-chung Red Flag Commune were soon at loggerheads.

The direction of the transition from August to September 1967 was similar to that made one half year earlier from February to March. But instead of now supporting the left, the PLA was instructed to take the side of "alliance." To the Red Flags who hoped to convert their ascendancy into "victory," this was anathema.

During August the Red Flags and East Winds in our school had matched strength on innumerable occasions. Since we saw each other all the time, arguments broke out repeatedly and hatred between the two sides grew deeper every day. Disputes would always begin with a few people from one side confronting a few from the other. As other students gathered around, the Red Flag majority would swing into high gear. Our debating tactic was the "method of exhaustion by rotation" (*ni-lao lun-liu fa*). We used ten of our people to surround one of theirs. Sometimes we brought in a relief team to allow the first ten to go off for a meal. Yet by September such a style of debate had become fruitless, even though it had been so effective before.

After Huang Yung-sheng's self-examination was propagated, MTP members who happened to be at the school were totally unwilling to aid the East Wind group, no matter how much they might have wished to do so. Some platoon members went so far as to offer open support to the Red Flags. But all this changed in September when the prestige of the MTP was revived. Thereafter, the platoon's duty was to end the confusion of our struggles and bring the two sides together.

During this period, Acting Chief of the General Staff Yang Ch'eng-wu[6] mounted the stage, and the PLA's responsibility in the movement was defined as "support the left but not any particular faction" (*chih tso pu chih p'ai*). The formula was generally interpreted to mean maintaining public order rather than actively taking sides in disputes between mass organizations.[7] In the context of Canton, however, it meant our MTP need no longer render assistance to the Red Flags. They were now supposed to support whichever individuals were active in pursuing great alliance.

Generally speaking, our rebel faction had little interest in a great alliance since we felt the conservatives had not yet acknowledged their mistakes. Under an alliance we would have to accept equal footing with the East Wind faction. Our failure to be active in pursuing an alliance naturally led to considerable friction between us and the MTP. The East Winds, on the other hand, once again cemented their relations with the platoon by expressing enthusiasm for the policy of alliance. Thus, from October to December, the interests of East Wind and MTP corresponded, and the Red Flags were again suppressed. Not until Yang Ch'eng-wu was overthrown (in March) was there a reversion to the previous condition of disorder, always favorable to the flag faction.

Dai's last comments are particularly interesting as they relate to the frequently heard hypothesis that the majority faction should be most open to the idea of forming great alliances, since by holding a majority of seats on the new organ of power, they could continue to discriminate against their opponents. Dai's analysis supports a different line of interpretation, one that projects a relatively minor role for mass organizations in the new structure of power, and thus views alliance formation as an effective loss of status for the majority faction.

Not surprisingly, a furious internal debate arose within the ranks of the flag faction itself over how to regard Peking's exhortations to form great alliances. One group wanted to implement the new appeal from the center; the other opposed making even the slightest concession to the conservative East Wind group. Dai recalled that pressure from Peking increased and internal debate grew more intense following Chairman Mao's "latest instruction" to "fight self, criticize revisionism," first publicized after National Day (October 1), 1967.

Indeed, it seemed that the more the center tried to promote unity, the more divided the Red Flags became. Even the twelve-point agreement concluded by the Kwangtung factions on November 12 in Peking failed to end the bickering. Dai illustrated this fact by citing the progress of the debate at Chung Shan University after the negotiators had flown back from the capital.

Members of the CSU Red Flag Commune were divided between peace advocates (*chu ho*) and war advocates (*chu chan*). The hawks argued that Canton and the whole country were in the midst of an "adverse current of rightist reversal of verdicts" (*yu-ch'ing fan-an ni-liu*). Enemies were scheming to use the great alliance both to suppress the rebel faction and to wipe out its illustrious achievements in the movement to date. Furthermore, the East Winds were preparing for even more violent struggle; the Red Flags should reply in kind.

The doves argued that the revolutionary situation everywhere was not only good but very, very good. They conceded the existence of an adverse current of reversal of verdict in Canton, but insisted it was an isolated phenomenon incapable of justifying further opposition to the agreement. The best policy would be to establish the absolute authority of Chairman Mao in a big way by immediately setting up a great alliance. More struggle by force would only demonstrate the flag faction's indifference to Chairman Mao's repeated instructions. Since both hawks and doves argued cogently, it was difficult to sort things out. Only when Wu Ch'uan-p'in himself declared in favor of alliance (peace) was the two-day standoff resolved in favor of the doves.

Kaochung's Red Flag students were similarly divided. Unable to win consensus on their own, Dai and a few other leaders again sought help from their seniors at Chung Shan University.

Since the East Winds were still provoking fights, I went to CSU with several members of the Kaochung Middle School Red Flag Commune's Standing Committee to ask for advice. We wanted Wu Ch'uan-p'in's permission to counterattack, but instead he gave us a lecture: "Even if the East Winds want to start a fight, we must undertake 'fight self, criticize revisionism.' If we ignore small problems struggle by force can be avoided." He further cautioned us: "At present there are several leaders of the August 1 Combat Corps who continually violate the general principles of the Red Flag faction by satisfying their own interests. You must be very wary of them, and refuse to give them your support indiscriminately."

Dai indicated when probed on the point that while both sides wished to be active in obeying the instructions of Chairman Mao, each required assurance in advance that their sacrificial action would be reciprocated. Those Red Flags most reluctant to surrender their arms in early fall 1967, as shown by Dai's account of the faction's internal debate, were those who thought the East Winds were plotting more struggle by force. And those least willing to accept the new twelve-point agreement were the ones who thought the East Winds would thereby be rescued from oblivion.

Evident from Dai's account is a two-step process through which Chairman Mao's "latest instructions" were transformed into a tactical decision for a particular group at the local level. Mao's words enjoyed high prestige among both factions, but were far too general to constitute a direct call to action. A person at the basic level like Wu Ch'uan-p'in, who could authoritatively make an appropriate local interpretation, was absolutely necessary. For all practical purposes, his decision would then itself become the "latest instruction" to people in his own group.

Wu Ch'uan-p'in was clearly one of Dai's heroes. When Chou En-lai publicly rebuked Wu one year later in fall 1968, Dai (then in Hong Kong) was inspired to express his indignation by defending Wu in the pages of a Hong Kong newspaper.[8] Dai emphasized in particular the support Wu had given to Chou in fall 1967, before the great alliance issue was solved.

> By October, the most difficult place in all Canton to form a great alliance was Kwangtung Technical College (KTC). Three major groups had organized there, belonging to three separate headquarters: 1) Yenan Commune, under Red Headquarters (Red Flag); 2) Chingkangshan Commune, under Third Headquarters (Red Flag); and 3) August 12 Commune, under Red First Headquarters (East Wind). One KTC student, Yi Tso-ts'ai, was the commander of Canton Red First Headquarters, and August 12 Commune was the majority faction at the college.

Serious trouble began there in August, when in one incident of struggle by force the two minority Red Flag groups were physically booted off the campus by the August 12 majority. Their belongings were thrown out behind them, and the whole group had to take up temporary residence at Chung Shan Medical College. Since the Red Flags had not yet been readmitted by October, Chou En-lai himself appointed one representative from each faction (in Peking at the time for negotiations) to arrange a compromise at KTC. The delegation included Wu Ch'uan-p'in from Red Headquarters, Kao Hsiang from Third Headquarters, and Yi Tso-ts'ai from Red First Headquarters. The trio went to KTC on October 19. They had no sooner entered the campus, however, when Wu and Kao were attacked and severely beaten. Wu nearly suffered a broken arm.

When this news spread to the flag faction throughout the city, we reacted immediately by assembling vehicles of all sizes and by bringing out guns, ammunition, and spears hidden away previously against just such an eventuality. We were prepared to wash KTC with blood. Before long an announcement was issued that our faction intended to destroy the college.

But to the surprise of all Red Flags, Wu Ch'uan-p'in refused to give his consent: "We Red Flags should be models in fighting self, criticizing revisionism. We cannot take the path of seeking revenge just because two of us were wounded. If the East Wind faction will absorb a lesson from this incident, realize their mistakes, and quickly undertake great alliance, then the deaths of both of us would not be too great a cost to pay."

Chou En-lai, extremely pleased when he heard about this in Peking, sent a special telegram of condolence to Wu Ch'uan-p'in and Kao Hsiang. Significantly, it was the first instance of such a telegram being sent to wounded Red Guards by a central leader.

In the fall 1967 atmosphere, dominated by themes of re-establishing the PLA's prestige and creating revolutionary committees at all levels (Kwangtung's came into being on February 21, 1968), this incident constituted one of the last threats of further mass violence. The movement's pendulum was destined to swing "left" again the following March, but for Dai Hsiao-ai, this strange life of interminable struggles, victories, and defeats had come to an end. Dai's decision to leave China at this point for an uncertain existence sixty miles away in colonial Hong Kong, as sudden as it was irrevocable, had been brewing for a long time. The development of the decision comprises the last chapter in our story.

CHAPTER ELEVEN

Dai Hsiao-ai: Disillusionment and the Decision to Leave China

Dai Hsiao-ai suddenly, almost impulsively, decided to leave China one day in October 1967. Less than a month later, in Hong Kong, his relatives watched as he emerged from behind a stack of crates and jumped from a ship onto a wharf. It would be both mistaken and unfair to interpret his flight to Hong Kong merely as the impulsive act of a disaffected adolescent. In fact, the events of the previous eight months had forced Dai into an intensely difficult appraisal and reappraisal of conditions in China and of his own place in his country's future. The psychological complexities of his decision defy brief analysis.

Dai began his summing up in March 1967, when the dangers of the "seize power" struggle led him to fear for his personal safety.

Later in the month, Huang Yung-sheng's suppression of the Red
Flag faction caused him to abandon his previously unquestioning
obedience to Party authority. For Dai, the Party could no longer fulfill its role as the main source of his values, attitudes, and direction.
But he needed direction desperately. Not surprisingly, he decided to
disengage temporarily from the movement and return to his home
in the countryside for a period of rest and reflection.

The comfort and support of family and friends soon partially
filled the emotional gap left by Dai's disillusionment with the Party.
His outraged resentment turned to a pronounced skepticism, which,
with the aid of his family, he applied to a close analysis of rural life.
The peasants had turned his world upside down by challenging the
very legitimacy and effectiveness of Mao Tse-tung, the Party, and the
policies of the last twenty years. Thus, torn between his allegiance to
the people whose word he knew could not be denied, and his commitment to the Communist ideas and symbols with which he had
been raised, he fell into a state of bitter disillusionment and depression. The conflict between his love for his family and his commitment to China's future, on the one hand, and his recognition
that it would be impossible to reorient the policies and programs of
the Party, on the other, became intolerable. In mid-October, he
temporarily resolved this tension by seizing an opportunity to escape.

In the first week of March 1967, Dai and his Red Flag followers
at Kaochung were chafing under the restrictions imposed by the
military training platoon. The March 1 order banning the Provincial
Revolutionary Alliance and the March 15 proclamation of military
control, placing the PLA at the apex of provincial authority, made
it impossible for the rebels even to seek, much less obtain, redress
for their grievances. Whether his one-sided estimate was correct or
not, Dai felt the rebels had been outflanked and could only roll
with the punches thrown by the new power holders. His outrage at
that time was reflected nearly eighteen months later as he continued
to fume:

> Nothing can describe my anger at the way the situation had
> developed in March. Those sons of bitches had thrown us
> all out the window. In January and February we had risked

our lives. Several of my fellows had been injured. I helped them to get medical aid. We had been through all of that and now we were penned up in the school while the army, our former heroes and models, consorted with conservative bastards. We had virtually succeeded in seizing power, in making a true revolution. Now the bastards had thrown it all away. It was unbearable to think about at the time. It is still so, even now. It was ironic that my hatred should reach its peak when directed against those who had previously been my heroes. Of course, the rank and file weren't at fault. It was the leaders, particularly Huang Yung-sheng. I think I could still kill him if I were to meet him face to face.

Had he enjoyed the opportunity to vent his resentment in verbal or even physical exchange with the opposition, Dai might well have overcome his outrage and continued his active participation, particularly when the pendulum swung back to the rebel side after Chou En-lai's April visit. But the MTP and the conservatives had boxed him in and he remained "penned up in the school" with virtually nothing to do. Thus, circumstances forced him into a period of brooding rumination which proved to be the first step in his decision to leave China. He began with an examination of his relations with the Party.

One might say that the first two weeks of March marked my political coming of age. It was the first time that I ever really sat down and independently questioned politics in China. Before that time, it would probably never have happened. But now I had personally been hurt and I wanted to know why. That is how it is. Everyone in China decides to participate in a movement or not according to how it will affect his life. If you feel you have something to gain, you go in with all of your strength. Participation is active or passive in direct proportion to rewards. I don't mean just material things; there are also emotional and psychological rewards which mean just as much. I don't know whether or not I felt it consciously at the time. I just knew that it was time for a summing up.

I had entered school at the age of seven. Because I was of worker background, and because I had a good recommendation from my Street Committee, I was appointed a class monitor. I immediately joined the Young Pioneers and from that day I considered myself to be a loyal servant of the Party. My highest ambition was to join the Party myself. Later, I joined the Young Communist League and entered Kaochung, where I participated in nearly every activity open to me. I did this because I thought it would be good training for the day when I was finally admitted to the Party. As a member and a cadre, I could really serve the people by building the country. I cared about nothing else.

I had the same attitude toward participation in the Cultural Revolution. It was part of serving the Party. Criticizing the teachers, the school Party committee, and the work teams wasn't really much of a test. I was never in any personal danger. But "seize power" was different. Many students were killed and injured. I myself could have been killed or injured at any time. Even so, my loyalty persisted. I felt I was doing the very least that I could. Perhaps I would have given my life had it been necessary.

What did I get for this? Nothing! I was stuck in school while the movement unfolded around me. I was actually being attacked and suppressed by the very authorities to whom I had dedicated my life. It seemed they had used me and then cast me aside when I had ceased to be of value to them. My bitterness knew no bounds.

Eventually, I concluded that using people in this way was really a standard tactic. Take the woman literature teacher who had been branded as a rightist by the school Party committee back in June 1966. True, she had a capitalist class background, but she had also renounced her family, joined the YCL, and given her all to teaching. We students idolized her. Yet the Party committee had turned their back on her and thrown her to the Red Guards just to protect themselves. That was her reward for years of dedication and service. This incident indicated to me the real character of so many Party leaders. On the surface, they were warm, sympathetic, and dedicated. Most of them probably were really sincere. But they had to get ahead and could do so only by climbing on other people. If another example is necessary, you might consider the

Kaochung Party committee members themselves. All of them were old cadres. Certainly all of them had joined the Party before liberation. As despicable as they were to me, they had given long years of service. Yet they too were struck down as soon as the higher Party leaders decided the time had come. Perhaps Liu Shao-ch'i and the other high Party officials were victimized in the same way. It certainly seemed to reflect a consistent pattern. Actions of this sort simply did not square with all I had been taught about mutual help and comradeship. All of my lessons on that point seemed to be complete hypocrisy when viewed in light of the actual conduct of Party members. Yet because I had taken such lessons seriously and could see no reason to deny them, I began to feel that I could not associate myself with such people. As the point struck home, I began to lose my desire to join the Party.

As Dai then turned to a more specific consideration of his own future, the high quotient of idealism in his earlier thoughts gave way to a flood of self-interest. He decided to scale down the intensity of his participation in the movement with a view toward ultimate withdrawal.

I considered my future as a Party member. I had never endured any storms like the "Long March." I had rendered no outstanding services to the cause of the revolution. If men who had done so could be so severely censured for having made one mistake, what chance could I have?

I saw myself ten years in the future confronted by a mob of rampaging students. Really for the first time, I began to imagine what it might be like to be the object of a struggle meeting. I was afraid.

I could see no point of devoting myself to a cause when its leaders were likely to shunt me aside in the most arbitrary manner. Indeed, I was so afraid of making a mistake and subjecting myself to censure, that I immediately resolved to play a passive role. Although I continued to function as a leader of my organization, I did so passively. I had concluded that, in a society like my own, it was safer to do nothing. I had made the evaluation that all Chinese must make sooner

or later and opted for safety. I had been transformed from
an activist positive element to the worst kind of what the
Party calls a backward element. However, it meant very little.
I felt that I would be safe and that was all that seemed to
matter.

At first reading, Dai's decision to be passive, in fact to do
nothing for fear of making a mistake, when coupled with his declaration that he continued to lead his group, seems absurdly contradic-
tory. Yet in the context of Cultural Revolution China, such impossible behavior was not only possible, it was eminently feasible.

In practice his tactic was to blur gradually his public image
as a rebel leader by avoiding photographs, signed newspaper articles,
and controversial public speeches. Within the school, his aim was
obviously impossible to realize, but outside the compound, he could
and did lose himself amid the formless mass of struggling Red Flag
students.

Thus, after the attempted rectification of the Chih-tien Chiang-
shan Rebel Headquarters in early March, he and his rebel colleagues
made no response to the attacks of the MTP-backed conservatives.
Rather, they bore the criticisms with stoic patience and only later,
in the privacy of their rooms, expressed their anger freely and swore
one day to even the score. Dai took the oaths, but knew that he
would never openly take his revenge.

Even during the period of the "March Black Wind" and after
the Red Flag position had been buttressed by Chou En-lai's April
visit, Dai remained true to his decision. As factional strife increased in intensity, he stood to one side. His editorials remained
unsigned and his speeches became fewer and fewer in number. He
might lead his group into a confrontation, but he always took care
to fade into the background once the dispute reached its full pitch.

So it went through the struggles of April and May, the relative
quiet of June, and the bitter battles of July and August. Dai led,
but only in a formal sense. He remained an active participant only
out of a feeling of duty to his friends and colleagues. Whenever
possible, he found excuses, usually writing or administrative duties,
for not joining in active struggle. His colleagues were either too

caught up in their own participation to notice his changed behavior or simply accepted it without question.

Of course I could not, despite my desire, withdraw completely. After all, I had been a founder of the Chih-tien Chiang-shan Rebel Headquarters and I felt a sense of responsibility for what might happen. Also, my very closest friends were in the Headquarters. I felt a deep loyalty to them. As disgusted as I was, it seemed dishonorable for me to desert them. I must also admit that I was afraid of what people would say if I were simply to turn and run. Physically it was possible but I couldn't have borne the censure of my friends. I suppose that I was too proud, or perhaps not proud enough. In any case, I could not abruptly disengage.

I did continue to speak in private and to offer criticisms and ideas when I could. But I gradually reduced my activities. On several occasions, I made excuses for not participating in struggle sessions within the city. At such times, others naturally took over. Sometimes I would tell the group to start without me because I had to finish an editorial or something. Usually, I joined them after things had already begun or did not show up at all. When they questioned me, I would make another excuse and ask to hear what had happened. After doing this for the four months between April and July, I succeeded in creating a vacuum of leadership that was filled by others. It happened as I hoped it would, automatically and gradually. Nobody ever questioned me about it. It appeared to them only that I had redefined my job. Some of my close friends may have guessed what I was doing. But in China such things aren't discussed even between friends. In reality, I was always looking for an opportunity to break my association with the movement entirely.

The long-awaited excuse, a telegram from his family, arrived late in August at the height of the 1967 "summer of violence." They had heard reports of large-scale conflict in the city and, fearing for his life, ordered Dai to return home without delay. Dai needed no orders. He left the next morning.

Our family was extremely close and I was regarded as its most promising member. I did not usually disobey them. Even so, had the telegram arrived at any time before March, I would probably have ignored it and dispatched a letter advising them to remember their responsibilities to the revolution. I might even have gone to the head of the Student Department to discuss how I could help them to see the error of their ways. But that era was light-years away. I left on the next day just as soon as I could get a bus ticket.

Actually such telegrams had been arriving in Canton all summer. Many parents were afraid for their children's lives and nearly all sent telegrams or letters. Some even came to the city to collect their sons and daughters. Early on, some refused to go, but as things grew more dangerous, there was a regular stream of students out of the city. I would estimate that at least 80 per cent of my classmates received similar telegrams around the same time as I did.

Of course, I was overjoyed. I didn't tell my friends that I had in effect been ordered home. I simply told them that I was needed there and that I would take the opportunity to make an investigation into the Cultural Revolution in the countryside. I even promised them a report after I returned. In fact, I did plan to return and make a report.

There were no parades and no garlands to mark the soldier's return home on the following day. But his thankful relatives and a hamlet full of peasants, all eager for news from the city, did give him a warm welcome. Dai Hsiao-ai had planned to investigate conditions among the peasants, but he found that the peasants were investigating him. It was their probing which forced him to continue to analyze the sources of his discontent and thereby forge another link in the chain of conclusions that was to prompt his flight to Hong Kong. Dai found the peasants to be naïve and poorly informed. But he readily admitted that they had a knack for raising the right questions.

During my ten days in the village, the peasants plied me with all sorts of questions. Since the Cultural Revolution had not really touched them at all, they were full of curiosity. Also, they all knew I had been a direct participant and regarded me as a good source of information.

It was obvious that they had no feeling for the real dynamics of the struggle. Nearly all thought that the conflict was between the forces of Mao and the forces of Liu. When I told them that Liu had in effect been defeated long ago, and that the fighting was between groups all of which claimed allegiance to Mao, they were incredulous. If Liu had been defeated, why should there be any fighting at all? Wasn't a Maoist a Maoist? Why didn't Mao stop the fighting?

These questions were naïve, even stupid, but I was hard pressed to satisfy them. When I finally did come up with something, I realized that I had pinpointed a major problem of politics in China, Mao Tse-tung himself. In my opinion, all of the factionalism, fighting, the shifting alliances, and the different positions arose because the instructions from Chairman Mao just didn't work. He might say that all members of the "left" should unite, but we were never told how to determine who was "left" or "right." His statements were so general that everybody, even those who opposed him, could find something to justify his own position. Remember, we rebels considered ourselves to be loyal Maoists just as the conservatives did. We each cited Chairman Mao as our authority. There was no way to interpret his vague directives and implementing them proved impossible. The peasants brought me to this conclusion; I will always thank them.

Once I had reached this state of knowledge, my admiration for the Chairman had to fade. He ceased to be the conquering hero of my *ch'uan-lien* days. Rather, I saw that he was just another man—intelligent, dedicated, and forceful to be sure—who made mistakes like the rest of us. Had he not been so deified, my shock and disillusionment would not have been so intense. Naturally, it occurred to me that vagueness was a tactic deliberately employed to see how different people would react. I didn't really believe that this was true, but because I had a suspicion that it might be, I began to like him even less. It meant that he was playing God and actually causing people to die so that he could maintain his power. I didn't confide these things to the peasants because they could never have understood them. They saw things more simply. To them life was good or bad according to how much or how little they had to eat.

That was another eye-opening experience. During those ten days of September, I looked at peasant problems through different eyes. Remember, I was no longer the enthusiastic revolutionary I had been. Of course, I had been on farms many times in the past and never failed to notice the poor living conditions, the lack of food, and the seeming lack of improvement. But I always explained this to my own satisfaction by recalling that we were a poor country, that much effort had yet to be expended, that our resources had to go to industry, that the peasants were backward, and other such reasons.

This time, however, I suspected that the real causes for lack of improvement were inherent in the system. The peasants confirmed this for me.

They ceaselessly complained about their hard life. They said they had little food to eat, even in good crop years. Two thirds of them could not marry for lack of resources. There was a shortage of teachers and opportunities for their children to attend school. Even what little cash they had was useless since there was nothing to buy. Their list of complaints was endless. Times had been better, they felt, even under the Kuomintang, when a man could work, save some money, invest it, and improve himself. True, the rich were a minority, but people at least had a chance. They also preferred Liu Shao-ch'i to Mao because they identified Liu with the private plots which gave them a chance to put some savings ahead and move up the ladder. To them Mao meant only compulsory grain deliveries, long hours of work for little reward, and movements which wasted the nation's time and money. The peasants particularly hated Chiang Ch'ing. They were certain the nation would collapse if put into the hands of a woman.

Even in my state of disillusionment, I couldn't stand for that kind of talk. It made me very angry. Some of their comments, like the one about Chiang Ch'ing, reflected their natural backwardness. Also, all people in China have a tendency to make things sound worse than they are. I told them that they were selfish and too much attached to the old ways; they had failed to grasp the meaning of the revolution and were hopelessly backward. I talked about the end of exploitation by landlords, new crops, new techniques, and other benefits of communism. True, the system had its faults, but they must think of the good of all. We were now working for ourselves and this was much better than before when officials were corrupt and rents impossibly high. I tried to get them to see that we had made a revolution. Everybody now had a chance and it didn't depend upon connections or graft. If we lacked material things, it was because the country was poor and not because of the system. I was furious with them!

They quickly broke down even this last defense with simple but sincere arguments. One older man, a friend of my family, who had been a Party member since the liberation, the head of the Peasant Association, and a production team leader took me aside. He knew all about the Party and its workings, at least in the countryside. He was more than a cut above the others. Because of this and his friendship with my relatives, I was willing to listen.

He said that in the beginning, all the peasants had tried to grasp the new standpoint and to think of things from the socialist point of view. They had worked hard for it. But communism had failed to fulfill the expectations it had raised. His own life had not substantially improved since the liberation. He had had no land in 1949, and he still had no land. No matter how hard he worked, he received the same amount in wages and food.

How, he asked, could a country be run when so much time was spent in movements and in plans like the Great Leap Forward? All the peasants were bitter about that. Several villagers had died of starvation when the new methods had failed to work and bad weather damaged the remaining crops.

By then I had nothing to say. Perhaps the same would have happened even if we were not under a Communist system, but the fact remained that the peasants felt that communism had not helped them one bit. Frankly, it seemed to be so. What else could I say now that the old answers had lost their value for me? These people had tried and given the system a chance.

Even if they were being selfish, they just wanted basic necessities and the chance for improvement that everyone has a right to expect. They had grown tired of struggling in a system that seemed to deny them this.

The same peasant advised me to return to the city, resign all my offices, and forget about joining the Party. He also said that most of the members in the village were planning to withdraw and that I should too or face the condemnation of history.

I had thought that only capitalist roaders and counter-revolutionaries had such thoughts. But I had just heard them from the mouth of a revolutionary poor peasant who had worked for the Party for more than twenty years. Furthermore, he was speaking for all of the other lower-middle and poor peasants, the classes whose outlook was, according to Chairman Mao, the most revolutionary. What could I say? In ten short days, my world outlook had been challenged by the reality of peasant life and attitudes. With communism it is all or nothing, and once I had admitted the truth of the challenge, the whole system collapsed around me.

Even after this disillusioning experience, Dai did not consider leaving China. That alternative had yet to be suggested. As he rode back to Canton after his visit home, Dai the idealist turned his thoughts to rectifying the Cultural Revolution by reorienting it toward the peasants. Although he recognized the hopelessness of the situation, the revolutionary spark continued to glow.

I considered what I might do. The fighting and the hypocrisy of the Cultural Revolution had caused me to lose faith in the Party and in Mao Tse-tung as its leader. My visit to the countryside had completed the process of disillusionment. I knew that the Cultural Revolution was not really a revolution, but just a power struggle between men at the top. No matter who won, things would remain substantially the same for the peasants, even though forms of organization might change.

I felt that if the Red Guards really wanted to make revolution, they should go to the countryside and see the bitterness of the people as I had done. Then we could have a true revolution that would really touch the people.

Then I considered the impossibility of it all. How could I organize something like that? I would have to petition the Central Committee, the Central Cultural Revolution Group, or the Military Control Committee. The moment I did that, I would be branded as a counterrevolutionary.

Even if it could have been organized, I had no hopes for my fellow students. They were so much prisoners of their education that they wouldn't have been able to understand. They would have dismissed it all as so many complaints of backward peasants just as I had done at first. Don't forget that it took a Party man who was virtually a member of my family to set me straight. My experience had been intensely personal. Certainly it wasn't the starting point for a mass movement of any kind. I was all too aware that I had moved out of the main current of Red Guard thinking and activity. I gave up the idea of starting a revolution directed toward the peasants.

Dai's perception of the Canton scene early in September confirmed his sense of a vast gap separating him from his Red Guard colleagues who were caught up in forming revolutionary great alliances and debating the usefulness of revolutionary committees. Because he had no wish to become further involved in what he considered to be misguided, misdirected, and futile activities, he immediately laid plans to leave Canton for good and return to the family's village. He would pass his days as an ordinary agricultural laborer.

My friends weren't interested. To them it was more important that they try to consolidate the Red Flag position in the budding great alliance. They said that my perceptions had become confused because I wanted to go back to the countryside. In their view, the action was in Canton. They continued to think and speak in the old terms that I now thought had no meaning. We were worlds apart with nothing whatever in common.

I was also convinced that the days of the Red Flag were

numbered. Once Wang Li, Kuan Feng, and Lin Chieh were
purged, we lost our influence in Peking. Who would now represent our view? The army, which had oppressed us in the
past, was on the rise once again and everyone was talking about
the formation of revolutionary committees. With the loss of
influence in Peking, there was no doubt that we would be
submerged under a tide of criticism. Many people resented
us and I feared that some of the East Wind faction members
might use their new influence to cause us harm. Frankly, I
was frightened and wanted no part of it. I resolved to get out.

Besides, what did it all matter anyway? No matter who
won, things would be the same for the people. Similar policies would continue as long as the same kind of thinking
prevailed at the center; that couldn't change. Ordinary men
would continue to direct the lives of other ordinary men in
the interests of something called "communism." That they were
sincere made no difference to me. Every social system has its
own injustices and communism is no exception. I understood
that at last and wanted to be done with it. I resigned myself
to returning to the village to spend my life as a farmer. I
would not delude myself and continue to cheat my people by
joining the Party and becoming a cadre. That dream had been
irrevocably shattered.

Dai never again played a truly active role in the movement, although he did continue to bicycle about the city in search of news.
He adopted a new routine of sleeping late, reading, discussing the
implications of new developments, and occasionally writing something for his group when nobody else was available for the job.

By mid-October 1967, he succumbed to a deep depression
which led him to seek the aid and advice of a long-time family
friend, a Party member who worked in the city. He frankly confessed
his feelings, described his plan to retire to the countryside, and asked
for an evaluation. The family friend stunned him with a strong
recommendation to flee to Hong Kong. He had, he said, all of the
necessary connections and could arrange things without delay. Dai
was even more amazed by the speed with which he himself agreed
to the plan.

As soon as my friend put the idea into my head, I knew that it was the answer. I had never considered running away before because I simply had no idea that it could be arranged. It was so far out of my range of possible alternatives that it never occurred to me. But I trusted my friend and knew about his wide contacts. If he said it could be done, I knew it was possible, and as soon as I accepted the possibility, it seemed the ideal solution. It actually seemed strange that I hadn't thought of it before.

I did not want to leave my family or my friends. I was also frightened about living in a foreign colony where life was supposed to be so bad. But by then, I had developed such doubts about Communist statements that I was willing to take the chance. Besides, I knew that I could live with my relatives there and that they would make things as comfortable for me as they could.

The advantages outweighed the disadvantages. First, I knew that I would be safe. Of course, I could have weathered the storm in the village and come through it relatively unscathed, but Hong Kong seemed safer. Second, I could no longer build my life around conflict. I wanted peace, stability, and physical safety of the kind I thought might exist with relatives in Hong Kong. Third, I felt the time had come to see life under a different kind of social system. I wanted to try to find some new answers and to explore other alternatives. I thought I could start a new life. Thus, my reasons for agreeing to the suggestion, which literally came out of nowhere, to flee to Hong Kong were really very personal. Overlaying these, however, there were more idealistic reasons which had little to do with my immediate personal safety or my future. Whether I was right or wrong, I still don't know. I had concluded that China's Communist society was a lie. It wasn't the injustice so much as it was the way that the leaders denied its existence and instituted policies which made the injustices worse. These were my reasons for leaving.

Dai immediately wrote to Hong Kong to ask if he could find sanctuary there. Within a week, having received an affirmative answer, he wrote to his family in Kwangtung and bade them farewell. He has not seen them since August 1967. In mid-November, the old family friend escorted him to a Canton wharf where he was smuggled aboard a small coaster bound for Hong Kong. Two days later, the vessel's captain, HK$500 richer, brought Dai Hsiao-ai ashore, slightly baffled, but ready to come to terms with his new environment.

EPILOGUE

The Aftermath
of the Revolution

During his first month in Hong Kong, Dai Hsiao-ai did little more than sleep, eat, and occasionally go out to familiarize himself with his new surroundings. Gradually, as he found employment and was introduced to young people of his own age, he was able to adapt himself, at least partially, to the rather cold style of life in Hong Kong. Having transformed himself from activist into observer, he devoured newspaper reports of events in China with avid interest. From his tantalizingly close position, just sixty miles removed from his former life in Canton, he watched as the Cultural Revolution drew, not to a triumphant close, but to a slow halt. Factional conflict was to end.

Beginning in fall 1967, strong pressure to achieve unity was exerted upon mass revolutionary organizations by central and provincial leaders alike. Both now called for an end to violence. They

urged factional leaders to concentrate upon achieving the Cultural
Revolution's original aim of repudiating Party authorities who
had opposed Chairman Mao's policies and his mass-mobilization
style of social-political control. Despite the private admissions of
central leaders that some capitalist roaders could still be found in
the army, the official line also now included the highest support
for the People's Liberation Army. The PLA would "help" further
the cause of re-establishing order and creating "provisional organs
of government" (revolutionary committees). Obviously, the independent political role of the mass organizations was to be reduced.
In response, many leaders of workers' and students' groups were
persuaded that the new line would ultimately prevail; hence, they
did as the center asked. For example, following the announcement
on November 21 in *Nanfang Jih-pao* (*Southern Daily*) that a
"preparatory group for a Kwangtung provincial revolutionary committee" had been brought into being, students, workers, and other
groups of all descriptions throughout the city quickly concluded
the required agreements with one another. The same newspaper
reported one month later that "During the five days from December
23 through 27, revolutionary great alliances were formed in thirty-
two factories, thirty-eight [government] organs, and five institutes
of higher learning. Up to the present, more than a thousand units
in Canton Municipality have formed revolutionary great alliances."[1]
The new policy came to ultimate fruition on February 21, 1968,
with the formation of both city- and provincial-level revolutionary
committees. Kwangtung's committee, interestingly enough, was
presided over by Dai's bête noire, Huang Yung-sheng, the controversial commander of the Canton Military Region. His willingness
to "support the left" actively, as the PLA had been instructed a
year earlier, was still regarded by many factional leaders as doubtful
at best.

As progress toward at least an outward show of unity and
alliance continued, however, there was precious little substantive
agreement on basic issues. The residue of bitterness over the struggles which had left several hundred people dead in Canton alone
was not so easily overcome. Also, members of various groups, and

especially the leaders, were naturally highly concerned over future official interpretations of positions they had advocated in the preceding months. Consequently they hedged their commitments as much as possible, notably by preparing hidden arms caches against the likelihood that street fighting would break out anew. Finally, some factional leaders were justifiably frightened that they would suffer personal harm in the event the opposition managed to increase its political influence in the post-alliance phase. Such discrimination might range from physical injury, to assignment to labor in a distant rural commune, or to "capping" as a serious counterrevolutionary criminal.

The center, of course, was not unaware of such fears. Chou En-lai seemed to be responding to them directly when he told stubborn representatives from feuding groups of industrial workers in January 1968 that under the new rules "No one is now permitted to call himself leftist and others conservative. Various departments under military control now give support to the left, but not any particular faction."[2] The Premier took pains to emphasize that each group of self-professed revolutionaries should concentrate on keeping its own house in order and not worry about the purity of the opposition's ranks:

> . . . all bad people should be dragged out by their own organizations and not by others. . . . I simply don't believe that genuine proletarian revolutionaries are not able to form alliances. And I don't believe that bad people haven't mingled with the revolutionaries.[3]

To ease the hoped-for transition from open violent struggle to co-operative alliance, Chou promised the center would not insist upon disbanding the mass organizations:

> Lowering the banners [of different factions] when an alliance is formed means that banners are temporarily not lowered *during* the formation of an alliance. . . . However, this does not imply that in the course of forming an alliance, more should be hoisted; otherwise, three-man factions or five-man groups will emerge.[4]

A separate and now quite familiar problem associated with the general crackdown on independent factional activity was that large numbers of youth involved only on the fringe of the movement simply dropped out. The Premier complained in particular of several groups of students who had been

> . . . quite daring in the early stage of rebellion. But after alliances have been formed, two thirds of the members have left. Can this be called revolution? This is a manifestation of petit bourgeois vacillation. They think they should take a rest and take things easy after making revolution for a year or so. Some have gone back home, some have turned to love, played poker, [and] degenerated. A few have pasted up reactionary slogans. . . .[5]

Despite these problems, as the policy of "military control" was implemented more effectively over the ensuing months, factional fighting declined significantly. In general, it appeared that problems among workers' groups were more easily settled than those dividing students. Accordingly, student groups received special attention. In summer 1968, teams of workers and peasants were dispatched to assist the PLA military training platoons already stationed in schools and colleges. On August 5, the first Worker-Peasant Mao Tse-tung's Thought Propaganda Team, residing at Tsinghua University in Peking, was presented with a "treasured gift" of mangoes from Chairman Mao himself, thereby indicating priority for the workers' mission from China's highest source of authority. To underscore the message, the Chairman's symbolic act was widely publicized throughout the country. Later in the month a new slogan, "The working class must exercise leadership over all," was advanced in the media. The effects of the center's move were immediately observable. Early in the fall, for example, most Red Guard tabloids ceased publication altogether.

The Chinese Communist Party's Ninth National Congress, held in April 1969 (the first convened since 1958), marked the effective end of the Red Guard movement. Although they continued to exist in organized form, and were represented on revolutionary committees at all levels, their approved role had changed. Now they were to lead their schoolmates in carrying out "meaningful" political activities *in their leisure time* and especially to take the lead in going out to settle down permanently in the countryside for a life of agricultural labor. Significantly, the relatively few articles about Red Guards which did appear during this period claimed that former factional leaders had "taken the initiative in setting a good example for continuing the revolution under the dictatorship of the proletariat by undergoing re-education in places where conditions are most difficult."

Actually, this large-scale movement to send middle school and college graduates to rural areas, begun in spring 1968, was conceived as merely one part of a more encompassing reform program inaugurated as the Cultural Revolution sputtered to a close. Not only students and teachers, but medical personnel and facilities, commercial services and small factories as well were pressed by the center to reorient themselves toward China's vast rural sector. Dai Hsiao-ai was undoubtedly correct in predicting his minimal chances of avoiding the fate of his 100,000 cograduates (his estimate of the middle school senior class in Canton). Had he stayed in China he would likely have been destined to head for the farm with the rest.

In a signed article written in Hong Kong, "A Discussion of the Movement to Send Intellectual Youth Up to the Mountains and Down to the Countryside,"[8] Dai gave his bitter attention to the miseries of students who had taken part in similar programs before the Cultural Revolution, and correspondingly belittled the result achieved by movements of this type. He recalled, for instance, that sometimes his schoolmates wrote letters reporting that no living accommodations had been provided for them, and that they had been forced to find habitable caves, or to build makeshift straw huts that were freezing cold in winter and often blew down during heavy storms. He recalled how painful it was to think about leaving one's family in the city at age nineteen for a life no better than that of "early primitive man." From one occasion when he himself had participated in *hsia-fang* ("sending down") he remembered vividly how the local peasants had scorned their city cousins: For example, they had humiliated a teacher because the fellow was unable to lift a 110-pound load as directed by a peasant. Since in 1968–69 approximately four or five times the number of youths were being "sent down" compared with previous *hsia-fang* campaigns, many earlier problems were undoubtedly magnified. On the other hand, concomitant reforms of rural education, public health, commerce, and industry all probably acted to offset somewhat the Spartan living conditions found in rural China. In any event, Dai's original ambition to "be a cadre" would certainly have been postponed for at least a few years until after his successful "re-education" by peasants in a relatively long period of agricultural labor.

Even though China's attempts at further reform in the mid-1960s were officially described in the language of continuing revolution, the over-all situation at the time was different from that which existed after the 1949 civil war victory over the Kuomintang. In 1949, a group of "outs" had successfully fought their way "into" a new system. Now, twenty years later, a group of "ins," many of whom had undergone extreme sacrifice while participating in the Cultural Revolution, were being asked to remove themselves "out" of a newer system and to sacrifice themselves further for goals not yet won. Because China's students have enjoyed the sense of significant participation and the satisfaction of being "in," the old leadership's task of motivating millions of Dai Hsiao-ais to continue to carry the center's torch will not be easily accomplished. In making continuous revolution, it appears, success does not necessarily breed success.

Dai Hsiao-ai has obviously been deeply influenced by the Cultural Revolution. Even after eighteen months' residence in Hong Kong and countless hours of discussion with the authors, he continues to fight old battles and to analyze China's present course. He articulates his acceptance of the fact that he has cut himself off from China and that he must find something new about which he can center his existence. However, in May 1969 he still remained far from internalizing this realization. One looks in vain for any evidence of enduring peace and contentment in his daily life.

While more than pleasant in conversation and very willing to enter into the activities of the moment, he remains essentially introverted, moody, and confused.

It is obvious that Dai continues to question the soundness of his decision to leave. With hindsight, he wonders if he should not have recognized his troubled state of mind in November 1967 and paused for further reflection before opting to flee to Hong Kong. He gives the strong impression of feeling that he could have remained safe from personal harm had he just held fast in the countryside under the protection of his family. The news that his old hero Wu Ch'uan-p'in was active again at Chung Shan University, and a member of its revolutionary committee, reinforced this tension. Perhaps the Red Flags were not doomed to destruction after all.

In the same way, he questions his evaluation of Mao Tse-tung and the Chinese Communist Party. Despite his ostensible distaste for Maoist methods of leadership, Dai continues to regard Chairman Mao as a genius. No one else, he feels, could have aroused, mobilized, and led the Chinese people as he did. Dai does not fail to recognize that Mao and the Party have unified China and made her a significant force in world affairs. He remains intensely proud of China's progress, and because he is Chinese, he feels that he should be making some contribution. If, as he says, all social systems have some injustice, why should he have fled just because the injustice of the Communist system was manifested as it was? Perhaps he should not have been so idealistic but rather should have remained and worked within the system. In other words, Dai feels as though he may have reneged on an obligation. But he cannot resolve the question to his own satisfaction.

His frustration is intensified by the fact that he sees no real alternative elsewhere. At present, Dai has acquired many of the characteristics of Hong Kong's typically middle-class Chinese young adults. He explores new restaurants with satisfaction, proudly displays his new suits, and eagerly discusses the latest films. Yet he regards all of these things as frivolous; he is unwilling to devote himself entirely to the acquisition of material comfort. This is precisely the source of his negative reaction to life in Hong Kong. Nobody, he says, seems to care about important things. There is no sense of co-operation in seeking to attain some higher and ultimately more worthwhile goal. He seems strongly convinced that this holds true elsewhere, particularly in the West. Thus, he does not to date find in the Western system a viable alternative to life in China.

If the Cultural Revolution was a political happening, its social and psychological ramifications were even more all-pervasive. The events of May 1966–April 1969 caused Dai Hsiao-ai to reject not the values expressed by the Chinese political system, but the institutions and personalities which constituted the system. Because of this, in justifying his continuing commitment to these values, Dai has been forced to elevate his conception of them to the very highest level of idealization. Accordingly, and he does not realize this yet, he can be satisfied in his present frame of mind with nothing short of perfection and total commitment. When he does understand this, he may well resolve it by means of cynical rejection or simply lapsing into the comfortable middle-class life of Hong Kong, or both. On the other hand, he may accept what he sees as a challenge and continue to strive for perfection. Then, as Dai makes revolution anew, perhaps success will breed success.

CHRONOLOGY OF EVENTS

DATE	CULTURAL REVOLUTION— GENERAL	CANTON—KAOCHUNG
1966		
late May		First attacks on Kaochung teachers
June 1	"Sweep Out All Monsters and Ghosts" editorial, *PD*	
June 4	Reorganization of Peking city Party committee announced, *PD*	
July		Work team in residence at Kaochung
July– November		Preparatory Committee in authority at Kaochung
August 1–12	Central Committee's Eleventh Plenum	
August 8	Sixteen-Point Decision passed	
August 18	Mao's first Red Guard review	
early September		Middle school students make contact with workers
October 1	National Day	Kaochung delegation travels to Peking
November– December		Dai's second trip north to *ch'uan-lien*

DATE	CULTURAL REVOLUTION— GENERAL	CANTON—KAOCHUNG
November 16	Central Committee's first Circular to terminate Red Guard traveling	
1967		
January 9	Official introduction of Shanghai "revolutionary rebels" as new model to imitate in "opposing economism" and "seizing power"	
January 21		Provincial Revolutionary Alliance "seizes power" in Kwangtung
February– March	"Military control" declared where no "revolutionary committee" existed	
April 14–18		Chou En-lai's first visit to Canton
July 18–20	Wuhan Incident	
late July, August	PLA heavily criticized	Canton Military Region's examination of mistakes
early September	New campaign to re-establish authority of PLA	
mid-September	Renewed emphasis on need for mass organizations to set up "great alliances" leading to "revolutionary committees"	

FOOTNOTES

PROLOGUE

1. This phenomenon is not surprising considering the wide diversification of local customs and language dialects in Kwangtung Province. It seems natural that students of similar origin should seek each other out to gain support and reinforcement in an unfamiliar environment. Shant'ou on Kwangtung's northeast coast is about one day's journey from Canton by bus. T'aishan is a coastal county located just south of Canton. Hainan Island separates the South China Sea from the Gulf of Tonkin and lies off the southern tip of Kwangtung. The Hakkas are a minority group in south China who originated in the north. Scattered throughout the province, but with concentrations in northern Kwangtung, they remain a significant minority who retain their own speech and customs.

2. The organization and propaganda members of the Party committee had the same functions as their counterparts on the YCL committee. The organization member, whom Dai could not identify, administered Party affairs such as the induction of new members, Party discipline, transfer of Party membership to and from other units, and reports on the performance of Party members. He also had general charge of the personnel files for the entire school. The propaganda member supervised political study for Party members and the dissemination of Party policies throughout the school. Dai could not identify this individual either. The YCL member was the head of the Student Department, whom Dai knew well. This member formed the link between the Party and the League. All League decisions, indeed, the entire League program, required his approval.

3. This concept was borrowed and adapted from the "Four-Good

Companies" and "Five-Good Soldiers" movement within the army. A class that achieved a certain standard in "being good in politics, studies, relations with their classmates, and in labor" was designated a "Four-Good Class." Similarly, individual students who were "good in politics, study, labor, daily life, and personal cleanliness" became known as a "Five-Good Student."

CHAPTER ONE

1. Wu Han, a specialist in Ming dynasty history and deputy mayor of Peking, had enjoyed extensive experience in work in the educational, cultural, and literary fields. His play is based upon the supposedly true story of a famous Ming dynasty official who was dismissed from office when other corrupt officials objected to his reforms, particularly his return of illegally extorted land to the original peasant owners. The play was written in 1961, after the dismissal of P'eng Teh-huai from his post of Minister of Defense in 1959 as a result of his criticisms of Mao's military, economic, and agricultural policies. The theme of restoration of land, particularly since it followed so closely upon the forced collectivization of the commune era, later led many to interpret the play as a not so veiled attack upon Mao and as a defense of P'eng. The parallel between the erstwhile P'eng and the persecuted Hai Jui is undeniable and was probably intentional. Unfortunately for Wu Han, his allegory was too explicit and he was now being called upon to pay the price.

Yao Wen-yuan was a young man whose star seemed to be in the ascendancy. Since 1958 he had been active in the All-China Youth Federation Committee, a relatively minor position. In late 1964, or early 1965, he appears to have been lifted from relative obscurity and drafted by Chiang Ch'ing (Mrs. Mao) to serve as a public spokesman for her radical group, which was committed to a rigorous reorientation of prevailing literary and artistic currents to emphasize class struggle. In early 1966 he was rewarded with an appointment to the editorial department of Shanghai's *Wen Hui Pao*. Shortly thereafter, his name appeared as editor of the equally prestigious Shanghai *Liberation Daily* and as director of the Propaganda Department of the Shanghai Municipal Party Committee. He emerged as a member of the Cultural Revolution Group after July 1966. His position was consolidated by his election as a full member of the Party Central Committee Politburo at the ninth Party Congress in April 1969.

2. *CCP Documents of the Great Proletarian Cultural Revolution,* 1966–1967, Hong Kong: Union Research Institute, 1968, pp. 3–12. (Hereafter referred to as URI, *Documents.*)
3. Teng T'o was a vice-secretary of the Peking Municipal Party Committee and general editor of *Front Line Magazine,* its journal. It has been reported that he was demoted from his position as editor of *People's Daily* after the anti-rightist campaign of 1957.

   Liao Mo-sha was director of the United Front Work Department of the Peking Municipal Party Committee, a position which afforded him constant contact with Wu Han, who was a member of the Democratic League, one of the "minority parties," and with Teng T'o, who was responsible for publishing news of United Front activities in *Front Line Magazine.* Later, the term "Three-Family Village" came to refer to these three men themselves as well as to the volume they published together.
4. URI, *Documents,* pp. 13–28.
5. Ibid., pp. 26–28.
6. Sung Shih was assistant chief of the University Work Department of the Peking Municipal Party Committee.

   Lu P'ing was president of Peking University and secretary of its Party committee.

   P'eng P'ei-yun was a vice-secretary of the Peking University Party committee and a cadre of the University Work Department of the Municipal Party Committee.

   All three worked closely together and in effect were the link between the university and the Party.

   Nieh Yuan-tzu was a lecturer in the Philosophy Department of Peking University.

CHAPTER TWO

1. The concept of "rebellion" was undergoing a fascinating transition at this time. Dai remembered hearing Principal Chen only a few weeks before using the word to reprimand students who had criticized the school leadership in a way he disapproved: "What are you trying to say? Do you want to rebel?" Now, like the Yankees of the American Revolution, student activists co-opted the term, saying in effect, "Yes! That's precisely what we want!" Later some alert reader in Peking found an old article by Mao not included in his *Selected Works* which contained the phrase: "In the last analysis, all the truths of Marxism can be summed up in one sentence: 'To rebel is justified.'" It was subsequently revealed in

the *People's Daily* that Mao had made this statement to a meeting of "all Circles" in Yenan to celebrate Stalin's sixtieth birthday, presumably in 1939. Publicized as Chairman Mao's "teaching" and the slogan of "all proletarian revolutionaries," the aphorism "To rebel is justified" seemed to rise and fall in prominence according to the vacillating political status of the Central Cultural Revolution Group (CCRG) in Peking. Sometimes it was modified to read "To rebel against reactionaries is justified," thus making it less a blanket endorsement of indiscriminate rebellion.

2. URI, *Documents,* pp. 73–76.
3. Ibid., pp. 113–19.

CHAPTER THREE

1. The term "Five Kinds of Red" is the semiofficial and discriminatory idiom of this stage of the Cultural Revolution probably originated at Peking's Tsinghua University. The reader will note that the Five Reds corresponds exactly to Dai's portrayal of the five "good" classes introduced in the prologue. The analysis assumes that children of Five Red parents will also be revolutionary. This, in turn, illustrates the Principle of Family Lineage (*hsieh-t'ung lun*) and the concept of Naturally Red (*tzu-jan hung*), both of which hold that the revolutionary character of the parents is passed to the children or that some people are naturally more revolutionary than others.

The natural enemies of the Five Kinds of Red are the Seven Kinds of Black, or landlords, rich peasants, counterrevolutionaries, bad elements, rightists, monsters and freaks, and capitalist roaders. These broad categories contain all of the "backward class" elements mentioned in the prologue. According to the Principle of Family Lineage, children of Seven Black parents will also be Black, or non-revolutionary. The concepts of the Five Kinds of Red and the Seven Kinds of Black along with the Principle of Family Lineage and Naturally Red (or Black) provoked a debate which was settled only after months of bitter struggle. The issues of that debate are described in Chapter Six.

2. *Peking Review,* No. 35, 1966, p. 8.

CHAPTER FOUR

1. Wang Wei was a member of the Standing Committee of the Youth League's Central Committee, and a secretary of the League's Central Secretariat.

2. Nieh Yuan-tzu, it will be recalled from Chapter One, had written the big-character poster "Sung Shih, Lu P'ing, P'eng Pei-yun, What Are You Up To in the Cultural Revolution?", which marked the beginning of the Cultural Revolution at Peking University.

3. Literally, "a peach orchard away from the world" (*shih wai t'ao-yuan*). The allusion derives from a story of a man who, while passing through a peach orchard, discovered a secluded valley in which people were living in peace, quite ignorant of passing events and changes of dynasty. Hence, the term connotes a harbor of refuge from oppressive governments.

4. Literally, a "water vehicle." A long wooden trough is divided into upper and lower channels. Wooden slips attached to a rotating cord, after pushing water through the lower channel, would then return through the upper one. It was powered by a person standing at one end of the device turning a wheel attached to the circulating cord.

CHAPTER FIVE

1. URI, *Documents*, p. 110.
2. Ibid.

CHAPTER SIX

1. The phrase is untranslatable. The words *Chih-tien Chiang-shan* are taken from a poem by Mao Tse-tung. *Chih-tien*=to direct or directing; *Chiang-shan*=lit. rivers and mountains, hence, the landscape, scene, or world. The spirit of the phrase might be rendered as "the All-Directing Rebel Headquarters." This powerful phrasing and the fact that the lines were written by Mao account for the organizational name's significance. It will be referred to hereafter simply as the Headquarters.

2. Although it is impossible to verify the exact nature of T'an Li-fu's involvement, the authors are inclined to agree with Dai's interpreting the wide distribution of T'an's speech as one of many efforts by various provincial Party committees to maintain their status. First, T'an Li-fu's father had been head of the People's Procuracy until his death. This meant that he had enjoyed close contact with children of other high-ranking Party and government officials and, by extension, with the officials themselves. Second, this close relationship is supported by accusations appearing in

Red Guard newspapers republished in Hong Kong. See Ting Wang (ed.), *Compilation of Materials on the Chinese Communists' Great Cultural Revolution* (*Hong Kong: Ming Pao Monthly Publishers*, 1967), pp. 663–67 to the effect that T'an and Liu Shao-ch'i's daughter, Liu Chou, were frequent guests in the home of Ho Lung, a vice-premier of the State Council and a vice-chairman of the National Defense Council. Considering the close relationship between T'an Li-fu, Ho Lung, Liu Shao-ch'i, and their children, it is not improbable that, in defending the work teams, T'an was acting with the support of the very elements within the central leadership that had been responsible for the posting of the work teams and who were now being attacked.

Similarly, since the work teams had been sent out with the support of the provincial Party leaders, these latter individuals had every reason to support T'an in his defense of the teams. In doing so, they were, like their counterparts at the center, deflecting criticism away from themselves.

Dai recalled a big-character poster he saw while buying tickets for his second journey north. Under the title "How Was the News of T'an Li-fu's Speech Spread So Rapidly Through Kwangtung?", the Provincial Committee was accused of acting with "certain persons in authority" to forestall criticism of the work teams. It seems safe to assume that the provincial Party leaders in Kwangtung and elsewhere were in fact "Waving the Red Flag While Opposing the Red Flag." This seems typical of the kind of rear-guard actions the provincial authorities had been fighting since the first criticisms of the work teams in June–July 1966.

3. In 1968, in Hong Kong, Dai read that T'an Li-fu had been sentenced by the Peking Technical University Revolutionary Committee and the Peking Municipal Revolutionary Committee to a term of reform through labor (*lao kai*). Dai expressed satisfaction at the news. He also observed that in his opinion T'an had indeed gone "as a good proletarian should."

4. Dai reported that dissatisfied Five Red elements from many Canton schools joined together for one last demonstration. When they were largely ignored, they went to the Pearl River Bridge, where they threw stones at portraits of Ch'en Po-ta and Chiang Ch'ing. Most students, according to Dai, simply laughed when they heard about the demonstration.

5. These rebel and conservative groups, in somewhat different form, later emerged as the nuclei of respectively the Red Flag and East Wind factions which led the struggles of 1967. The process of

their transformation and their activities are described in Chapters 7-10.

6. Dai first heard mention of a bourgeois-reactionary line implemented by certain persons in authority in a report of a speech made by Chiang Ch'ing in mid-October. He recalled that this seemed to be a prelude to the intense criticism which began in November.

CHAPTER SEVEN

1. As officially explained, this meant to struggle "to overthrow those persons in authority who are taking the capitalist road," to criticize "the reactionary-bourgeois academic 'authorities' and the ideology of the bourgeoisie and all other exploiting classes," and to transform "education, literature and art and all other parts of the superstructure that do not correspond to the socialist economic base." See *Peking Review*, January 1, 1967, p. 9. Dai remembered that extensive publicity was given to this "task" in late 1966, but he had forgotten it appeared in the Sixteen-Point Decision.

2. *Peking Review*, January 20, 1967.

3. Ibid., p. 5.

4. Ibid., p. 15.

5. Li Chia-jen was first secretary of Chung Shan University's Party committee. He was also a member of the standing committee of the Kwangtung Provincial Party Committee, and a vice-governor of Kwangtung Province.

6. T'ao Chu was first secretary of the Central-South (including Kwangtung) Bureau of the Chinese Communist Party (CCP) Central Committee. He had been promoted to membership on the Standing Committee of the Central Committee's politburo, and to head of the Central Committee's Propaganda Department, after the purge of Lu Ting-yi in July 1966.

7. U. S. Consulate General, Hong Kong, *Survey of China Mainland Press*, No. 4029, p. 9. Hereafter referred to as SCMP.

8. When Premier Chou En-lai visited Canton in April, he said, " 'Swear to Die . . . General Headquarters' is troublesome to pronounce. Names should not be so long and difficult to remember. It would be better just to call yourselves the Workers' Alliance." Dai recalled that members of this organization were so proud of the attention given them by the Premier they could be heard daily quoting his words in public.

9. This group was the least committed of the eight, and it retreated from the alliance once military control was imposed in Kwangtung Province.

10. These students were civilians, not members of the air force.

11. These students were not on active duty (military) either, but rather training to engage in military engineering work after graduation. They were the most active of all student groups in making contact with rebels inside the Canton Military Region organization, according to Dai.

12. Ou Meng-chueh (female) was a member of the Standing Committee of the Kwangtung Provincial Party Committee, one of the provincial Party secretaries, and an alternate secretary of the Central Committee's Central-South Bureau. She was later purged as a close associate of T'ao Chu and Chao Tzu-yang. This use of Ou's home provided critics with more evidence of collusion between the PRA and Chao.

13. Dai did not know just who constituted these groups. A search of available Red Guard publications for the information proved unrewarding.

14. The August 1 Combat Detachment (*pa i chan-tou ping-t'uan*) was one of the larger revolutionary mass organizations of workers in Canton. When it was first set up in mid-January 1967, it had about 5000 members. From late January to early February, its membership in urban areas expanded to some 80,000 (plus about 30,000 persons recruited in the counties outside the urban areas). At the time it was disbanded on March 1 by the Kwangtung Provincial Military District Command, its urban membership had fallen to 40–50,000. The Detachment began as an organization of army veterans, but later included large numbers of workers as well as handicapped servicemen, many members of the cadre militia and armed militia, and Party members. The Detachment's Chuai district branch, for example, was reported to have more than 110 units under it. Of the 98 investigated later in the year, 69 were found to be distributed in industry and communications, accounting for 70 per cent of the total; the remaining 30 per cent were scattered in finance and trade enterprises, schools, neighborhood organizations, and farms.

Of the more than 350 persons in one barber-instrument-manufacturing factory investigated, 75 joined the Detachment. Of these, 11 were Party members, representing over one third of the Party members in the factory, and 9 were League members, representing two thirds of the League members in the factory. Fif-

teen of the factory's 24 propagandists joined up, as did all production activists and trade union group leaders.
See *SCMP*, No. 4096, pp. 1–7; *SCMP*, No. 4029, pp. 12–14.
15. Before military ranks were abolished in China in May 1965,
Huang was a general (*shang-chiang*). Huang was later to be made
head of the Kwangtung Province Revolutionary Committee (February 1968) and Chief of Staff of the PLA (March 1968).
16. A Cultural Revolution group under the CCP Central Committee's Military Affairs Committee was set up probably in summer
1966. It was headed by Lieutenant General Liu Chih-chien, a
deputy director of the PLA's General Political Department.
17. URI, *Documents*, p. 96.
18. Hsu, a marshal, was probably elected to the politburo at the
Central Committee's Eighth Plenum in August 1966. In mid-April
1967, he was dismissed from his new post as head of the PLA's
Cultural Revolution Group when that body was reorganized a
second time. He survived the later purges, however, and was
restored to his former prominence by spring 1968.
19. URI, *Documents*, pp. 195–97.

CHAPTER EIGHT

1. *SCMP*, No. 4096, p. 4. Dai and his friends drew no distinc-
tion between the views of the Military Region under Huang Yung-
sheng, the Military District under Huang Jung-hai, or even the
Canton Municipal Garrison Command (*kuang-chou shih ching-pei
ssu ling pu*) on matters relating to "support the left" work (in
this case the dispatch of MTPs or the suppression of the PRA).
In the eyes of the students all such policies were approved by
Huang Yung-sheng.
2. It will be recalled that Dai thought such liaison personnel had
been the chief instigators behind the February 7–8 attack upon
the Canton Military Region Headquarters.
3. In response to a follow-up question on this point, Dai argued that
every military organization must have a Party representative, or
commissar. For authority he referred to passages from the little
red book of *Quotations from Chairman Mao*. When the authors
countered that those quotations had been selected and compiled
by the PLA's General Political Department, to popularize their
own view of military organization, Dai refused to qualify his
belief that the idea had been a consistent tenet of Mao's writing.
In fact, Dai further claimed that he had read Mao's *Selected*

Works from beginning to end and felt the *Quotations* to be an unbiased sample. He further noted that this view was shared by the forty per cent or so of his classmates who had received copies of the *Quotations* in 1965. He could not remember anyone questioning how the passages had been chosen. Dai's opinions on this point lend some support to the argument that the PLA's General Political Department had been propagandizing students from the very earliest days of the Cultural Revolution.

4. Dai's concept of "neutralists" was not used in debate in China. He adopted it in the course of our interviews.

5. *SCMP*, No. 3893, pp. 1–10. The text was originally published in a Shanghai tabloid, *Physical Education Combat News* (*t'i-yü chan-pao*).

6. The so-called "mass line" subsumes several of Mao's ideas on leadership, all of which caution leaders not to forget those led. First, it indicates that leaders should act in accordance with the needs of the "broad masses" and not with the interests of individuals. Secondly, leaders must not simply think about the needs of masses, they must also make frequent contact with them for firsthand knowledge. Third, actions proposed by leaders should ideally be implemented only after the group's consent has been secured. Very few specific institutional forms for giving practical expression to these ideas can be found in Mao's writing. He probably believes that only through constant experimentation and struggling with the ambiguities in light of each place's own circumstances can the general ideals be approximated in real life. For several references to Mao's writing on this point, see Section Eleven on the "Mass Line" in *Quotations from Chairman Mao*.

7. Receiving a political "hat" in China can lead to considerable personal suffering. Those who are "capped" as a landlord or rightist or other variety of political "criminal," limited to 3–4 per cent of the population in most areas, are those people the Communist regime considers to be its most dangerous enemies. They are subjected to endless ideological exercises in class struggle as well as discrimination. An elaborate though not formally prescribed procedure, involving accumulation of evidence and a round of struggle meetings, must usually be utilized to place a "hat." Accusations appearing in wall posters represent only an early stage in the process, and may not come to fruition. A specific accusation appearing in an official newspaper usually indicates the process has reached completion for the named individual.

8. "Ch'ing-ch'u T'o-p'ai," *Ch'ing-hua Ching-kang-shan*, Nos. 13–14,

February 1, 1967. One copy of this newspaper is held by the URI, Kowloon, Hong Kong.

9. This name literally translates as "bind the giant dragon." It means to do something beyond one's powers, to accomplish the impossible.

10. All of them would become members of the standing committee of Kaochung's own Red Flag Commune when it was formed in late April.

11. T'an Chen-lin was a vice-premier and director of the State Council's Agriculture and Forestry Staff Office. In the Communist Party, T'an was a member of the politburo, and a secretary of the Central Secretariat. For CSU Red Flag's version of this episode, see *SCMP*, No. 4169, pp. 7–10.

12. "Decision of the CCP Central Committee, the State Council, the Central Military Control Commission, and the Central Cultural Revolution Group Concerning the Question of Tsinghai" (March 24, 1967), URI, *Documents*, pp. 383–87.

13. Dai failed to mention the April 6 Order of the Central Military Commission, which clearly restricted local commanders. This order, which was widely disseminated throughout the army, has been reprinted in URI, *Documents*, pp. 407–11. The Military Affairs Committee prefaced its several points by pointing out that "Recently we have examined the work of supporting the left in some military districts, in some of which it is well done and in others not well done." Specifically:

1. In dealing with mass organizations . . . shooting is forbidden. Only political work may be conducted.

2. Arbitrary arrests are forbidden . . . the evidence must be conclusive and the arrests must first be approved.

3. It is forbidden to declare arbitrarily a mass organization a reactionary organization and repress it. . . . When it is absolutely necessary to declare them reactionary organizations and repress them, approval must first be obtained from the center.

4. No action shall be taken against the masses who intruded into or assaulted military organs in the past, regardless of whether they are the left, the middle, or the right. . . .

5. Before deciding on what attitude to take toward the large mass organizations, profound investigation and study should be made locally and class analysis should also be made. Before taking any important action, a report should be made to the Central Cultural Revolution Group and the All-PLA Cultural Revolution Group and their advice sought.

CHAPTER NINE

1. In 1967, the one-month fair opened on schedule on April 15. Some seven thousand foreign businessmen from over sixty countries attended, about a thousand more than came the year before. Over twenty thousand different items were reportedly on display.

2. All members of the Doctrine Guards in Canton were middle school students of a conservative persuasion, and thus most of them were less than twenty years old. Like the notorious United Action Committee (*lien tung*) in Peking, they included among their membership sons and daughters of high-ranking cadres. Dai remembered that Huang Yung-sheng's son (Huang Chun-ming) and the sons of Chao Tzu-yang, Canton Mayor Tseng Sheng, and Ch'en Teh, a deputy political commissar of the Kwangtung Province Military District, were members.

3. Beginning as early as 1953, cadres native to Kwangtung openly resented the fact that leadership posts in their province were dominated by northerners who came into Kwangtung during the land reform campaign (Dai called them the *nan-hsia ta-chün*, or "great army marching south"). Among the most prominent local protesters during the mid-1950s had been Feng Pai-chu and Ku Ta-ts'un, both vice-governors of Kwangtung at the time. Peking's response had been to mount a campaign against "provincialism" led by T'ao Chu, the provincial governor and himself an outsider. A permanent solution, however, was not found.

   When T'ao Chu came under fierce attack during the Cultural Revolution his associates on the Provincial Party Committee lost prestige. Local cadres took advantage of the situation to attack the outsiders once again, this time in the legitimate guise of attacking T'ao. The leaders of this offensive most visible to Dai were Lin Chiang-yun, Yi Lin-p'ing, and Feng Shen. But however much it wished to pursue its attack on T'ao Chu, the center could not tolerate this revival of provincialism. Hence, Chou En-lai's criticism. The Premier's words were incidentally critical of the Red Flag side on this point, since the self-styled rebels had generally supported the local cadres, even to the point of advocating a "reversal of verdict" for them.

4. In the past, a few conservative groups had used the term "Red Flag" in their names as well. It was merely coincidental that the three rebel student groups Chou had cited all had chosen the same name.

5. See Chapter 1.
6. *Hung Wei Pao* (*Red Guard News*) was the new name given to the *Yang-ch'eng Wan Pao* (*Canton Evening News*) in September 1966. This was one of three popular evening papers in China, the other two being Shanghai's *Hsin-wen Wan Pao* (*Evening News*) and Peking's *Pei-ching Wan Pao* (*Peking Evening News*). All three maintained a higher than average literary standard to appeal to intellectuals, but *Yang-ch'eng Wan Pao* was by reputation the best of the three and could claim a loyal readership in all parts of China. It was officially managed by the Kwangtung Provincial Party Committee's Propaganda Department, and located in the same office as the organ of the Party committee, *Nan-fang Jih Pao* (*Southern Daily*). The connection with the Propaganda Department of the Central Committee's Central-South Bureau (formerly led by T'ao Chu) was undoubtedly strong if indirect.
7. Canton Municipality is divided into urban districts (*shih-ch'ü*) and suburban districts (*hsiao ch'ü*), besides two counties of largely rural make-up. Dai's school was in the suburbs. In the past it had been unusual for students there to carry on propaganda activity in the urban districts.
8. These throwing knives (*fei tao*), as represented by Dai in a diagram, looked more like darts. They were six to eight inches long and adorned with a strip of red cloth tied to the tail. In combat they would be carried in the mouth.
9. When asked if he was speaking figuratively, in the sense of "armed to the teeth," Dai emphasized that *fei tao* were literally carried in the mouth, whence they could be quickly taken and thrown.

CHAPTER TEN

1. Canton Military Region Command Party Committee, "An Examination of Mistakes Made in the Work of Supporting the Left in the Canton Area," *SCMP*, No. 4082, pp. 1–5. Dai thought the original from which this translation was taken corresponded with the version he read while still in China.
2. "The Proletariat Must Firmly Grasp the Barrel of the Gun," *Hung Ch'i* 1967, No. 12, p. 47 (emphasis added).
3. Mao's action suggests that he wished to qualify or hedge his concurrence with criticism of Huang by eliminating the commander's personal apology. This would have been useful at a later time, if he and Huang had been forced into a close relationship. (This, in fact, may well have already happened.) However, other

people at the center seemed intent upon publicizing the more abject and perhaps more damaging version.

4. China's air force is roughly 90,000 strong within a total PLA complement estimated at 2,600,000 men. The air force commander Wu Fa-hsien had been prominent and active throughout the movement, though he was not a member of the CCRG. As mentioned above, Peking Aviation Institute had one of the strongest Red Flag contingents in the capital. And in March 1968 rightist Yang Ch'eng-wu would be charged with having tried to seize and other clues pointing to general air force support for the Cultural Revolution, Dai recognized no special connection between attitudes of the central air force leadership in Peking and the greater activism of air force units in Canton.

5. Foshan lies about fifteen miles southwest of Canton. The boy mentioned had been shopping there when he got wind of a local Red Flag plan to raid the Public Security Bureau, whereupon he decided to join in. The gate was locked when they arrived, but they were able to scale the wall and make off with a number of firearms anyway. All other members of the party were from Foshan itself, hence the action was essentially a neighborhood raid by locals. Dai claimed it was very rare for groups to forage outside their own "territory."

6. Yang was promoted to acting secretary of the Central Committee's Military Affairs Commission in August 1967, replacing Hsiao Hua, whose purge at the same time accompanied the fall of the PLA's General Political Department. Seven months later, in March 1968, Yang himself was purged as a "rightist."

7. Dai remembered the flag faction raising objections to this slogan as early as October 1967, although to the best of the authors' knowledge it was first unveiled publicly in the *Liberation Army Daily* on January 28, 1968.

8. Pan Ping, "I Am a Flag Faction Red Guard," *Sing Tao Daily News*, November 3 and 4, p. 4. Subsequently he contributed two other articles to the same paper, signed with his chosen pseudonym Dai Hsiao-ai: "Ch'en Yi After the Cultural Revolution Swept Away His Prestige" (December 22, 1968) and "A Discussion of the Movement to Send Intellectual Youth Up to the Mountains and Down to the Countryside" (February 28 to March 2, 1969).

EPILOGUE

1. *Nanfang Jih-pao,* December 30, 1967; *SCMP,* No. 4155, p. 7.
2. *SCMP,* No. 4148, p. 6.
3. Ibid.
4. Ibid. (emphasis added).
5. Ibid.
6. *Sing Tao Jih-pao,* February 28–March 2, 1969, p. 4.

SELECTED BIBLIOGRAPHY

The following books and articles represent but a mere fraction of the available works in English concerning the Cultural Revolution. They have been chosen to provide a short list of readily accessible sources on this important topic. It is hoped that the general reader and the beginning student will find this bibliography a useful starting point for exploring the Cultural Revolution in greater depth.

BARCATA, LOUIS. *China in the Throes of the Cultural Revolution.* New York, 1968.

BAUM, RICHARD. "Ideology Redivivus," *Problems of Communism,* XVI, iii (1967), 1–11.

———. "China: Year of the Mangoes," *Asian Survey,* IX, i (January 1969), 1–17.

Bulletin of the Atomic Scientists. China After the Cultural Revolution. New York, 1970.

CHANG, PARRIS H. "Mao's Great Purge: A Political Balance Sheet," *Problems of Communism,* XVIII, ii (1969), 1–10.

CHENG, CHU-YUAN. "The Root of China's Cultural Revolution: The Feud Between Mao Tse-tung and Liu Shao-chi," *Orbis,* II, iv (1968), 1160–78.

Current Scene—Editor. "A Year of Revolution: Mao Tse-tung and the 'Anti-Party' Struggle," IV, xxii, pt. 1 (1966); IV, xxiii, pt. 2 (1966).

———. "In the Name of Revolution: Peking's Campaign to Crush the 'Anti-Party' Line," IV, xii (1966).

FRIEDMAN, EDWARD. "Cultural Limits of the Cultural Revolution," *Asian Survey,* IX, vi (1966), 188–201.

GRAY, JACK, and CAVENDISH, PATRICK. *Chinese Communism in Crisis.* London, 1968.

HO PING-TI, and TSOU, TANG, eds. *China in Crisis:* Vol. I: *China's Heritage and the Communist Political System.* Vol. II: *China's Policies in Asia and America's Alternatives.* Chicago, 1968.

HUNTER, NEALE. *Shanghai Journal.* New York, 1969.

JOFFE, ELLIS. "China in Mid-1966: Cultural Revolution or Struggle for Power," *China Quarterly,* xxvii (1966), 123–31.

LIFTON, ROBERT J. *Revolutionary Immortality: Mao Tse-tung and the Chinese Cultural Revolution.* London, 1969.

NEE, VICTOR. *The Cultural Revolution at Peking University.* London, 1969.

OKSENBERG, MICHAEL; RISKIN, CARL; SCALAPINO, ROBERT A.; VOGEL, EZRA; *et al. The Cultural Revolution: 1967 in Review.* Ann Arbor, 1968.

TSOU, TANG. "The Cultural Revolution and the Chinese Political System," *China Quarterly,* xxxviii (1969), 63–91.

GEORGE ALLEN & UNWIN LTD

Head office:
40 Museum Street, London, W.C.1
Telephone: 01-405 8577

Sales, Distribution and Accounts Departments
Park Lane, Hemel Hempstead, Herts.
Telephone: 0442 3244

Athens: 7 Stadiou Street, Athens 125
Barbados: Rockley New Road, St. Lawerence 4
Bombay: 103/5 Fort Street, Bombay 1
Calcutta: 285J Bepin Behari Ganguli Street, Calcutta 12
Dacca: Alico Building, 18 Motijheel, Dacca 2
Hornsby, N.S.W.: Cnr. Bridge Road and Jersey Street, 2077
Ibadan: P.O. Box 62
Johannesburg: P.O. Box 23134, Joubert Park
Karachi: Karachi Chambers, McLeod Road, Karachi 2
Lahore: 22 Falettis' Hotel, Egerton Road
Madras: 2/18 Mount Road, Madras 2
Manila: P.O. Box 157, Quezon City, D-502
Mexico: Serapio Rendon 125, Mexico 4, D.F.
Nairobi: P.O. Box 30583
New Delhi: 4/21-22B Asaf Ali Road, New Delhi 1
Ontario, 2330 Midland Avenue, Agincourt
Singapore: 248C-6 Orchard Road, Singapore 9
Tokyo: C.P.O. Box 1728, Tokyo 100-91
Wellington: P.O. Box 1467, Wellington